Regulation of Entry and Pricing in Truck Transportation

Regulation of Entry and Pricing in Truck Transportation

Edited by Paul W. MacAvoy and John W. Snow

Ford Administration Papers on Regulatory Reform

American Enterprise Institute for Public Policy Research
Washington, D.C.

Paul W. MacAvoy is professor of economics at Yale University and an adjunct scholar at the American Enterprise Institute.

John W. Snow is a visiting fellow at the American Enterprise Institute.

ISBN 0–8447–3261–3

AEI Studies 162

Library of Congress Catalog Card No. 77–89167

Printed in the United States of America

CONTENTS

FOREWORD

Early in 1975, I called for the initiation of a major effort aimed at regulatory reform. Members of my administration, and the Congress, were asked to formulate and accelerate programs to remove anti-competitive restrictions in price and entry regulation, to reduce the paper work and procedural burdens in the regulatory process, and to revise procedures in health, safety and other social regulations to bring the costs of these controls in line with their social benefits.

My requests set in motion agency and department initiatives, and a number of studies, reorganization proposals, and legislative proposals were forthcoming last year. A number of these resulted in productive changes in transportation, retail trade, and safety regulations. Nevertheless, much remained to be done, in part because of the time required to complete the analysis and evaluation of ongoing regulations.

This volume provides one set of the analytical studies on regulatory reform that were still in process at the end of 1976. Necessarily, these studies would have undergone detailed evaluation in the agencies and the White House before becoming part of any final reform program. They do not necessarily represent my policy views at this time, but they do contribute to the analyses that must precede policy making. I look forward to the discussion that these papers will surely stimulate.

Gerald R. Ford

GERALD R. FORD

PREFACE

The Ford administration's proposal to reform economic regulation of the trucking industry, the Motor Carrier Reform Act, was submitted to Congress on November 13, 1975. In his message accompanying transmittal of the bill, President Ford said that "the basic thrust of this proposed motor carrier legislation is to improve performance of our transportation industry by replacing Government regulation with competition." The proposal sought to accomplish this objective by liberalizing entry into the industry, providing greater pricing flexibility, and reducing antitrust immunity for collective rate-making activities of carriers.

The motor carrier industry originally came under federal regulation in 1935, when it was made subject to the jurisdiction of the Interstate Commerce Commission. The Ford administration's view was that ICC regulation of trucking causes serious inefficiencies and inequities, and that the industry would perform better in a less regulated environment. During the preparation of the Motor Carrier Reform Act, a number of background studies and analyses were undertaken dealing with the trucking industry and the effects of economic regulation on its performance. Further studies and analyses were carried on during the ensuing public debate over the proposal.

This volume presents a number of these background studies and analyses. These papers provide insights into the major issues in the debate over trucking deregulation. They indicate the type of research which served as the foundation for the development of the administration's legislative proposal and for the debate which followed its introduction. They also present some findings on the economics of motor carrier regulation that have previously not been generally available. In proposing reform of the economic regulation of the airline industry, the administration was able to draw upon a rich academic literature on the subject. Although a number of useful studies had been made on motor carrier regulation, the academic literature on the effects of economic regulation on the trucking industry was not as comprehensive as that on the airline industry. Thus, the work undertaken within the administration to evaluate trucking regulation was of great scope and significance.

Hearings on the Motor Carrier Reform Act were held in the House during the 94th Congress. The Senate Commerce Committee undertook an extensive internal review of the matter but held no hearings of its own. Other legislative proposals to reform regulation of trucking were also introduced in the 94th Congress. The chairmen of the appropriate committees in both the House and the Senate have indicated that trucking regulation will be considered in the 95th Congress, and President Carter indicated during his town meeting at Clinton, Massachusetts, that he intends to pursue reform of trucking regulation.

We trust that these papers will contribute to the continuing debate on this major public policy issue. As President Ford has stated: "The importance of regulatory reform in improving our transportation system cannot be overemphasized."

PAUL W. MACAVOY
Yale University

JOHN W. SNOW
American Enterprise Institute

July 1977

PART ONE
OVERVIEW OF THE ISSUES

For an overview of the motor carrier regulation controversy, we present a paper by one of the editors, John W. Snow, drawn from testimony on the Motor Carrier Reform Act before the Surface Transportation Subcommittee of the House Public Works Committee. The paper reviews the major problems resulting from regulation of the motor carrier industry by the Interstate Commerce Commission and analyzes how the proposed legislation would address those problems. The paper also briefly reviews a number of the major issues in the debate over deregulation of the trucking industry. The papers in succeeding parts of this volume explore these issues in more detail.

1

THE PROBLEM OF MOTOR CARRIER REGULATION AND THE FORD ADMINISTRATION'S PROPOSAL FOR REFORM

John W. Snow

An Introduction to the Motor Carrier Industry

The motor carrier industry is both large and complex. Although the exact number of intercity trucking firms is not known, the total is believed to be in excess of 100,000 firms. More than 15,000 motor carriers are regulated by the Interstate Commerce Commission. The trucking industry hauls thousands of different commodities to and from tens of thousands of different communities. Total expenditures on intercity truck transportation in 1974 were $48.8 billion. Trucking accounts for 23 percent of all intercity freight transportation measured in terms of ton-miles, or about 64 percent measured in terms of expenditures. The industry employs about 1.2 million people and the labor force is heavily organized, principally by the Teamsters Union.

Despite the large number of motor carriers, an individual shipper of regulated commodities generally has a limited choice of carriers available to him. Not even the largest ICC-regulated carriers have authority to carry all freight everywhere in the country. The number of carriers available depends on the commodity being shipped and the location of the shipping and receiving points. For shipments between large cities, a number of carriers are usually available, perhaps a dozen or more. For smaller cities, especially if they are located in parts of the country which have experienced substantial growth in

On September 14, 1975, John W. Snow, who was then administrator of the National Highway Traffic Safety Administration, U.S. Department of Transportation, gave oral testimony on motor carrier regulatory reform before the Subcommittee on Surface Transportation of the House Committee on Public Works and Transportation. This paper is edited from the written extended testimony which was submitted on October 1, 1975.

the years since motor carriers became regulated, the number of carriers available may be quite small, sometimes only one or two. In many cases, no carrier has authority to serve both the shipping and the receiving points. When this occurs, two or more carriers must combine to perform the service, with each carrier moving the shipment part of the way.

The regulated sector of the industry earns profits which compare favorably to the rest of the U.S. economy. Less information is available about the exempt sector of the industry, but it is known that exempt carriers earn sufficient profits to allow them to attract capital, operate good equipment, and provide reliable service. The turnover rate for exempt carriers is comparable to rates for other similar industries.

All sectors of the industry, regulated and unregulated, are affected by the regulatory system which forms a crazy-quilt pattern of highly restricted truck transportation. Common carriers must provide their services to anyone, but they are prohibited from entering into contracts with their customers and are limited in the commodities they can carry and the places they can serve. Contract carriers can provide service only by contract and only to a strictly limited number of customers. A private carrier may haul goods for its own company, but not for any other company, including its own corporate affiliates and subsidiaries except in very limited circumstances. Agricultural carriers are exempt from federal economic regulation, but only as long as they are hauling unprocessed agricultural products, such as cabbage or livestock. They are not allowed to compete for regulated freight.

Regulated Carriers. The regulated sector of the industry, consisting of common and contract carriers, accounts for about 40 percent of total intercity ton-miles of truck freight. The ICC regulates the rates a common carrier may charge, the commodities it may carry, and the routes over which it may operate.

Entry by new firms into the industry is extremely limited, as evidenced by the fact that most ICC operating authorities are so-called grandfather rights. These are operating authorities granted to firms already in existence when the motor carrier industry originally came under federal regulation in 1935. Entry is granted, in general, only when the ICC determines that the existing carriers cannot provide adequate service for the traffic under consideration. Expansion of existing carriers into new routes often requires the purchase of another carrier's operating authority.

Firms are generally regulated in one of two ways: (1) they are closely regulated as to the commodities they may carry, but they are allowed latitude as to the routes over which they may operate; or (2) they are allowed latitude as to which commodities they may carry, but they are closely regulated as to where they may operate. Typical of the first category are "specialized commodity carriers," which are limited to a narrow range of commodities and often have irregular route authorities. This means that they may haul specified commodities between a number of different points over any particular road. "General freight carriers," which compose the second category, usually have regular route authorities. This means that they serve a limited number of points and that the routes between the points are explicitly specified. In some cases the specific road to be traveled, including turnoffs for pickups and deliveries, is spelled out in the carrier's operating authority.

The specialized commodity carriers generally are smaller firms that specialize in truckload shipments (ones large enough to require an entire truck) which do not require the use of terminals. These carriers often rely on owner-operators (drivers who own their own trucks) to provide the actual transportation of the freight. General freight carriers usually specialize in smaller shipments which require terminal facilities to consolidate the shipments into loads large enough to utilize their trucks efficiently. These carriers also carry large shipments, but in many cases such freight is handled by a separate truckload division. General freight carriers account for about two-thirds of the total revenue of the ICC-regulated trucking industry. The truckload shipment carriers compete to a significant extent with the railroads. The carriers of smaller shipments do not compete with railroads, since railroads do not carry small shipments to any significant extent.

Rate regulation applies to both truckload (TL) and less-than-truckload (LTL) traffic, but it particularly affects LTL general freight traffic. Almost all LTL shipments move under rates determined collectively by associations of carriers called rate bureaus and sanctioned by the ICC. This results in a situation where LTL shippers generally have only one rate available to them. Thus, despite the large number of carriers, price competition on LTL traffic is almost completely stifled. Private carriage and railroads place a competitive discipline on truckload rates. Many TL rates are negotiated individually between carrier and shipper, and they are essentially competitive prices.

Unregulated Carriers. The nonregulated sector of the trucking industry, which accounts for the remaining 60 percent of the traffic, consists essentially of two separate parts: exempt carriers and private carriers. The exempt carriers operate under a section of the Interstate Commerce Act whereby the motor carriage of unprocessed agricultural goods is exempt from federal economic regulation. Private carriers are companies which carry their own goods in furtherance of their nontransportation business interests. For example, a large manufacturer which used its own trucks to deliver its product to wholesalers would be a private carrier, as would a small wholesaler which used its own trucks to deliver to its customers. Unregulated carriers are simply carriers which have no ICC operating authority and therefore may not carry regulated commodities on a for-hire basis. Thus, although not directly subject to economic regulation, they are, nevertheless, severely restricted by it. For example, exempt carriers haul unprocessed agricultural products from rural areas to manufacturing and consuming centers (often larger cities), but they are prohibited from competing with regulated carriers for shipments moving in the reverse direction. A carrier that hauls peaches to a cannery cannot haul canned peaches back to the growing area. This causes exempt carriers to have excessive empty mileage, increases the cost of transporting agricultural commodities, and reduces the availability of truck service to haul manufactured goods to rural areas.

Private carriers are faced with additional unnecessary restrictions. A private trucking organization of one company may not haul goods on a for-hire basis for another company, even if it is entirely owned by the other; that is, intercorporate hauling is prohibited. Private carriers are prohibited from leasing their trucks and drivers to regulated carriers for periods shorter than thirty days. This effectively denies them the ability to lease their trucks on a one-way (backhaul) basis and results in unnecessary empty mileage.

Passenger Carriers. Like the trucking industry, the intercity bus industry is subject to detailed economic regulation. There were 1,067 regulated intercity bus firms in 1973. They received $884 million in revenue. In spite of the large number of firms, the bus industry is dominated by two companies which account for approximately 70 percent of total industry revenue. Most routes are dominated by one carrier, and even the most heavily traveled routes have no more than two or three carriers. Despite the high industry concentration, entry is tightly restricted. One large carrier admits to a policy of protesting every application for entry into its markets. Rates are also tightly regulated.

Motor Carrier Rates

The pricing system of the regulated motor carriers is highly regulated both by the industry itself and by the ICC. It is a system that lacks substantial competition and results in rates which are too high.

Description of the Present System. Motor carrier rate regulation particularly affects LTL general freight traffic. Most LTL rates are initiated by associations of carriers called rate bureaus which are granted antitrust immunity by the ICC. Almost all LTL shipments move under these rates. Price competition is virtually inoperative. Individual carriers are permitted to file independent rates, but important rates are almost always set through the bureaus. Moreover, if an important rate is set by independent action, the ICC normally suspends the rate pending a hearing on its ultimate lawfulness. The ICC has broad powers to supervise rates through its authority to find a rate unlawful. But its powers are usually exercised in enforcing the cartel price-fixing of the rate bureaus rather than in encouraging price competition or innovation in rate making.

Most LTL traffic moves under class rates. Under this system, commodities are grouped into broad classes, and average rates based on average costs are published for each class. The class into which a commodity is placed can substantially affect the shipping rate. It is not unusual for two commodities with essentially the same transportation characteristics to move under widely different rates simply because they have been artificially grouped into two different classes. The classification of particular commodities ostensibly reflects transportation characteristics, but it also reflects nontransportation factors such as the value of the commodity. A large element of arbitrariness also enters in. For example, the same product may be classified differently according to the process by which it was produced.

These class rates are only loosely related to costs through industry-wide or system-wide averages. Thus, a shipper does not generally pay the specific costs incurred in transporting his traffic, and shippers' and carriers' incentives are distorted. No allowance is made for a range of rates varying with the quality of service provided, and the range of choices available to shippers is restricted. Rates do not usually vary according to the balance of traffic or seasonal factors. Fronthaul and backhaul rates are usually the same, as are peak and off-peak rates. As a result, there is little encouragement to use the empty space on a backhaul or to ship in an off-peak time.

Truckload shipments, by contrast, frequently move on rates which reflect the actual costs of the specific movement. Private carriage and railroad transportation often provide alternatives to common carrier TL trucking and place an important competitive discipline on TL rates. The ICC sanctions cost-based rates in this situation by allowing individual carriers to publish commodity rates or exceptions to classification rates. These rates, which are usually restricted to shipments above a certain minimum weight (that is, TL shipments), are often negotiated between individual carriers and shippers and apply to specific commodities moving between specific points. They reflect the actual costs of the particular movements to which they apply, as well as the degree of competition from substitute methods of transportation.

Economic Effects. Under the present regulatory system, rates are high, inflexible, irrational, and discriminatory, and the whole rate structure is needlessly complex.

Rates are too high. The present system of regulation causes rates to be higher than they would be if greater reliance were placed on competition and if carriers were given increased freedom to manage their operations unencumbered by detailed economic restrictions.

Rates are too high partly because unnecessary regulatory restrictions cause carriers to operate less efficiently than they could without the restrictions. Regulation causes carriers to use circuitous routes and to have empty backhauls. We will discuss these restrictions in detail later. At this point, suffice it to say that, because costs are inflated by regulation, rates must be higher than they otherwise would be to compensate for the increased costs.

Rates are also higher than they should be because competition has been suppressed. LTL rates, in particular, are set collusively by rate bureaus. Price-fixing leads inherently to higher than competitive rates. Firms will use the power to set rates collusively to their own advantage, and price-fixing is therefore illegal in almost all other industries. There is nothing unique about the physical or economic attributes of the motor carrier industry to justify anticompetitive practices such as collective pricing.

There is considerable evidence that rates are higher than they should be. Perhaps the most convincing evidence arises from actual experience with the removal of economic regulation. In the mid-1950s fresh and frozen poultry and frozen fruits and vegetables were changed from regulated to exempt commodities. The U.S. Department of Agriculture conducted a "before" and "after" study of rates and service.[1] Rates dropped by 33 percent on poultry and 19 percent on fruits and vegetables, and service actually improved.

The study also found that private carriage usage dropped significantly after the commodities were made exempt. Shippers turn to private carriage when common carrier rates are too high, or service is poor, or a combination of both conditions exists. In this case, for-hire rates dropped and service improved, so the need for private carriage decreased for many shippers and they returned to for-hire transportation.

Equally convincing evidence of an entirely different sort comes from a recent American Trucking Associations (ATA) submission to the ICC concerning the accounting treatment for the value of motor carrier operating rights.[2] The ATA states that operating rights often have great value and that the value has been increasing over time. According to ATA, "Recent acquisitions in the motor carrier industry indicate that amounts paid for operating authorities are approximately 15% to 20% of the annual revenue produced by those authorities." And after examining a sample of 43 percent of all transactions, they conclude: "motor carrier financial statistics indicate that the value of these rights tends to increase rather than diminish in the ponderance of cases."

The fact that operating rights have value *is* strong evidence that the present regulatory system works to the detriment of the consuming public. Operating rights would only have value if carriers were able to earn higher than competitive returns on motor carrier service. Thus, the value of rights indicates that shippers and ultimately consumers are paying more for motor carrier service, and are receiving less service, than they would under competitive market conditions. Operating rights have value only because the ICC has suppressed competition.

It is important to recognize that the value of operating authority does not represent the value of "goodwill" earned through superior

[1] James R. Snitzler and Robert J. Byrne, *Interstate Trucking of Fresh and Frozen Poultry under the Agricultural Exemption*, U.S. Department of Agriculture, Marketing Research Division, MRR-224, March 1958; idem, *Interstate Trucking of Frozen Fruits and Vegetables under the Agricultural Exemption*, U.S. Department of Agriculture, Marketing Research Division, MRR-316, March 1959; and J. C. Winter and Ivan W. Ulrey, *Supplement to Interstate Trucking of Frozen Fruits and Vegetables under the Agricultural Exemption*, U.S. Department of Agriculture, Marketing Research Division, Supplement to MRR-316, July 1961.

[2] American Trucking Associations, *Accounting for Motor Carrier Operating Rights*, Brief and Petition of American Trucking Associations, Inc., before the Financial Standards Board of the Financial Accounting Foundation, Washington, D.C., 1974; and letter from Peter T. Beardsley, general counsel of ATA, to John A. Grady, director of the Bureau of Accounts, Interstate Commerce Commission, "re: Accounting for Intangible Assets, File AMC 72-1," July 14, 1972.

performance and market acceptance. In fact, the ATA submission explicitly states: "Operating rights are not goodwill."[3] They represent solely the value of the monopoly power conferred upon certificate holders by the present regulatory system.

Other evidence also supports the conclusion that regulated rates are higher than they should be. A study which compared trucking rates in unregulated Canadian provinces against rates in regulated Canadian provinces and in the United States found that revenues per ton-mile were about 7 percent lower in the unregulated provinces than in the regulated areas.[4]

Finally, case studies of the reasons firms turn from common to private carriage frequently show that they do so because they can provide the same service for a lower cost.[5] This would only be true if common carrier rates were inflated or otherwise distorted, since private carrier costs are essentially the same as common carrier costs for the same operation, and private carriers are not allowed to solicit traffic to fill up their empty backhauls.

Because regulated motor carrier rates are too high, shippers' distribution costs are too high and consumers end up paying more for goods than they should. Inflated common carrier rates also distort shippers' modal choice incentives and cause them to use private carriage in the hauling of regulated goods more than they otherwise would. In motor carrier markets where price competition has been stifled but service competition has not been suppressed by overly restrictive entry limitations, carriers engage in wasteful service competition. That is, since they are unable to compete for traffic by lowering rates, they compete by providing more frequent service, for example, than they otherwise would. This raises costs because trucks run less fully loaded than they otherwise would. Although this added service may be of value to some shippers, others are forced to pay more and to receive more service than they would choose to receive if carriers were free to offer lower rates.

---

[3] American Trucking Associations, *Accounting for Motor Carrier Operating Rights*, p. 9.

[4] James Sloss, "Regulation of Motor Freight Transportation: A Quantitative Evaluation of Policy," *Bell Journal of Economics and Management Science*, vol. 1 (Autumn 1970), pp. 327-66. There are several reasons why the findings seem to understate the actual difference in rates. For a discussion of these findings, see Thomas G. Moore, *Trucking Regulation: Lessons from Europe* (Washington, D.C.: American Enterprise Institute, 1976).

[5] See Robert M. Sutton, Donald W. Weitz, and Ronald S. Potter, *Case Studies of Private Motor Carriage*, final report prepared for U.S. Department of Transportation, November 1973; and Drake Sheahan/Stewart Dougall, Inc., *Private Carriage Motivation and Impact of Rural Location PS-50367*, prepared for U.S. Department of Transportation, March 28, 1975.

Rates and service are not flexible. There is little provision in this regulated rate system for a range of rates which vary according to service quality. Since rates are not allowed to vary, service quality is similarly constrained. Carriers are unable to recoup the higher costs of superior service by charging premium rates or to offset lower quality service with economy rates. As an analogy, the system operates as if all restaurants were required to charge five dollars for a meal. This would result in an excellent choice of five-dollar meals. But the person who wanted a ten-dollar meal or a one-dollar meal would be out of luck.

There is ample evidence that users of motor carrier services also want a diversity of price and service-quality alternatives. But they are prevented from obtaining it from the regulated common carrier industry by the system of rate regulation. The range of rates is too restricted to provide carriers with adequate incentives to offer a range of service quality.

Studies of the reasons shippers turn to private carriage show that often it is because of dissatisfaction with common carrier service, either because common carriage is overpriced or because it fails to provide service tailored to the individual shipper's needs. For example, a recent U.S. Department of Transportation survey of industrial shippers found that about 50 percent used private carriage.[6] When questioned about their reasons for engaging in private carriage, about 70 percent of the shippers cited dissatisfaction with common carrier service as their primary reason. It is important to recognize that the reason for this widespread dissatisfaction is not that common carriers are unable to match private carrier service, but that often the regulated rate structure is too inflexible to allow regulated carriers the proper incentives to provide diverse, responsive service tailored to shippers' needs.

There are numerous examples of shippers who are willing to pay premium prices for premium service but are unable to obtain such service from the common carrier industry. There are also examples of firms who receive more frequent service than they need. They go into private carriage because it is the only way to capture the cost savings of less frequent service. Common carriers are unable to respond by offering less service at lower rates because the system of rate regulation does not allow rates to vary according to service quality. A few specific examples may be illuminating.[7]

---

[6] U.S. Department of Transportation, Office of Transportation Planning Analysis, *Industrial Shipper Survey*, September 1975.

[7] The examples are taken from Drake Sheahan, *Private Carriage Motivation.*

A furniture manufacturer ships 85–90 percent of its finished products by private carriage even though it is able to generate backhauls on only 10 percent of its trips. It has two alternatives, specialized furniture carriers and general commodity common carriers. The latter have discouraged the business through equipment unavailability and long transit times because the rates are too low to make furniture transportation profitable. The specialized carrier rates are lower than private carriage costs but the service is decidedly inferior. The reason the rates are low is that the specialized carriers consolidate numerous small shipments to a single metropolitan area. This increases transit times substantially. The furniture company wants more timely service even though it costs more. Because the regulated rates are too low to enable the regulated carriers to supply timely service profitably on low-volume, low-density shipments, the shipper must enter private carriage.

A manufacturing plant in Oregon makes kraft paper bags which it sells in the San Francisco Bay area. Customers want, and competitors are prepared to provide, scheduled deliveries of small orders with short lead times. To meet the competitors' service, the firm must ship by private carriage even though with an empty backhaul its transportation costs are 35 percent higher than they would be with common carrier service. They state that common carriage is too inconsistent and unreliable to meet the competition. However, the common carrier cannot supply the high quality of service that the shipper wants at the present regulated rate and still earn a profit. Because of the inflexibility of the rate system, the manufacturing firm must turn to private carriage to obtain the price-service option that it wants.

A small ($5 million annual sales) job shop manufacturer of industrial glass products ships 85 percent of its output by private carriage because of lower costs. Cost savings are obtained by accumulating orders up to a week until a full truckload is obtained. Twelve to fifteen separate orders typically constitute a load. The firm's market area is limited to delivery areas which can be economically served by the private fleet. The firm generates some exempt backhaul traffic but runs 38 percent empty mileage. In spite of this, its costs are lower than they would be with common carriage.

A manufacturer of industrial and mining machinery saves costs by shipping via private carriage because its shipments are predominantly LTL with high common carrier rates. The firm relaxes shipment time-standards to accumulate loads and achieve high equipment utilization.

A textile manufacturer located in the Southeast uses private trucking selectively where cost savings can be obtained. The firm routinely holds private carriage shipments twenty-four to forty-eight hours in order to consolidate loads, but it schedules same-day shipments where it uses common carriage.

As these examples indicate, shippers' private carriage usage is often highly conditioned by the inflexibility of the rate system which makes it difficult for regulated common carriers to provide a flexible range of services and charge appropriate prices. The first two examples illustrate cases where shippers wanted premium service even though it would increase their shipping costs. They were unable to obtain such service because of the inflexibility of the regulated rate system. The last three cases show examples where shippers would prefer lower cost service even at some sacrifice in service quality. They turn to private carriage because the inflexible rate system does not allow regulated carriers to offer lower quality service at economy rates.

A series of interviews by the department with retail shippers and receivers showed the same pattern of shipper dissatisfaction with the diversity of options regarding rates and quality of service. To cite an example: A California clothing and fashion goods manufacturer uses air freight on shipments to Portland, Oregon, even though it costs 40–50 percent more than motor carrier service. The firm cannot buy overnight delivery service from regulated motor carriers because it is not offered.

The USDA studies of poultry and frozen fruit and vegetables referred to above also confirm this point. The studies found that private carriage was used extensively when these products were regulated and decreased substantially when they became exempt. The reason is that exempt carriers were able to adjust rates and service to the individual needs of shippers. The exempt service became far more flexible and responsive than regulated common carrier service had been. Trucks were readily available, and there was greater willingness to haul less-than-full loads, to schedule deliveries by appointment, to make multiple stops for pickups or deliveries, to change a destination in the middle of a route, and to serve small, out-of-the-way places. As a result, the use of private carriage dropped substantially.

The consequence of this limitation of the range of rate and service-quality options is not only that shippers' choices between private and common carriage are distorted. Their overall distributional decisions—such as production scheduling, inventory policies, and locational choices—are also made less efficiently than they could be if the common carrier system were able to match rates to costs adequately and thus offer a suitable diversity of services. As a result, distribution costs are higher than they should be and consumers pay more for goods than they should.

Many rates are irrational. Because rates, especially class rates, are not tied to the actual costs of the service provided, rates are frequently irrational; that is, there may be no rational relationship between the rates charged and the service provided. A study of rates in the Rocky Mountain region found that rates for a given commodity class are often higher for shorter distances than they are for longer distances in the same direction or even traveling over the same route.[8] A few examples will illustrate this. The study examined the LTL rates for a given commodity from Dallas to various points in Colorado. In the southeastern corner of Colorado a group of towns are charged $8.22 per hundred pounds for shipments from Dallas, whereas another group of towns just north of the first group on the same highway and closer to Dallas are charged $7.53 per hundred pounds. In the southwestern portion of Colorado a group of towns starting in the vicinity of Alamosa are charged $11.75 for shipments from Dallas. Beyond this group and farther from Dallas are two groups of towns charged lower rates. One group, which center on Salida, are charged $10.98; the other group, which center on Grand Junction, are charged $11.50.

The Rocky Mountain study found further that rates for service between an interchange point and a final destination (so-called arbitrary rates) are almost always different for trips with different origins, regardless of the fact that the portion of the trip from the interchange point to the final destination is the same. In other words, the cost of shipping goods from Trinidad, Colorado, to Allenmine, Colorado, is more than 20 percent higher if the trip originally starts in Dallas than if it originally starts in Los Angeles. And the physical journey from Trinidad to Allenmine is the same in both cases.[9]

---

[8] Paul T. McElhiney, *Motor Common Carrier Freight Rate Study for Nine Western States,* final report prepared for Federation of Rocky Mountain States, Inc., in cooperation with U.S. Department of Transportation, May 1975 (hereinafter cited as Rocky Mountain study).

[9] For instance, the total Class 100 LTL rate from Los Angeles, California, to Allenmine, Colorado, is 1443 cents per 100 pounds. This is rated over Trinidad, Colorado. The rate is made up as follows: Los Angeles to Trinidad is 1306 *plus an arbitrary of 137 from Trinidad to Allenmine* for a total of 1443. The rate from Dallas, Texas, to Allenmine is 936 cents per 100 pounds, made up as follows: Dallas to Trinidad is 768 *plus an arbitrary of 168 from Trinidad to Allenmine* for a total of 936.

This report contains about seventy pages of such examples of rate relationships in the nine-state Rocky Mountain region. It concludes that regulated rates are frequently irrational, capricious, and inconsistent because they are determined by regulation, not by competition. In a competitive market, rates would be cost-based. If rates exceeded costs, the business would be lost to a competitor. This competitive discipline would force rates into a more consistent and rational pattern. Inequities that now result from an artificial rate structure would be eliminated.

Many rates are discriminatory. The Interstate Commerce Act requires that all motor carrier rates and fares be reasonable and not unjustly discriminatory. The commission has interpreted this provision to mean that the same rates should apply to all shippers moving similar traffic between specific points. But in many cases the costs are not the same. When costs differ, the principle of equal rates results in actual discrimination. Some shippers are charged more than the cost of their traffic and some are charged less. The discrimination is inequitable and it leads to economic inefficiencies.

The most prevalent examples of systematic price discrimination of this type concern prime haul and backhaul rates and peak and off-peak rates. Where traffic is greater in one direction than in the other, rates should be higher on the prime haul and lower on the backhaul. This is because the costs of backhaul traffic are lower due to the availability of excess capacity. The commission and the industry have resisted the application of lower backhaul rates because such action would inevitably open up much of the nation's shipping to competitive pricing. But attempting to hold rates equal regardless of traffic imbalances causes severe, long-lasting economic inefficiencies.

Perhaps the most serious consequence is that shippers' long-run locational decisions are distorted. If rates were properly related to costs, manufacturers would have an economic incentive to locate in the direction of the prevailing backhaul. This would enable them to take advantage of lower backhaul rates. Although there will probably always be some natural traffic imbalances, they need not be as large as they presently are. The current rate policy discourages shippers from locating in areas where they would add to backhaul traffic. In fact, it is completely perverse. Since prime haul shippers are cross-subsidized by backhaul rates under the present rate policy, growth in prime haul traffic is encouraged and backhaul traffic is discouraged. Traffic imbalances are stimulated rather than moderated by the present rate policy.

This policy also induces shippers with balanced traffic to shift to private carriage. In essence what happens is that shippers with an unbalanced load are subsidized by shippers with balanced loads. A simple numerical example may clarify this complex issue. Consider a route with only two shippers. Shipper A has balanced traffic, moving five loads outbound and five inbound each period. Shipper B moves fifteen loads outbound and five inbound each period.

	Shipper A	*Shipper B*	*Total*
Outbound loads	5	15	20
Inbound loads	5	5	10
Total	10	20	30

The total traffic on this route requires twenty round trips, dictated by the twenty loads on the prime (outbound) haul. If rates on the route were cost-based, Shipper A would pay for the five round trips required to haul his loads or five-twentieths of the total and Shipper B would pay for fifteen round trips or fifteen-twentieths of the total. He should pay for the additional capacity he causes. However, the ICC attempts to hold backhaul rates up to prime haul rates, especially in the case of class rates. This is equivalent to acting as if there are thirty one-way trips, with each one-way trip bearing one-thirtieth of the cost. On this basis Shipper A is charged ten-thirtieths and Shipper B twenty-thirtieths of the total cost of traffic on the route. Since one-third is greater than one-fourth, Shipper A is paying more than his share of the cost. Shipper B is subsidized by the rate policy because he incurs three-fourths and pays two-thirds of total costs.

The results of ICC rate regulation are:

(1) Shippers with balanced traffic (or shippers whose prime haul moves in the direction of the route's backhaul) pay part of the costs of unbalanced traffic. They thus have an incentive to shift to private carriage.

(2) If Shipper A switches to private carriage, Shipper B's rates must eventually increase to cover fifteen round trips. In this situation, the carrier and B accuse A of becoming a private carrier to "skim off the cream." They would argue that A has removed his balanced traffic from the route and aggravated the imbalance on the remaining common carrier traffic. The implication of the "cream-skimming" allegation is that A's action has somehow made the remaining traffic more costly to haul. But, in fact, the remaining traffic requires fifteen round trips just as before. A's action has eliminated a distortion in the rate system, not changed costs.

(3) The rate structure distorts shippers' incentives and contributes to empty backhauling. Prime haul shippers using common carriage want more service and backhaul shippers less service than they would if rates were properly related to costs. The long-run impact is to distort locational decisions and add to basic traffic imbalances. This problem particularly affects rural areas which generate a greater volume of outbound agricultural traffic than inbound traffic in manufactured goods. Eliminating this rate distortion would stimulate economic development in rural areas. If rates were reduced, materials needed for rural businesses and industries could be obtained more inexpensively.

Evidence of rate distortions of this type is readily available. For example, case studies of private carriage show that firms often switch their balanced traffic to private fleets to avoid cross-subsidizing those with unbalanced prime haul traffic.[10]

The study of the Rocky Mountain area shows that commodity rates often differ substantially by direction of haul. Because of competitive pressure from private carriers and railroads, these rates are generally set competitively and, unlike LTL rates, are cost-based. For example, commodity rates on outbound (backhaul) traffic moving from Denver to Dallas are often about half the inbound (prime haul) rates on selected manufactured goods.[11]

Systematic rate discrimination is also found in peak and off-peak movements when shippers with large seasonal demands for service are charged the same rates as shippers with stable traffic flows. In this case, peak movements should be charged higher rates. This would be more equitable because peak shipments would then bear the additional capacity costs required to meet seasonal demands. As was recognized in the Railroad Revitalization Regulatory Reform Act, this would be more efficient because the tendency for equipment shortages would be reduced. Under the present policy, chronic seasonal shortages are likely because carriers are not allowed to charge higher rates for short-term seasonal use. Hence, shippers have no incentive to avoid the peak period and carriers have no incentive to invest in equipment that can be used only in peak periods.

A final example of serious systematic rate discrimination caused by the present rate policy is that high-valued goods are often charged

---

[10] See Drake Sheahan, *Private Carriage Motivation.*

[11] See Rocky Mountain study, table 7-1.

higher rates than low-valued goods—even though the transportation and handling characteristics of the goods are identical.[12] The rates on nylon hosiery, for example, are twice as much for shipments out of the Carolinas as the rates on cotton hosiery, even though the shipping characteristics are the same. Many shippers and receivers complain that for many goods it makes no difference to the trucker what he is carrying. Why should goods be classified differently and carry different rates just because the values of the goods differ? In some cases different insurance risks may account for a small portion of the rate difference, but often the difference is almost entirely attributable to differences in product values.

Again, where rate distortions of this sort occur, shippers make adjustments which are often uneconomic and would not occur if rates and service were set by competitive market forces. For high-valued, high-rated items, it may in fact be cheaper to switch to the traditionally more expensive alternatives such as air freight or deliveries by salesmen. Where these decisions are made simply because rates are distorted and not for service reasons, shippers, motor common carriers, and ultimately consumers are needlessly harmed. This process is well recognized in the trucking industry and takes the form of loss of "good freight," that is, freight with rates which are particularly high relative to cost. Members of the industry now regard this problem as the most serious one they face.

The rate structure is needlessly complex. Many shippers and receivers complain that the motor carrier rate system is cumbersome and needlessly complex. The industry claims that this complexity results from the need to develop rates for so many different commodities traveling between so many different communities. But other, unregulated industries offer large product lines to tens of thousands or even millions of customers. They do so without creating a demand for specialized services such as rate audit firms to ensure that customers receive the correct price, and without generating the frustration and confusion voiced by so many users of motor carrier services.

The real problem arises from the endless artificial distinctions in the rate classification system which is strictly a product of the regulatory system. Under a competitive pricing system, a simplified rate structure would evolve based on genuine cost difference. Given a choice, customers would not long tolerate the present cumbersome system. They would allocate their business to carriers which charged

---

[12] Josephine Olson, "Price Discrimination by Regulated Motor Carriers," *American Economic Review*, June 1972, pp. 395-402.

understandable, cost-based rates. Thus, such a system would rapidly evolve based on such characteristics as distance, weight or volume, special handling characteristics, insurance risks, and so forth.

Restrictions on Entry

Description of the Present System. To operate as a common carrier of regulated goods, a motor carrier must have a certificate from the Interstate Commerce Commission. These certificates have been obtained in one of two ways. According to the ATA: "The vast majority of operating rights existing today arose under what is referred to as the 'grandfather' clause in the Act."[13] That is, when the motor carrier industry was first brought under the Interstate Commerce Act in 1935, some 18,000 or more existing carriers were granted "grandfathered" operating authority, and these grants of authority still make up the vast majority of operating rights today. Through mergers, acquisitions, attrition, and a severely restrictive entry policy, the current number of certificated carriers has decreased to about 15,000, even though output and revenues of the industry have grown enormously.

Those authorities not originally granted under the grandfather clause have been obtained by satisfying a statutory test of "public convenience and necessity." This is an extremely difficult test to meet because the commission has interpreted the statute to mean that new carriers should not be certificated as long as the existing carriers are able to provide adequate service for the traffic under consideration. In a leading case the ICC clearly enunciated its policy: "It has consistently been held that existing carriers should be afforded the opportunity to transport all the traffic which they can handle adequately, economically and efficiently in the territory they serve before a new service is authorized."[14] The policy primarily safeguards the interests of existing carriers and only secondarily considers the interests of the public in an innovative, more responsive, or more efficient service. The inequity of denying persons the opportunity to engage in the business of their choice in order to protect the interests of existing carriers is not considered at all.

Many applications for operating authority are made each year and a large fraction are granted. In recent years some 4,000 grants were made from about 5,000 applications. However, very few of

[13] American Trucking Associations, *Accounting for Motor Carrier Operating Rights*, p. 1.

[14] 110 M.C.C. 180, 184-85.

these certificates were new carriers, and of this small number very few were for authority that was broader than one commodity or one place.

Economic Effects. We will consider three effects of the market entry restrictions imposed under the present regulatory system.

Market concentration and monopoly power. One result of the severe limitation on new entry and the imposition of detailed certificate restrictions on existing regulated carriers is to convert a naturally competitive industry into one in which there are numerous instances of monopoly (or oligopoly) power. Although there are some 15,000 certificated carriers, the number available to carry any particular shipment is often very limited. On high-density routes where a number of carriers may have been operating before regulation was imposed in the mid-1930s there may be a dozen or more. But on many routes, particularly in rural areas or in regions that have grown rapidly, the number of available carriers may be far fewer. Only two or three or even one carrier may be authorized to carry a particular shipment in these areas.

The best evidence of the widespread existence of market power caused by the ICC's restrictive entry policy is that operating rights have market value. They only have value because they have been artificially restricted. The value of rights consists of the capitalized value of the excess over normal competitive returns. It arises from the certificate holder's ability to charge higher rates and provide less service on the average than he would in a competitive market. Thus, the policy operates to the detriment of the public and to the benefit of the original holders of these rights.

The aggregate statistics on industry concentration in the regulated motor carrier industry are also revealing. In 1972 the top four and the top eight firms' shares of total industry operating income were 17 percent and 23 percent respectively.[15] Although this is low relative to most manufacturing industries, it must be viewed in the perspective of individual routes. Since even the largest firms have limited authority and are unable to serve the entire market, concentration on individual routes is much higher.

Evidence of concentration on individual routes is found in the Rocky Mountain study.[16] From this study it appears that about one-

[15] Interstate Commerce Commission, *Transport Statistics in the United States,* Part 7. The figures here refer to the shares of Class I and Class II operating income.

[16] Rocky Mountain study, p. 44.

fourth of the towns in the nine-state region are served by no more than one carrier and more than half (56 percent) are served by no more than two. Interviews with retail shippers and receivers conducted around the country by DOT staff indicate further that there are substantial regional inequities in the extent to which the number of competitors has been restricted. For example, retailers interviewed in New Orleans reported that for more than half of their shipments two motor carriers at most were authorized to serve them. By contrast, shippers interviewed in the Denver area reported that they were limited to no more than two motor carriers on only 10 percent of their shipments.

A breakdown of the top four and top eight firm concentration ratios for the top four and top eight firms by ICC regional districts shows further evidence of the regional inequities in market concentration referred to above. For 1972 the concentration ratios were as follows:

ICC District	*Top Four Firms*	*Top Eight Firms*
Eastern	32	41
Southern	27	40
Western	17	26

Operating inefficiencies. Competition among certificated carriers is limited by restricting the authority granted. These certificate restrictions not only limit competition, they also cause regulated carriers to operate less efficiently than they could if they were free to manage their own internal operations. Commodity-restricted authorities, the most prevalent kind, limit the types of cargo that can be carried. Carriers with this sort of authority are legally prevented from filling up their trucks with other cargo even if it can be hauled for very little additional cost.

In addition, according to a study done by the ICC, about 30 percent of all commodity-restricted authorities provide only one-way authority.[17] This is true even after allowing for combinations of grants to the same carrier. Carriers subject to the one-way restriction are not legally able to carry a load on their return trips even if cargo is readily available to be shipped. This restriction wastes resources by causing unnecessary motor carrier capacity and excessive empty mileage.

Route-restricted authorities specify the routes over which carriers must travel. They waste resources by adding unnecessary mile-

[17] Interstate Commerce Commission, Bureau of Economics, *Profile of Motor Carriers of Property Subject to ICC Regulation*, July 1965, p. 43.

age to trips. Permission for modest deviations in routing to eliminate circuity is routinely granted by the ICC. But in considering requests for large deviations, those which would produce the most substantial savings in mileage, the commission gives primary weight not to the improvements in efficiency or customer service but to the effects on competitive relationships on the route. For example, in February 1974, during the height of the energy crisis, the commission denied a request by Consolidated Freightways to reduce its circuity by 37 percent on movements between Minneapolis-St. Paul and Dallas. The commission held that the mileage savings would reduce transit time and thus adversely affect competing carriers in the market.

Route restrictions also cause inefficiencies by adding to excessive interlining. In many cases no single carrier has the necessary operating authority to carry a shipment its entire journey. When this happens, two or more carriers participate in the movement by transferring the cargo between carriers at selected interchange points along the way. Excessive interlining raises transportation costs and frequently adds substantially to transit times.

Shippers and receivers complain about excessive transit times caused by interlining because it adds to their distribution costs. They must carry more inventory and provide more warehouse and storage space than they should because of interlining caused by arbitrary route restrictions. In addition, there is the psychic toll from the sheer frustration of dealing with a cumbersome, inflexible, unjustified, and frequently irrational system. For example, on one recent occasion a wholesaler of school and church furniture located in Salt Lake City ordered some lamp shades to be delivered from Union City, Indiana, to the University of Utah. Discovering they were the wrong size, he attempted to send them back. The shipment somehow ended up in Indianapolis. It waited there because no carrier had operating authority between Indianapolis and Union City. Eventually, the shipment was sent to Chicago where it could be routed to Union City.

Reliable estimates of the total effect of route and commodity restrictions on the cost of regulated motor carrier operations are not available.[18] But the effect of these restrictions is undeniable. By preventing carriers from making the most efficient use of their resources,

---

[18] One estimate is given in Stephen Sobotka and Thomas Domencich, *The Energy Use Implications of the Rail and Truck Regulatory Reform Bills*, prepared for the U.S. Department of Transportation, October 1975. This study, which is included in the present volume as Chapter 8, estimates efficiency savings in common carrier trucking from eliminating operating restrictions to be on the order of 3 percent, but the estimate is admittedly based on a series of highly tenuous assumptions.

they add to the amount of fuel, labor, and equipment required to move the available freight and they increase transit times. Ultimately, because of these inefficiencies, consumers must pay more for the goods they buy.

Inequities. The restrictions on entry into the regulated motor carrier industry inevitably result in gross inequities among individuals. Persons who happened to be in the motor carrier business in the mid-1930s have been awarded, free of charge, valuable property rights. The ATA estimates that through 1970 about $300 million in operating rights had been transacted.[19] This represents only a fraction of the property rights that have been conferred because only those authorities that have actually been sold are included in the figure.

Other individuals, no less capable, have been prevented from engaging in the business or occupation of their choice. This is inherently undemocratic. Individuals have been denied the right to enter the motor carrier industry, not because of any failing on their part, but simply to protect those already in the industry from competition.

Still others, who wanted either to enter the industry or to expand, have been forced to pay large sums to those who already possessed operating authority in order to do so. To quote the ATA:

> Consider, for example, a relatively small carrier with a limited set of operating rights that desires to expand. Virtually the only way for it to obtain additional operating authorities is to buy them from other motor carriers, either by direct acquisition of a particular authority or by acquisition of the entire carrier and all of its assets, including operating authorities.[20]

Needless to say, newcomers, including members of minority groups, have been most disadvantaged by the exclusionary entry practices of the present regulatory system. They were not in the motor carrier business when the vast majority of existing authorities were granted in the 1930s. Minorities and small businessmen would find the motor carrier industry particularly attractive because of its modest initial capital requirements if it were not for the limitations on operating rights and the scarcity values that these rights command.

---

[19] Beardsley to Grady, July 14, 1972.

[20] American Trucking Associations, *Accounting for Motor Carrier Operating Rights*, p. 6.

Restrictions on Nonregulated Carriers

Description of the Present System. Nonregulated carriers account for about 60 percent of total intercity trucking ton-miles. Nonregulated carriers are simply carriers that are not required to obtain ICC operating authority and may not carry regulated goods on a for-hire basis. Rather than being free of economic regulation, they are severely restricted by it.

As was noted above, the nonregulated sector of the trucking industry consists essentially of two separate parts, exempt carriers and private carriers. The so-called exempt carriers operate under an exemption from the Interstate Commerce Act which allows unprocessed agricultural goods to be carried by truckers free of economic regulation. Private carriers are corporations and businesses carrying their own goods with their own trucks.

To limit competition from private carriage, the commission has interpreted the Interstate Commerce Act to place restrictions on private carriage operations. The commission creates inefficiencies in one sector of the motor carrier industry and then mitigates the effects on regulated carriers, not by eliminating the inefficiencies, but by creating offsetting inefficiencies elsewhere in the industry.

ICC rulings prevent private carriers from hauling goods for other firms. They are not even allowed in most cases to haul for subsidiaries and affiliates within their own corporate family. They are also prohibited from leasing their equipment to common carriers for periods of less than thirty days. This effectively eliminates their ability to lease equipment on empty backhaul trips.

Exempt carriers are allowed to haul unprocessed agricultural goods from farm areas to manufacturing and consuming areas. But they are not allowed to compete against regulated carriers for the carriage of manufactured goods. Exempt carriers are allowed to lease equipment to regulated carriers for individual trips. So, the exempt carrier who hauled peaches to a cannery would be allowed to haul canned peaches on his backhaul as long as he did not compete for the cargo against regulated carriers but instead leased himself to the regulated carrier.

Economic effects. The restrictions on private and exempt carrier operations add to transportation costs by preventing these carriers from utilizing their equipment as fully as they could. They result in unnecessary motor carrier capacity and unnecessary mileage. Two specific examples illustrate the wastefulness involved.[21]

- A firm interviewed in a study of private carriage operations reported that it ships from New Jersey to St. Louis by private carriage and the trucks return empty. The firm's subsidiary in Georgia uses its trucks to ship goods to the Northeast and these trucks return empty. The firm's St. Louis plant sends products to the South by common carrier. If the prohibition on intercorporate hauling were eliminated, this firm would operate a round trip from the Northeast, to St. Louis, to the South, and back to the Northeast. The empty backhauls from St. Louis to New Jersey and from the Northeast to the South would be eliminated. The firm estimates that annually it would save 200,000 empty miles and 50,000 gallons of fuel.
- Another company ships two loads per week from North Carolina to New England and the trucks return empty. A subsidiary firm ships a like number of truckloads from New England to Georgia. These also return empty. Total annual mileage is 330,000, almost half of which is needlessly empty because of ICC restrictions on intercorporate hauling by private carriers. If these artificial restrictions were eliminated, either of the present fleets could pick up the other's cargo on its return haul. Total annual mileage would be 170,000, of which 5,000 miles would be empty. Fleet capacity would be reduced by half, mileage savings would be 160,000 per year, and fuel savings would be 40,000 gallons per year. There would be no impact on regulated traffic.

The best indication of the wasted resources caused by backhaul restrictions on private and exempt carriers comes from Federal Highway Administration (FHWA) data on trucks traveling empty.[22] The primary effect of these restrictions is to add to empty travel. Comparing the percentage of empty mileage for regulated and unregulated carriers using like equipment gives a conservative estimate of the additional empty travel caused by these backhaul restrictions.

In the 1972 survey, 27.7 percent of the ICC-regulated vehicles stopped were found to be empty. Because of the large number and

---

[21] See Drake Sheahan/Stewart Dougall, Inc., *Evaluation of Potential Changes to Federal Economic Regulations Governing Private Carriage*, prepared for U.S. Department of Transportation, Industry Analysis Division, December 6, 1974, pp. C-I-1 and C-I-6.

[22] See Federal Highway Administration, *Annual Truck Weight Study*.

careful selection of the checkpoints used for this study, this percentage can be extended to all ICC-regulated vehicles.

The 27.7 percent figure applies to all ICC-regulated vehicles stopped. It includes vehicles operating on prime hauls and on backhauls, and it includes both specialized and unspecialized equipment. Since a vehicle normally would not make the fronthaul unless it had a load, all of the empty vehicles must be on backhaul. Thus, an alternative interpretation of the data is that 55.4 percent of all ICC-regulated backhauls are empty.

Of the ICC-regulated semicombination vans (the unspecialized truck types typically used in hauling general freight), 19.3 percent of the trucks stopped were found to be empty. This implies that 38.6 percent of such vehicles were traveling empty on their backhauls since all are presumably loaded on their fronthauls. By comparison, 33.2 percent of private carriers' semicombination vans that were stopped were reported empty. Hence, we can infer that on backhauls these trucks run empty 66.4 percent of the time, compared to 38.6 percent for ICC-regulated vans. Thus, restrictions on private carriage utilization cause private van-type trucks to run empty on their backhauls about 70 percent more than ICC-regulated van-type trucks.

The data on semicombination vans not regulated by the ICC—primarily exempt carriers—show that 26.7 percent of those stopped were empty. Thus, on backhauls 53.4 percent were empty. These trucks run empty on their return trips almost 40 percent more often than regulated vans do because of ICC restrictions on their operations. Exempt carriers are less severely affected than private carriers because of their ability to trip lease. Nevertheless, the effect is sizeable.

Private and exempt carrier restrictions also cause them to operate less fully loaded than they could. Often these trucks have unused space which they could fill if they had greater freedom to solicit loads. The statistics on empty mileage do not reflect this, so they actually understate the extent of the inefficiencies caused by restrictions on nonregulated carriers. In the FHWA survey a vehicle is counted as loaded as long as it carries some cargo. It need not be fully loaded.

The economic consequences of these restrictions are easy to see. Costs of private and exempt carriage are higher than they should be. Regulated common carriers are partially sheltered from competition. Market pressures which would normally eliminate inefficiencies in regulated carriage are not allowed to operate fully. The restrictions help preserve common carrier monopolies where they exist and help support a noncompetitive rate structure. As a result, the costs of manufactured goods whether carried by regulated or private carriers are inflated. Restrictions on exempt carriers drive up the costs of agricultural goods and reduce service on manufactured goods moving back to rural areas.

Service to Rural Communities

It is frequently alleged by supporters of the present regulatory system that, unless competition is restricted, motor carrier service to small rural communities will deteriorate. One argument is that the commission's current restrictive entry policy confers both benefits and obligations upon certificated carriers. They benefit from protection from new entrants, and in return they have a "common carrier obligation" to provide service to the towns covered by their operating authority. Without this obligation, it is alleged, small rural towns would not receive service. A related argument is that rural service is inherently unprofitable and that motor carriers can only afford to provide it if they are able to earn profits elsewhere which they can use to support service to rural areas.

The first argument implies that competition should be restricted in rural areas on a quid pro quo basis because carriers undertake the common carrier obligation to provide rural service. The second implies that competition should also be limited in high-density interurban corridors so that common carriers will have the wherewithal to support rural service.

The DOT has analyzed the rural service issue and has concluded that, far from providing a justification for the current restrictive regulatory policy, the present system has impaired rural motor carrier service. Rural towns would be much better served by a regulatory program which placed greater reliance on competitive market forces and which eliminated unnecessary and wasteful operating restrictions.

The so-called common carrier obligation to serve is not an effective guarantee of rural service, and it provides no justification for the continuation of restrictive entry and rate regulation. The evidence shows further that cross-subsidies to rural motor carrier service are not needed and they are not an appropriate means of ensuring rural service.

Common Carrier Obligation to Serve. The Wyoming Public Service Commission (PSC) studied the extent to which the common carrier obligation is honored in this largely rural state.[23] The Wyoming PSC selected eleven towns to study: Casper, Cheyenne, Cody, Gillette, Jackson, Laramie, Newcastle, Rawlins, Riverton, Rock Springs, and Sheridan. The points surveyed are among the largest towns in the state and thus, if anything, overstate the extent to which service is actually provided in the small towns.

The Wyoming PSC found that only half of the carriers authorized to provide service in these towns actually do so. Of these, the larger carriers appear to be serving in truckload lots only. Clearly, certification does not confer an obligation to serve.

A study was also made of the number of authorized carriers in the rural Rocky Mountain region.[24] All cities and towns in the nine-state region were included. Based on the Wyoming study, the number of authorized carriers is twice the number actually providing service. On this basis, the study shows that about one-fourth of the towns in the nine-state region are served by no more than one carrier. More than half (56 percent) of the towns are served by no more than two carriers. In view of the route and commodity restrictions which generally prevail, the choice of carriers to ship a particular load to a particular destination is very limited in these rural areas.

To check on the quality of service received by rural shippers, a mail questionnaire was circulated by state regulatory officials for the Federation of Rocky Mountain States to shippers in three states—Utah, Wyoming, and Idaho.[25] The service was unfavorably rated by 55 percent of the respondents. Many individual comments on truck service were volunteered. They ranged from calling the service erratic to stating that "the stagecoach would be faster." One respondent in Idaho commented that private carriage from California is $400 a trip cheaper than using common carriage.

The mail questionnaire results also showed that 66 percent of the respondents used private carriage. The high incidence of private carriage usage is highly indicative of the poor quality of the regulated common carrier service. Shippers usually switch to private carriage because of dissatisfaction with the available common carrier service.

These findings in the rural Rocky Mountain region are confirmed by U.S. Department of Agriculture studies of transportation in rural

---

23 The Wyoming Public Service Commission study is included in the Rocky Mountain study, pp. 45-52.

24 Rocky Mountain study, p. 44.

25 Ibid., pp. 64-67.

parts of Iowa.[26] These studies found that rural regulated common carrier truck service is of uncertain quality and that residents in smaller Iowa communities are highly dependent on private trucking for the movement of goods.

Regulated Rates in Rural Areas. As discussed above, the investigations of the rate structure in the Rocky Mountain area found rates to be irrational and capricious. A particular problem for rural shippers and receivers of regulated commodities arises because many small towns do not generate enough traffic to justify publishing separate rates for them. In this case nearby small towns are sometimes grouped into "rate groups" and a single-factor through rate is published for the group.

Nevertheless, many rural towns are not included in the rate groups, and a rate has to be "manufactured" for any shipment moving to such a point. In the Rocky Mountain region it was found that this is usually done by applying arbitrary rates from an interchange point to the final destination. According to the study, the problem with the use of arbitraries is that they appear to be truly arbitrary.

> The establishment of freight rates is generally supposed to be based upon economic factors, the ultimate of which are the cost to the carrier for providing the service and the need or demand of the customer to have it. The major rate theory behind arbitrary rates, however, is summed up in their name—they are established arbitrarily. Economic factors may be considered in their establishment but probably only in an intuitive way.[27]
>
> Frequently an arbitrary will be imposed on top of a group rate. This situation is particularly observable in Colorado. For instance, from Los Angeles, California, Colorado Springs is shown as being in its own rate group taking a through rate of 1306 cents per 100 pounds. . . . In practice, however, motor freight patrons are assessed a rate of 1306 plus an arbitrary of 48 cents per 100 pounds to cover the service of breaking bulk at Denver and delivering the freight from there. This occurs even though the carrier passes through Colorado Springs on his way to Denver.[28]

---

[26] Iowa State University, Engineering Research Institute, *Integrated Analysis of Small Cities Intercity Transportation to Facilitate the Achievement of Regional Urban Goals*, prepared for the U.S. Department of Agriculture, June 1974 and December 1975 (hereinafter cited as Iowa State University study).
[27] Rocky Mountain study, p. 123.
[28] Ibid., p. 126.

The report also found that arbitraries are applied to some shippers but not others and to some towns but not others. For instance:

> Several carriers "flag out" or choose not to apply the arbitrary at Golden, Colorado. Several carriers remove application of the extra charge only for one large industry located at Golden. There are, however, several industrial sites along the route between Denver and Golden to which the arbitrary rate is applied.[29]

The study of motor carrier service in rural Iowa supports these findings. It was found that about two-thirds of the rural communities in the study region were subject to arbitrary rates. The December 1975 report concluded: "a study of arbitrary rates indicated that they often were inequitable and tended to induce distributional patterns that could be inhibitory to the potential for growth in rural regions." [30]

The overall picture that emerges on rates to rural communities is that they are by no means fair, or consistent, or related to costs. And the small rural shipper has little recourse under the present system. The cost and inconvenience of a formal protest are out of the question. Moreover, the shipper has no opportunity to "shop around" for a more satisfactory alternative because price competition is effectively precluded by the regulatory system. He either accepts the situation or turns to private carriage. Again, these examples show that the present system places rural areas at a particular disadvantage.

Cross-Subsidies. The argument that motor carrier competition must be restricted to allow carriers to earn high profits on some routes so that they can subsidize rural service is contradicted by the facts. A study of carriers who specialize in rural service shows that they are profitable on rural service alone.[31] Since these carriers provide only rural services and are profitable, it can be deduced that rural service does not have to be subsidized. Additional evidence is provided by the American Trucking Associations who have surveyed their members to determine their attitudes toward rural freight. They found that thousands of firms wished to provide regular service to

---

[29] Ibid., p. 139.

[30] Iowa State University study, December 1975, p. 4.

[31] R. L. Banks and Associates, Inc., *Economic Analysis and Regulatory Implications of Motor Common Carrier Service to Predominantly Small Communities*, draft report submitted to the U.S. Department of Transportation, pursuant to DOT-OS-50096. (The final report was submitted on June 24, 1976, and an edited version of it is included in the present volume as Chapter 5.)

small towns.[32] Rural service is self-supporting and there is no need for a cross-subsidy.

Moreover, as shown by the evidence from the Wyoming study of the common carrier obligation, there is little reason to believe that common carriers would choose to use profits from high-density routes to pay for service on low-density routes. They are not effectively required to provide such service as a condition of certification, and they certainly have no private incentive to do so. Instead, they make every effort to avoid cross-subsidizing rural service, and excess profits are translated into high certificate values.

The facts suggest that the cross-subsidy argument is specious. But even if there were some substance to the argument, there would be good reason to oppose this mechanism as a basis for obtaining service in rural areas. First, if a cross-subsidy existed, it would mean that some shippers are being forced to pay part of the costs of other shippers' transportation. This is inequitable. Second, if a subsidy were required to ensure rural service, direct government subsidy would probably be preferable to the haphazard system of rate regulation and restrictive entry.

Some persons argue that, without the present system of regulation, transportation rates would rise substantially and retail prices in rural areas would rise astronomically. This argument implies that rural service is presently cross-subsidized. The evidence indicates that rural service is already profitable. Hence, a rise in rural motor carrier rates as a result of regulatory reform is unlikely. But even if there were a rise in rural shipping rates, it would not greatly affect retail prices. Shipping costs average only about 2–3 percent of retail prices, and only a part of this percentage is accounted for by the rural portion of the movement.

Comparison with Nonregulated Rural Service. An examination of the quality of service provided by the nonregulated truckers in rural areas also supports our argument that service in rural areas would improve if more reliance were placed upon the competitive market forces. As was discussed above, several agricultural commodities were changed from regulated to exempt goods in the mid-1950s and rates dropped substantially—by about 20–30 percent—when the commodities were exempted from economic controls. In addition to the price reduction and service improvements previously noted, it is particularly noteworthy that service on small lots, on less-than-full

[32] American Trucking Associations, *Small Town Blues* (Washington, D.C., 1976).

loads, and on partial loadings and unloadings improved. Service to small, out-of-the-way places improved.

Opponents of regulatory reform sometimes concede that truckload service might improve in a competitive environment, but they stress that service to small shippers or small, out-of-the-way communities would deteriorate. Actual experience shows, however, that this is wrong. Under competitive conditions, carriers are more willing to serve out-of-the-way places and to carry partial loads. As was pointed out in the Rocky Mountain study, today many of the larger regulated carriers are unwilling to carry less-than-truckload lots to and from small towns.

These findings are reinforced by recent USDA studies of exempt livestock trucking service.[33] A survey of users reported that more than 95 percent found the service to be satisfactory. It may be recalled that in the Rocky Mountain survey of regulated rural motor carrier service, 56 percent of users considered the service unsatisfactory.

These findings are further substantiated by data on private carriage usage. The USDA study of exempt livestock trucking found that private carriage accounted for less than one-fifth of the livestock trucked. The Rocky Mountain survey showed, by contrast, that 66 percent of the respondents used private trucking. Similarly, the Iowa study showed that rural shippers in Iowa rely heavily on private trucking to haul regulated goods.

USDA research on the effects of the exemption of poultry and frozen fruits and vegetables in the mid-1950s found a significant decrease in the use of private carriage after these commodities were exempted from ICC regulation. The only way shippers could obtain the flexible, responsive service they needed while the commodities were regulated was to turn to private trucking. After they were exempted, the type of service they wanted became available from exempt carriers responding to competitive initiatives. Private trucking diminished significantly.

These various studies on unregulated rural service also demolish several other myths. It is frequently argued that, unless rates are set through regulation, they will fluctuate wildly. USDA studies of the effect of exempting fresh fruits and vegetables in the 1950s found that rates were stable after the exemption, except for desirable seasonal fluctuations.

Opponents of regulatory reform also argue that under a

---

[33] L. A. Hoffman, P. P. Boles, and T. Q. Hutchinson, *Livestock Trucking Services: Quality, Adequacy, and Shipment Patterns*, U.S. Department of Agriculture, Economic Research Service, Agricultural Economic Report 312, October 1975.

liberalized entry system, the business will be overwhelmed by "fly-by-night" operators who enter and leave the industry at will. This argument has been thoroughly researched. USDA studies of the exempt livestock truckers show that the average firm has been in business for eighteen years. Another study of bankruptcy rates and business turnover in the exempt trucking industry shows that it is comparable to similar industries.[34]

Studies also show that exempt truckers operating under competitive incentives operate safe, modern equipment and have safety records as good as those found in the regulated industry.[35]

In summary, the evidence indicates that rural America has been poorly served by the present regulatory system and would be far better served by a competitive industry. Prices would be lower, there would be more carriers to choose from, service would become more flexible and suited to shippers' individual needs. The evidence shows further that by releasing common carrier managements from the many encumbrances of regulation and by providing them with proper incentives they would be able to compete far more vigorously with private carriage.

Intercity Bus Transportation

Under the same provisions of the Interstate Commerce Act which apply to the regulation of interstate motor carriers of property, the ICC is authorized to regulate interstate motor carriers of passengers, typically referred to collectively as the intercity bus industry. The ICC regulates rates, controls entry, and imposes numerous detailed operating restrictions on regulated carriers. A crazy-quilt pattern of detailed economic regulation has developed. The industry is fragmented into regular route carriers, charter carriers, contract carriers, and special service carriers. Each is limited to specific types of operation and is restricted to specific routes or operating territories. The effect of these detailed restrictions, as with the trucking industry, has been to limit severely competition within the industry.

As in the case with motor carriers of property, the majority of operating rights granted to motor carriers of passengers exist as

[34] Walter Miklius and Kenneth L. Casavant, *Stability of Motor Carriers Operating under the Agricultural Exemption*, prepared for the U.S. Department of Agriculture, August 1975. An edited version of this study appears in the present volume as Chapter 11.

[35] U.S. Department of Transportation, Federal Highway Administration, *Safety Road Checks, Motor Carriers of Property, January through June 1973*, June 1974; and U.S. Department of Transportation, Federal Highway Administration, *1973 Accidents of Motor Carriers of Property*, July 1975.

grandfather rights, dating back to 1935. In that year more than 2,100 intercity bus companies were granted operating authority by the commission. Today, as a result of mergers, acquisitions, attrition, and a restrictive entry policy, there are fewer than 1,000 such firms in existence.

Although the ICC's approach to regulation of motor carriers of passengers has remained the same, the intercity bus industry has changed dramatically in many respects in the forty-one years that have elapsed since the passage of Part II of the Interstate Commerce Act. Much of the interstate travel about which the commission expressed concern in the years preceding the passage of Part II of the act was intrametropolitan in nature (for example, Camden to Philadelphia and Newark to New York). Today, the bulk of this market is served by metropolitan and regional transportation authorities and not by the intercity bus industry.

In 1935 the industry comprised numerous small firms, no single one of which was dominant, although the foundation for the emergence of the industry giants had been laid. Today, the intercity bus industry is concentrated to an extent rarely seen in the U.S. business community. Over the years two names have become synonymous with intercity bus travel in the United States. Greyhound Lines and Continental Trailways and its score of affiliates clearly dominate the industry. Together, they account for approximately 75 percent of all revenues earned in regular route service by interstate motor carriers of passengers.

A DOT analysis of intercity bus routes shows that for service between major metropolitan areas about 20 percent receive regular route service from only one firm and about 80 percent from two or more. Of the 80 percent, virtually all are served by only two carriers. For rural routes, about three-fourths are served by only one carrier, the balance by two.

A DOT cost study of fifty-eight Class I intercity bus firms which derived more than 50 percent of their revenues from intercity regular route service during the 1971–1974 period showed that there are no economies of scale in intercity bus operations. The operating cost per bus-mile does not decrease as firm size and output (bus-miles operated) increase. This implies that there are no reasons, other than regulatory ones, why the industry should be dominated by one or two large firms, since large firms are able to realize no cost advantages over smaller firms.

The Motor Carrier Reform Act will liberalize entry into the industry and will introduce competitive pricing. This will allow new carriers into the industry, will encourage innovation, and will enable well-managed smaller firms to expand as market forces dictate. As a result of increased competition from new entry or the threat of new entry, passengers can expect to receive improved service at competitive rates. On sparsely traveled routes the threat of new entry will enforce an important competitive discipline on service and rates even though actual new entry may not occur.

It might be noted that improvements in intercity bus transportation are particularly important to the poor, the elderly, and the young since these are the persons for whom bus travel is most attractive.

Other Myths Used to Oppose Motor Carrier Regulatory Reform

Market Chaos. It is sometimes argued that under regulatory reform the market for motor carrier service will become chaotic. Carriers will rush around blindly, entering and leaving markets or concentrating only on the large, high-density markets. Prices and service levels will fluctuate drastically. Shippers will not know from day to day which carriers will be available at what rates. Long-range planning will be impossible for both shippers and carriers. Essentially, it is argued that the market for motor carrier services will not function.

Why the motor carrier industry is so different from other industries that are not regulated but function satisfactorily without regulation is not clear; nevertheless, the argument is made. Although there is no justification for such an argument, it is often made as a defense or an excuse for continued anticompetitive practices. It might be pointed out that the same argument has been made by the airline industry in response to proposed regulatory reform legislation.

Most markets are unregulated and these markets function in a generally efficient way without chaos. Firms make long-run commitments and customers are able to secure services. It is in the supplier's interest to give orderly and dependable service.

In the motor carrier industry, there is clear evidence that normal market incentives provide more responsive motor carrier service than regulation does. In the mid-1950s the carriage of several agricultural products which until then had been regulated were made exempt. The studies conducted by the U.S. Department of Agriculture found that rates dropped substantially, by 19 and 33 percent for the two products affected by the change. Moreover, unregulated motor carrier rates were found to be stable, except for seasonal influences.[36]

---

[36] Snitzler and Byrne, *Interstate Trucking of Frozen Fruits and Vegetables* and *Interstate Trucking of Fresh and Frozen Poultry.*

At the same time, service improved dramatically, becoming far more flexible and responsive to shippers' particular needs. Under regulation, the shipper had to have his own fleet of trucks to be able to reach small, out-of-the-way plants, to ship small loads conveniently, to make multiple stops or change a destination in the middle of a trip, or to arrange deliveries by scheduled appointment. When the products were made exempt, the shipper was able to obtain this flexible service from the for-hire carriers, and use of private carriage diminished.

It was found that not only did the exempt carriers provide a more flexible range of services than the regulated carriers did, but transit time also improved. In some cases transit time dropped by half. Under competition carriers no longer held goods to accumulate loads. They were more eager to please their customers.

The argument that there will be a headlong rush to provide service only on high-density routes is also clearly refuted by these studies. More service and better service became available to out-of-the-way places. Service is provided to these places because there is a market demand, not because of any regulatory requirement.

A related argument is that regulatory reform will result in destructive price wars during the period in which firms adjust capacity to the new regulatory environment. The argument is that regulatory reform will cause excess capacity by eliminating restrictions on efficient use of equipment. Faced with excess capacity, carriers will use the increased pricing freedom to drop rates to variable costs in order to attract freight from competitors. The end result will be widespread price wars, bankruptcies, and chaotic conditions in the motor carrier industry.

Regulatory reform may lead to temporary excess capacity by reducing wasteful operating restrictions and thus freeing resources for more efficient use. But this will not lead to severe price wars or to a situation of chronic overcapacity in the industry. Studies of motor carriers' costs and asset structures show that variable costs are not substantially below fully allocated costs. Fixed costs are low in the motor carrier industry. Thus, any price reductions in response to excess capacity would be mild. Moreover, the economic life of most fixed assets is short. Tractors have an economic life of a few years. A combination of natural attrition of operating equipment and normal market growth would soon absorb any temporary excess capacity. As a result, any tendency toward unsettled price conditions could be expected to be brief and mild.

Regulatory Reform Will Lead to Monopoly. It is sometimes argued that regulatory reform will lead to monopoly. Opponents claim that competition may lead to lower rates for a time, but eventually the industry will come to be dominated by a few large firms that will then raise rates higher than ever. Thus, they argue, the proposed savings from regulatory reform are an illusion.

The increased management flexibility under regulatory reform would lead to market dominance by a few large firms only if large firms had lower average costs than small ones. But careful studies of the costs of motor carrier operations show that there are no economies of scale in trucking.[37] That is, large firms have no cost advantage simply from being large. In fact, small firms even seem to have the advantage in some markets, especially the rural and truckload freight markets.

Moreover, for industry concentration to lead to monopoly abuses, the surviving firms would have to be able to bar new entrants. Otherwise, competing firms would reenter markets when the existing firms tried to raise prices. But other than regulatory barriers, there are no effective entry barriers in this industry. The technology is widely available. No unusual management skills are required other than the present need to understand the current, incredibly complicated regulatory system. Trucks and drivers are readily available. Terminal facilities can be built or leased. Capital requirements are modest by the standards of most manufacturing industries. The necessary management structure can be created. All this may not be easy, but it can be done by corporations where there are prospects of future long-term profitability.

It is important to recognize that under competitive conditions there may be only a few competitors on some low- and medium-density routes. But they will not be able to exploit their monopoly power because the threat of new entry will discipline their market actions.

Actual experience with unregulated conditions in the motor carrier industry confirms that increased market freedom will not lead to monopoly. Before the industry was brought under regulation in 1935, there were thousands of trucking firms and no tendency toward industry concentration. Indeed, some 18,000 firms were grandfathered into the industry when it was brought under the Interstate Commerce Act. Currently, the exempt trucking industry has many

---

[37] Richard Klem, *The Cost Structure of the Trucking Industry,* prepared for the U.S. Department of Transportation, Office of Transportation Regulatory Policy, 1975. An edited version of this report appears in the present volume as Chapter 4.

thousands of carriers, most of them small firms, and there has been no tendency toward dominance by a few large carriers.

Predatory Practices. Some opponents of regulatory reform contend that it will lead to predatory price cutting as firms try to drive others out of the market. Since predatory competition entails certain short-term losses, a rational firm would engage in such conduct only where there existed a strong prospect of obtaining monopoly profits either by driving other firms from the market or by disciplining the market. Two conditions are essential for predatory pricing. First, the predator firm must have superior resources that give it greater staying power to achieve the purpose of driving the rivals out of the market. Second, there must be high barriers to entry to enable the predator firm to recoup its losses.[38] In other words, the prospect of eventually realizing monopoly profits from the predatory conduct must be high. Where entry or reentry can occur relatively easily whenever prices return to levels at or above cost, the incentive to engage in such behavior is eliminated. There are no effective entry barriers other than regulatory barriers in the motor carrier industry, and large firms have no economic advantage which could give them greater staying power. Extensive studies of motor carrier costs show that the economies of scale needed for inherent monopoly power do not exist.[39] Thus, there would be no incentive to engage in predatory practices under regulatory reform.

Actual experience in exempt trucking confirms the absence of predatory behavior in an unregulated environment. There are thousands of exempt carriers. Rates tend to be stable except for seasonal influences, and they are high enough to attract people into the industry and keep them there. Bankruptcy rates are low and business turnover among exempt trucking firms is comparable to similar industries.[40] Studies of exempt livestock truckers, for example, show that the average firm has been in business for more than eighteen years.[41]

Finally, adequate safeguards against predatory pricing are contained in the act. The ICC will be allowed to rule rates below variable costs unlawful. Other laws also exist that operate in other industries to protect against predatory behavior.

---

[38] See the extended discussion in Phillip Areeda and Donald F. Turner, "Predatory Pricing and Related Practices Under Section 2 of the Sherman Act," *Harvard Law Review*, vol. 88 (1975), pp. 697-733.
[39] See Klem, *The Cost Structure of the Trucking Industry.*
[40] Miklius and Casavant, *Stability of Motor Carriers.*
[41] Hoffman, Boles, and Hutchinson, *Livestock Trucking Services.*

In short, this is not an industry which is inherently monopolistic, and the fear of emerging monopoly is unfounded.

Motor Carriers Are Like Public Utilities. A traditional argument for public utility regulation is that the industry is a natural monopoly. This argument requires that there be long-run economies of scale in the industry. If this is so, the industry will inevitably become concentrated in one or a few large firms unless there are legal restrictions which prevent it from happening. This is because the increasing returns to scale will give larger firms a competitive advantage over the other firms in the industry. Their unit costs will be lower and they will be able to underprice the smaller firms and drive them out of the market.

It would be inefficient to prevent the industry from becoming concentrated because then the cost savings from scale economies would not be realized. A logical solution is to let the natural monopoly evolve but to regulate it to prevent monopoly abuses.

This argument is not applicable as a justification for regulation of the motor carrier industry because motor carriers are not subject to increasing returns to scale. Large firms have no competitive advantage simply from being large. Large and small firms often compete side by side in many markets with neither having any particular advantage. Experience in the industry prior to regulation in the 1930s and in the exempt industry today is also available for comparison. There was no tendency toward natural monopoly in either case.

A related argument is that regulation is justified because the motor carrier industry, like a public utility, has an obligation to provide service. To balance the burdens of this obligation, it is argued, the industry should be sheltered from competition by restricting entry.

This is putting the cart before the horse. Public utilities are regulated because they have a natural monopoly. Because of this monopoly they are required to provide service to all customers and prices are regulated. The obligation to serve is imposed because the consumer has no alternative supplier, and price regulation is required because otherwise customers would be exploited by the monopoly. In other words, utilities are not regulated because they are required to serve; they are regulated *and* required to serve because they are monopolies. This is not the motor carrier situation because motor carriers are not natural monopolies.

The facts regarding the motor carrier's obligation to serve also contradict the "public utility" argument. The Wyoming Public Utilities Commission studied the extent to which motor carriers actually served the Wyoming towns they were certificated to serve.[42] They found that only half of the carriers authorized to serve the towns studied actually provided service. The motor common carrier "obligation to serve" is not honored and is not required to be honored as a condition for certification. In practice, motor carriers have wide discretion over the amount of service they provide and, as the Wyoming evidence indicates, they have great latitude over whether to serve a market at all. They provide service where there is an effective demand for it and where it returns a profit. This is what ensures service, not a public utility obligation to serve. The motor common carrier obligation to serve is not a burden and does not justify protection from competition.

Price Discrimination. Some argue that without the safeguards offered by the present regulatory system, carriers would practice price discrimination against shippers. Under the present system, they argue, all shippers, large and small, are charged the same rate for the same movement.

Regulatory reform will not lead to price discrimination in motor carriage. Only a monopoly is able to practice price discrimination. In a competitive industry any attempt to charge different prices to different customers—where not justified by cost differences—results in business being lost to competing firms. The motor carrier industry is naturally competitive even though competition has largely been suppressed by regulation. By liberalizing entry and providing price flexibility, the bill will stimulate competition and ensure that the prices charged by motor carriers are competitive and cost-based. There will be no opportunity for firms to engage in price discrimination without the threat of losing their customers to competitors.

By contrast, the current regulatory system causes price discrimination among shippers because rates are not based on the specific costs of the service being performed. Much of the discrimination is haphazard. Studies of rates have found, for example, that often there is no rational relationship between the distance shipped and the rates charged for a given commodity.[43] Rates may be higher for shorter than for longer distances in the same direction or even over the same route.

---

[42] See Rocky Mountain study, pp. 49-52.

[43] Ibid., chapters 4-6.

Moreover, there is a systematic discrimination against backhaul and off-peak shipments because they are charged the same rates as prime haul or peak shipments even though the costs are considerably lower. Costs are lower because of the availability of excess capacity on backhaul or off-peak movements. The commission and the industry have resisted the development of lower backhaul or off-peak rates because the use of such rates would open up much of the nation's shipping to competitive pricing. There is frequently discrimination against high-valued commodities.[44] Rates are twice as high on nylon hosiery shipped out of North Carolina as cotton hosiery even though the transportation and handling characteristics are identical. Examples of discrimination caused by the present system of rate regulation are commonplace. These inequities will be eliminated by price competition under the act.

How Can Motor Carrier Rates Drop If Costs Do Not Drop? Opponents of regulatory reform argue that it is illusory to think that it will result in lower shipping rates. They say, How can rates drop unless the costs of labor, fuel, and operating equipment go down? Rates will decrease with regulatory reform, not because the costs of inputs will go down, but because resources will be used more efficiently. The act will reduce wasteful route, commodity, and backhaul restrictions. As a result, there will be less circuity, fewer empty backhauls, and trucks will travel more fully loaded. Thus, costs per ton-mile will decrease because drivers and equipment will be more efficiently utilized, not because labor rates or equipment prices will go down. As carriers achieve efficiencies, the pricing and entry provisions of the act will assure that any cost savings resulting from those efficiencies are passed on to travelers and shippers. Consequently, average prices will be lower than they would be under a continuation of the present regulatory system.

Of course, if inflation continues, costs may continue to rise. But the important point is that motor carrier rates would increase less if the system were changed with regulatory reform than with the present wasteful regulation.

Danger that Liberalized Entry Will Lead to Increased Truck Traffic on the Highway. Some people are concerned that regulatory reform will lead to adverse external consequences such as increased traffic congestion, air pollution, fuel consumption, and accidents. It is argued

---

44 See Olson, "Price Discrimination by Regulated Motor Carriers."

that, by limiting entry, regulation holds down the number of trucks on the highway and thus serves to reduce the undesirable side effects of truck traffic.

This argument confuses an increase in the number of trucking firms with an increase in the number of trucks on the highway. The latter is determined by the amount of cargo to be shipped and the operating efficiency of the industry. Regulatory reform will improve the operating efficiency of the industry by enabling regulated carriers to rationalize their route structures—eliminating artificial backhaul restrictions affecting common, private, and exempt carriers; fostering price competition, which will place a competitive discipline on costs and operating efficiency; and allowing innovative and well-managed firms to expand and serve new routes. Although regulatory reform may lead to an increase in the number of firms in the industry, it will also stimulate efficiency in the industry and will result in less truck traffic on the highways. There will be less circuity, less empty mileage, and trucks will tend to travel more fully loaded.

One analysis of the effects of regulatory reform on the operating efficiency of LTL common carriage shows an increase of about 10 percent in load factors.[45] The efficiency gains in private and exempt carriage were also estimated to be substantial. The improvement in operating efficiency will result in a decrease in the number of truck-miles used to haul the available cargo. This in turn will reduce the undesirable external consequences of motor carriage such as congestion, accidents, energy consumption, and air pollution.

Impacts on Railroads. Some persons claim that an easing of economic controls on the trucking industry will help to worsen the severe financial straits of many of the nation's railroads. The bill will, in fact, have little effect on the railroad industry. The bill primarily increases the competitiveness of the less-than-truckload sector of the industry. Railroads do not compete for the business. The truckload sector of the industry, with which the railroad industry competes, is already substantially competitive and thus will not be greatly affected by regulatory reform.

The recently adopted Railroad Revitalization and Regulatory Reform Act gives railroads the pricing flexibility they need to compete more vigorously for larger truckload or carload shipments than they have been able to do in the past. That act also helps railroads by providing government funds and incentives to upgrade the railroads' plants and equipment. Almost all studies of the effect of regulatory

[45] Sobotka and Domencich, *The Energy Use Implications.*

reform of both the truck and railroad industries on intermodal competition conclude that it will shift traffic from truck to rail. Thus, the overall effect of the administration's regulatory reform program should be to strengthen the railroad industry and increase its share of the intercity freight market.

Recreate the Conditions of the 1930s. Some argue that regulatory reform will turn the clock back to the conditions of the 1930s when the industry was first regulated. This will not happen. The 1930s was a period of severe business depression and not a representative period in American life. Interestingly, the principal proponents of motor carrier regulation in the 1930s were the railroads who wanted to impose restrictions on a growing competitor. It was alleged that "chaos" then existed. But the "chaos" consisted of small truckers in a severe depression who preferred to work at low earnings because their alternative was unemployment.

The bill will strengthen the regulated industry and will enable it to compete more effectively with the unregulated sector of the industry. It will not bring about a return of the depression of the 1930s.

PART TWO

THE SOCIAL COSTS OF REGULATION

Advocates of motor carrier deregulation argued that regulation was imposing significant net costs on society from inefficiencies and higher transport rates. Critics of the reform proposals, such as the Interstate Commerce Commission, argued that the assessments did not take into account the benefits of regulation and that, while imposing some costs, regulation resulted in net social benefits. Thus, the issue of the benefits and the costs of regulation was drawn and it occupied a central place in the motor carrier deregulation debate.

The first paper in this part is an analysis by the ICC's Bureau of Economics on the benefits and costs of regulation. Although the ICC study is not a Ford administration paper, the paper is presented here to put the following study by W. Bruce Allen and Edward B. Hymson into context and to facilitate reading it. Allen and Hymson originally prepared their paper for the Council on Wage and Price Stability in response to the ICC study. They find little evidence in support of the ICC view that regulation results in substantial net social benefits. They conclude that the ICC view is erroneous and that, on the contrary, there are substantial net social costs resulting from surface transport regulation.

2

A COST AND BENEFIT EVALUATION OF SURFACE TRANSPORT REGULATION

Bureau of Economics, Interstate Commerce Commission

Cost of ICC Regulation: An Evaluation

Introduction. This analysis focuses heavily on an evaluation of Dr. Thomas Gale Moore's estimates of the cost of Interstate Commerce Commission regulation. Such heavy attention devoted to a single student of regulation seemed necessary because his work is the source of the monetary quantification most often quoted and used by critics of transport regulation. It was believed, therefore, that any "cost" evaluation must examine, probe, build upon, or refute this heavily cited source. Although economic literature does not lack for critiques of Dr. Moore's work, few have probed as deeply into the mathematical framework, the basic assumptions, and the validity of the logic as this review. In the course of this analysis, it was found necessary to question, and as a result to make adjustments to, Dr. Moore's cost figures because of detected faults in logic. The total cumulative impact of these faults on estimates of the cost of ICC regulation was rather significant. However, at no time was the review intended, a priori, to prove or disprove a particular point of view; instead, its purpose was to assess objectively Dr. Moore's analysis.

The basic assumption underlying Dr. Moore's studies is that the U.S. economy would be better off without ICC regulation. This is premised on the apparent conviction that the Interstate Commerce

---

This paper, which is not a Ford administration paper, is edited from a report that was prepared in 1976 as an element of a regulatory review program undertaken by the Interstate Commerce Commission.

Commission has created a negative effect on the economy through regulatory control of the surface transportation industry, and that this needless intervention can be translated into a cost to society (estimated to be equivalent to billions of dollars a year). In attempting to prove this, Dr. Moore's study hypothetically constructs a perfectly competitive market system which is free from any type of control and assigns cost estimates to the "distortions" in the present surface freight transportation system. While the author notes that these conditions do not necessarily represent what the actual transportation system would be like without ICC regulation, the difference between that ideal and the present system is, nevertheless, represented as the "cost of regulation."

Dr. Moore's ideal is not necessarily everyone's ideal. Rather, it is largely the product of subjective reasoning in which the overriding criterion is the minimization of the cost of transportation. Unfortunately, such a perception overlooks the somewhat unique manner in which transportation service is supplied and consumed. For example, it does not perceive the fact that shippers are often more sensitive to variations in service quality than to variations in rates and are often willing to pay a premium for speed and/or reliability. In a broader "public need" perspective, it has long been recognized that Dr. Moore's approach is too limited in scope to apply to an economy. The approach, therefore, is not only too narrow but also offers a result which is based on a flawed perception of the special characteristics of the surface transportation industry.

The Bureau of Economics' analysis, in contrast to Dr. Moore's ideal, evaluates the existing system of surface freight transportation against that system as it would operate without ICC regulation. It is believed that this approach is a more realistic and useful one. But it also requires use of more complex methodology since it compels an understanding of both the present system's structure and the pervasive role of ICC regulation. The fact is that regulation has, in the almost ninety years of its existence, come to be very much an integral part of the economics of our transportation system today. Consequently, evaluations of such a system and its alternatives must recognize this historically integral climate of interaction and must satisfactorily account for it.

Plan of Evaluation. In order to understand fully Dr. Moore's analysis, a brief discussion describing some of the work on intercity freight demand conducted by Dr. Alexander L. Morton is necessary, for Dr. Moore depends heavily on demand equations obtained from Dr. Morton's analysis.[1] Revised and updated versions of Dr. Morton's demand equations for railroads and trucks are therefore considered and evaluated. While such revisions are somewhat crude, they represent a substantial step forward. Moreover, they are useful in demonstrating the analytic process necessary to gain a better understanding of the transportation industry.

The analysis then examines the total demand for freight transportation for all commodities—a demand equation developed by the bureau from weighted averages of rates and tons shipped. Such aggregate demand equations often can lead to confusing results since truck and rail demand behavior varies greatly among regions and commodities, and depends heavily on the type of service required and the alternative modes of transportation available. Nevertheless, the results even with such possible flaws do provide new insight into the dynamics of demand.

Finally, Dr. Moore's estimates of the "cost of regulation" are analyzed in detail and are matched against alternative cost estimates developed by the bureau. Some of the revised estimates developed by the bureau result in negative figures, indicating a possible benefit from ICC regulation rather than a cost. Negative cost estimates are nevertheless quite appropriate in light of Dr. Moore's and the bureau's differing perceptions of the nature of the most likely freight transportation system alternative, absent regulation.

Demand for Freight Transportation. In 1969 Dr. Alexander L. Morton published the study entitled "A Statistical Sketch of Intercity Freight Demand." The study attempted to analyze the structure of the demand for railroad and truck transportation by statistically measuring the traditional determinants of freight demand with the aid of several statistical equations. Dependent demand variables were regressed against several explanatory variables, such as railroad rates, truck rates, and gross national product (GNP) for the period 1966 to 1974. The aggregate demand equation obtained for railroad traffic was as follows:

[1] Alexander L. Morton, "A Statistical Sketch of Intercity Freight Demand," *Highway Research Record 296* (1969), pp. 47-65; and Thomas G. Moore, "Deregulating Surface Freight Transportation," in *Promoting Competition in Regulated Markets,* ed. Almarin Phillips (Washington, D.C.: The Brookings Institution, 1975), pp. 55-98.

$$\log \text{RR Vol} = -0.537 \log \text{RR Rate} + 0.628 \log \text{GNP}$$
$$(2.658) \qquad (2.606)$$
$$-0.730 \log \text{TK Rate}$$
$$(1.330) \tag{1}$$
$$R^2 = 0.79$$
$$n = 20$$

where:

log = natural logarithm
RR Vol = railroad ton-miles
RR Rate = railroad rate index
GNP = gross national product (constant 1958 dollars)
TK Rate = truck rate index
R^2 = coefficient of determination
n = number of observations
( ) = t-statistic for coefficient.

The results of this analysis indicated that the demand for railroad transportation is inelastic relative to railroad rates. This occurs because the coefficient for the "log RR Rate" variable is less than 1, at a value of 0.537; hence, a general *reduction* in rail rates would *increase* rail traffic proportionately less than the rate reduction.[2] This indicates that railroads would reduce total operating revenue by reducing rates.[3]

The coefficients of the other two variables on the right side of equation 1 are intended to measure the sensitivity of rail demand to changes in GNP and truck rates. They show rail demand growing less rapidly than GNP over time and falling as truck rates increase. Dr. Morton suggests that growth in GNP stimulates proportionately smaller increases in rail traffic demand because "the economy is growing primarily in service fields (including government services), which have negligible freight requirements, and in areas of industry that produce highly fabricated outputs for which the truck is better suited to transport."[4]

Dr. Morton notes that the statistical relationship which was obtained between rail demand and truck rates is predominantly a time trend and not a cross-elasticity relationship. As a negative cross-elasticity phenomenon, it suggests that an increase in truck rates

---

2 A change in railroad rates results in a less than proportionate change in the quantity of railroad transportation demanded.

3 If demand were price-elastic, traffic would increase proportionately more than the rate would decrease; hence, total operating revenue would increase.

4 Morton, "A Statistical Sketch," p. 54.

would cause a reduction in rail volume. Obviously, this is not the case, since it would be illogical to expect trucks to drive railroads out of business by increasing truck rates. Nevertheless, since World War II, trucks have rapidly expanded their market share despite steady rate increases. Dr. Morton indicates that this time trend factor needs to be statistically measured and included in the regression equation to obtain a meaningful cross-elasticity. In light of more current observations of rail–truck dynamics, the bureau's analysis suggests that the trend variable Dr. Morton sought may be deteriorating rail service and improving truck service.

Dr. Morton also investigated truck demand. His study showed demand to be sensitive to changes in truck rates. It indicated that, as truck rates are reduced, the demand for truck transportation increases more than proportionately, as reflected in the equation below:

$$\begin{aligned} \log \text{TK Vol} = & -\underset{(5.367)}{1.841} \log \text{TK Rate} + \underset{(15.384)}{2.323} \log \text{GNP} \\ & +\underset{(7.397)}{0.932} \log \text{RR Rate} \qquad (2) \\ & R^2 = 0.996 \\ & n = 20 \end{aligned}$$

The results indicate that an overall reduction in truck rates would result in an increase in total truck operating revenues. This occurs since the 1.841 coefficient is greater than 1, signifying an elastic demand for truck transportation. The equation indicates that truck demand increases more rapidly than GNP; hence, trucks must be increasing their share of the total market of freight transportation. The equation also indicates that the "cross-elasticity" of truck demand to railroad price is approximately unity, signifying that an increase in rail rates would result in a proportionate increase in the demand for truck transportation.

Dr. Moore accepts Dr. Morton's truck demand equations but for his purposes reestimates the railroad demand equation. Such manipulation is based on the questionable proof that the cross-elasticity for railroad transportation demand to truck rates is assumed to be equal to the cross-elasticity of truck transportation demand to rail rates. Since the truck demand to rail rate cross-elasticity is approximately unity, he assumes the rail demand to truck rate cross-elasticity to be unity. He then regresses the log of railroad traffic volume on the logs of railroad rates, real gross national product, and truck rates, while holding the coefficient of truck rates constant at 1. With this regression, he obtained the following railroad demand equation:

$$\log \text{RR Vol} = \underset{(6.258)}{2.228} - \underset{(4.575)}{0.915} \log \text{RR Rate} - \underset{(1.090)}{0.097} \log \text{GNP}$$

$$+ 1.0 \log \text{TK Rate} \qquad (3)$$

Dr. Moore's methodology results in an elasticity of rail demand to rail rates of 0.915, or approximately unity. This is significantly greater than the elasticity of rail demand to rail rates obtained by Dr. Morton and has significant repercussions on his analytical results.

Dr. Morton's study and Dr. Moore's partial replication of his work both depend on data drawn from the 1947 through 1966 time period. In reviewing Dr. Moore's analysis, the Bureau of Economics performed regression analyses similar to the Morton-Moore analysis but used data for 1955–1974 to develop more representative demand equations reflecting more current trends for rail and truck traffic. These equations are offered as a critique/review of Dr. Moore's results rather than as a definitive study of the demand for freight transportation. Dr. Moore's technique for deriving cross-elasticities is employed in order to demonstrate that even if Dr. Moore's own tools are accepted as useful, updated data will significantly alter the results.

In the bureau's replication of the procedure described above, the log of truck traffic volume and the log of rail traffic volume were regressed against the logs of rail rates, truck rates, and GNP. The regression analysis of truck demand was performed first. Following Dr. Moore's procedure, the cross-elasticity obtained in this equation, 0.558, was then used in the rail demand regression equation. The coefficient of the log of truck rates was held constant at 0.558, while the log of rail traffic volume was regressed against the log of rail rates and GNP.

Although the bureau's procedure is similar to the Morton-Moore technique, the use of more current data alone resulted in significantly different elasticities. The bureau's equations are as follows:

$$\log \text{TK Vol} = -\underset{(1.704)}{0.861} \log \text{TK Rate} + \underset{(4.271)}{0.452} \log \text{GNP}$$

$$+ \underset{(2.299)}{0.558} \log \text{RR Rate} + \underset{(3.974)}{0.645} \log t \qquad (4)$$

$$R^2 = 0.991$$
$$n = 20$$

and

$$\log \text{RR Vol} = -0.232 \log \text{RR Rate} + 0.309 \log \text{GNP}$$
$$(1.501) \qquad (3.896)$$
$$+0.558 \log \text{TK Rate} \qquad (5)$$
$$R^2 = 0.749$$
$$n = 20$$

where:

t = time trend variable.

These equations, which measure transportation demand over the most recent twenty-year period, indicate that the demand for railroad transportation (see equation 5) is considerably less responsive to changes in rail rates than over the 1947–1966 time period. The truck demand equation (see equation 4) indicates that the truck traffic elasticity with respect to changes in truck rates is approximately equal to 1; this contrasts with an elastic value (a value greater than 1) using data from the earlier period. With an elasticity of 1, an overall reduction in truck rates would result in an approximately proportionate increase in truck demand; consequently, total operating revenue would not change in the face of a change in truck rates.

Clearly, the age of the data has led to conclusions regarding the transportation industry which do not reflect its current behavior. The original 1947-1966 Morton-Moore data base fails to account, for example, for the influence of an extensive superhighway system which has had substantial impact upon truck transport, the regional shift of industries, and the changing mix and nature of goods produced and shipped. It also fails to account for the massive inflation that has occurred since 1966 and the very significant impact it has had on the transportation industry. In view of these and other influencing factors, the use of a time period which reflects a more current transportation environment would seem to be critical. The time period can and does modify basic building blocks of the analysis and thereby provides significantly different results regarding the cost of ICC regulation.

The Cost of ICC Regulation. A principal contribution of Dr. Moore's work to the deregulationist philosophy is the accumulation of various cost-of-regulation figures and the aggregation of these figures into a total cost-of-regulation figure. This summation process has created a convenient and quotable number available for presentation. The interaction among regulation, the industry, and the economy, however, is not as simple, nor as easily quantified, as Dr. Moore suggests. As indicated previously, the subtleties of the regulatory climate which have evolved over time make it difficult to disassociate regulatory cause and effect from operating practices which, nevertheless, would have developed absent regulation. The bureau has attempted, however, to reevaluate each of Dr. Moore's cost figures in this light. Where appropriate, the bureau has offered what are believed to be more satisfactory estimates based on thorough evaluation of the factors. In the process, the bureau has found that much of Dr. Moore's information fails by being simply outdated, and that certain significant presumptions would not be applicable even if more current information were substituted.

A basic assumption used by Dr. Moore is that any deviation (upward) from the minimum dollar cost of transporting freight is because of the existence of regulation. This presupposes that without regulation the freight transportation industry would be perfectly efficient. This assumption leads to a result which overlooks those benefits of regulation intended to modify the problems of a less-than-perfect system, and at the same time overstates its costs.

The cost of regulation is designated by Dr. Moore as an "economic loss" and is divided into four basic categories:

(1) losses due to inefficient use of mode,

(2) losses due to traffic shifted to alternate mode,

(3) losses due to traffic not carried, and

(4) losses due to miscellaneous causes.

The first two categories account for about 95 percent of Dr. Moore's cost-of-regulation estimate. The third category accounts for the remainder, and the fourth is not quantified. The quantified costs are discussed in detail in the following review.

Inefficient use of mode. The following modes are considered: railroads, common carrier trucks, private truck carriers, and water carriers.

1. Railroads: Dr. Moore offers three cost estimates—high, medium, and low—for each item he quantifies. For railroads, under the category of "inefficient use of mode," Dr. Moore offers $2.4 billion as his high estimate. This estimate is taken directly from a paper by Dr. Ann Friedlaender, an early critic of regulation.[5] Even Dr. Moore considers this figure to be too high. Consequently, the analysis ought to focus more closely on the medium and low estimates.

---

[5] Ann F. Friedlaender, "The Social Costs of Regulating the Railroads," *American Economic Review*, vol. 61 (May 1971), pp. 226-34.

For his low and medium estimates of $1.7 billion and $2.0 billion, respectively, Dr. Moore depends on the supposition that trucks, if deregulated, would reduce their rates 20 percent, increasing their volume by more than 20 percent. This "20 percent theory" (a theory which will be disputed in a later section of this analysis) is based on a modification of Dr. Morton's demand equation.

Relying on the elasticities he obtained in equation 3, Dr. Moore states that in a deregulated environment a 20 percent reduction in truck rates (with rail rates remaining constant) will cause a 20 percent reduction in the demand for rail transportation. He assumes that railroad management would react by reducing rail rates in order to win back the lost traffic. Consequently, the railroads would be forced to trim their costs 20 percent in order to maintain their profit margins. It is this cost savings which, when aggregrated into an industry figure, yields the medium and low cost estimates of $2.0 billion and $1.7 billion.

This logic fails on at least two points. First, Dr. Moore assumes that without regulation railroads would behave as if the railroad industry were composed of only one firm. There is no evidence that this would be the case (in fact, history suggests that the opposite is probably closer to fact). Under regulation, rate decisions are developed through the rate bureau structure, which represents a composite and compromise of individual objectives. By contrast, in a competitive environment firms would act independently of one another and would tend to set their prices according to their own demand, costs, and competitive position in order to maximize profits. Consequently, the final level of industry prices cannot be predicted by looking only at the industry demand equation; rather, a review of individual firm demand curves would be required.

Second, even if one assumes an aggregate industry demand, the railroads, in attempting to maximize their profits, would not likely reduce their rates just to maintain traffic volume. Reducing rates would leave operating revenues unchanged.[6] However, operating costs would certainly increase as a result of a sudden increase in traffic, without the benefit of significant economies. In this case profit levels would actually be less compared to the case in which railroads refrained from attempting to capture the additional traffic.

As indicated earlier, Dr. Moore's cost estimates for the inefficient use of railroads not only are on precarious theoretical ground, but also

[6] Because of Dr. Moore's presumption that the price elasticity of demand is unity, according to equation 3, changes in price are offset by the same percentage changes in volume sold, thus leaving total revenue unchanged.

are based on structural equations which are outdated. The updated demand equations developed by the Bureau of Economics show railroad volume to be inelastic to both changes in its own rates and changes in the truck rates (see equations 4 and 5).

Given this inelastic demand equation and Dr. Moore's definition of what constitutes an economic loss, it is possible to surmise that regulatory effects upon railroad volume and efficiency are insignificant. One can only conclude, therefore, that the cost of regulation "due to the inefficient use of railroads" is zero.[7]

2. Common carrier trucks: Dr. Moore's estimate of loss in the common carrier truck sector is at least as questionable as the estimates developed relative to railroads. The high, medium, and low estimates for the loss are set at $1.9 billion, $1.7 billion, and $1.4 billion, respectively. The basic assumption underlying these estimates is derived from a single experience in the deregulation of the trucking of fresh-dressed poultry, frozen poultry, and frozen fruits and vegetables. This development is assumed to represent the entire scenario of deregulation relative to all commodities carried by common carrier trucks. This assumption is stated:

> Since there is no compelling reason to believe that the commodities deregulated by the court decision were atypical, it can be assumed, following Friedlaender, that rates would fall 20 percent generally if regulation of trucking were eliminated.[8]

This notion is based upon a U.S. Department of Agriculture study completed in 1958, which indicated that the weighted average of rates for these agricultural commodities decreased by 20 percent when they were deregulated in the early 1950s.[9] The Bureau of Economics has evaluated the relevant Department of Agriculture studies and believes there is substantial reason to question the assertion that a possible 20 percent reduction in freight rates can be attributed to deregulation. Nevertheless, using this limited benchmark, Dr. Moore concluded that total deregulation of the trucking industry would result in an overall rate reduction of 20 percent, representing a $2 billion cost

[7] This does not mean that inefficiencies do not exist in the rail industry—either in the use of energy or in the form of other costs—but that any such inefficiencies are not likely to be cured by deregulation.

[8] Moore, "Deregulating Surface Freight Transportation," p. 8.

[9] J. C. Winter and Ivan W. Ulrey, *Supplement to Interstate Trucking of Frozen Fruits and Vegetables under the Agricultural Exemption*, U.S. Department of Agriculture, Marketing Research Division, Supplement to MRR-316, July 1961.

savings to the consumer. This reflects a far too simplistic conclusion respecting a very complex rate environment.[10]

Sound comparative bases for quantifying the results of possible rate deregulation must be developed. Today most comparative analyses are flawed by differences in the assumed regulatory structure, the economic characteristics of the area or industry, the various deregulation alternatives, rail–truck relationships, and other factors. Nevertheless, one respected contemporary student of the motor carrier industry has determined, while observing the experience of deregulation of the British transport system, that a substantially different result occurred than that asserted by Dr. Moore. Dr. D. Daryl Wyckoff has noted that rates on truckload traffic decreased only about 10 percent, and actually increased 40 percent on less-than-truckload traffic (LTL) after deregulation in the United Kingdom.[11] If deregulation in the United States were to have a similar impact on truckload and LTL rates and were to result in operating revenues from truckload traffic decreasing 10 percent and those from LTL increasing 40 percent, the overall effect on the total traffic mix would be approximately a 20 percent increase in total dollars spent on truck transportation for a constant volume of shipment—a $2.2 billion increase.[12]

Testing Dr. Moore's theory in another way, there is considerable question whether today it would be feasible for carriers to reduce truckload rates by as much as 20 percent. In recent years, high-volume truckload traffic, to a certain extent, has been observed to be swinging away from regular route motor common carriers of

[10] Dr. Moore also supports the position that free entry into trucking would result in a flood of new carriers, causing lower rates because "there are no substantial economies of scale in any of the major modes of transportation, with the possible exception of pipelines"; Moore, "Deregulating Surface Freight Transportation," p. 93. However, this is a much disputed point. In fact, a number of studies have shown the opposite to be true or have at least criticized the arguments that no economies exist. See George N. Dicer, "Economics of Scale and Motor Carrier Optimum Size," *Quarterly Journal of Economics and Business*, Spring 1971; Edward Smykay, "An Appraisal of the Economies of Scale in the Motor Carrier Industry," *Land Economics*, May 1958; and John C. Spychalski, "Criticisms of Regulated Freight Transport: Do Economists' Perceptions Conform with Institutional Realities?" *Transportation Journal*, Spring 1975.

[11] From a speech entitled "Motor Carrier Deregulation—Some Unanswered Questions," by D. Daryl Wyckoff before the Joint Meeting of the Ohio Chapter of the Transportation Research Forum and the Eastern Central Motor Carriers Association, December 17, 1974.

[12] Operating revenues for Class I and Class II common carrier trucks for both truckload (TL) and less-than-truckload (LTL) traffic were used as "weights" to derive the 20 percent increase in overall truck rates. The 20 percent was then applied to the total 1968 motor carrier freight bill.

Table 2-1

THE EFFECTS ON OPERATING RATIOS OF MIDDLE ATLANTIC CARRIERS OF A 20 PERCENT DECREASE IN FREIGHT RATES AT 1974 TRAFFIC AND COST LEVELS

Combined System	1974 Revenue (1)	80% of Column 1 (2)	1974 Expense (3)	1974 Operat-ing Ratio (4)	Operating Ratio Based on Column 2 (5)
Minimum charge (MC)	215,300	172,240	265,690	123.4	154.3
Under 500 pounds	253,372	202,698	285,336	112.6	140.8
500 to 999	238,513	190,810	234,344	98.3	122.8
1,000 to 1,999	289,699	231,759	260,292	89.8	112.3
2,000 to 4,999	354,116	283,293	303,878	85.8	107.3
5,000 to TL	409,669	327,735	339,967	83.0	103.7
All LTL including MC	1,760,668	1,408,534	1,689,508	96.0	119.9
Truckload	1,088,707	870,966	1,048,373	96.3	120.4
Total	2,849,376	2,279,501	2,737,880	96.1	120.1

Note: Columns 1, 3, and 4 are taken from Appendix E, attachment 5, sheet 1 of Holt's verified statement in suspension case No. 63879. Columns 2 and 5 are based on constant traffic and expense levels but a 20 percent lower rate level. T. G. Moore argues that rates could fall by 20 percent on average and that the present modal shares would remain constant. Some additional traffic (presumably shared equally by each mode) would be generated by the lower rate level.

Source: Verified statement of David D. Holt, director of cost research, Middle Atlantic Carriers, in suspension case No. 63879.

general commodities to the benefit of limited service, irregular route, and specialized carriers.[13] Truckload rates published by regular route carriers appear to have been gravitating, under competitive pressure, toward more marginal profitability. Much of this truck traffic moves at a level close to the rail carload rates (at the same minimum weight) on the same traffic. The possibility of a rate level drop of 20 percent, if regulation were abandoned, does not appear feasible when examined relative to the level of truck traffic of the Regular Route Common Carrier Conference (Middle Atlantic territory), as demonstrated by Tables 2-1 and 2-2. On the basis of these figures, Dr. Wyckoff's revelations with respect to British traffic (a 10 percent reduction) would not seem to be inappropriate when applied to U.S.

[13] Charles A. Taff and David R. Rodriguez, "An Analysis of Some Aspects of Operating Rights of Irregular Route Motor Common Carriers," *Transportation Journal*, vol. 15 (Winter 1975).

Table 2-2

THE EFFECTS ON OPERATING RATIOS OF MIDDLE ATLANTIC CARRIERS OF A 20 PERCENT DECREASE IN FREIGHT RATES, A 12.5 PERCENT INCREASE IN TRAFFIC LEVELS AND A 10 PERCENT INCREASE IN TOTAL OPERATING COSTS

Combined System	1974 Revenue (1)	80% of Column 1 (2)	1974 Expense (3)	1974 Operating Ratio (4)	90% of Column 1 (5)	110% of Column 3 (6)	Revised Operating Ratio (7)
Minimum charge (MC)	215,300	172,240	265,690	123.4	193,770	292,259	150.8
Under 500 pounds	253,372	202,698	285,336	112.6	228,035	313,870	137.6
500 to 999	238,513	190,810	234,344	98.3	214,662	257,778	120.1
1,000 to 1,999	289,699	231,759	260,292	89.8	260,729	286,321	109.8
2,000 to 4,999	354,116	283,293	303,878	85.8	318,704	334,266	104.9
5,000 to TL	409,669	327,735	339,967	83.0	368,702	373,964	101.4
All LTL including MC	1,760,668	1,408,534	1,689,508	96.0	1,584,601	1,858,459	117.3
Truckload	1,088,707	870,966	1,048,373	96.3	979,836	1,153,210	117.7
Total	2,849,376	2,279,501	2,737,880	96.1	2,564,438	3,011,668	117.4

Note: Columns 1 through 4 taken from Table 1. Column 5 represents the effect on revenue of a 20 percent reduction in the rate level and a 12.5 percent increase in tonnage levels. Column 6 presumes that carrier costs will rise by only 10 percent as a result of the 12.5 percent traffic increase (which implies some economies in load factors, et cetera). Column 7 represents the revised operating ratios under the new conditions.

Source: Table 1.

rate levels. A 10 percent decline seems to be the absolute maximum reduction feasible in the United States.

3. Private truck carriers: Dr. Moore based the estimate of the "inefficient use of private carriers" on a presumption that the restrictions which the ICC imposes on private carriers are causing waste by way of empty backhauls. His estimated range of this loss, $100 million to $1 billion, assumes that with deregulation private carriers would operate at the same backhaul level as common carriers.

Private carriers differ significantly from common carriers in the type of service they provide. First, the average length of haul of private carriers is only 50 to 60 percent that of common carriers.[14] Second, private fleets usually exist because they provide speed, flexibility, and special services not otherwise available from common carriers as part of an operation not well suited for backhaul traffic. Also, many organizations use private fleets as distribution tools, employing drivers as salesmen in a comprehensive company effort which does not emphasize the acquisition of backhaul.

There is an element of speculation in any estimate of any deregulation effect on empty backhaul movements. But it is possible to accept the likelihood that private carrier empty backhaul would be somewhat reduced. It is clear, however, that much (or all) of this change would likely represent a shift in empty backhauls to common carriers.[15] The key question is whether under deregulation there would be a change in the overall level of empty backhauls by private and common carriers combined. It would be reasonable to expect that, at least in the period immediately following deregulation, empty backhauls would actually increase substantially as new entrepreneurs compete to offer new service for a relatively fixed volume of traffic. In subsequent periods, the precise level of empty backhaul would depend on the final market structure assumed by the transportation industry. But the ease of entry and the competitive, service-motivated scramble for available loads would likely lead to an aggravation of the empty backhaul problem to all carriers. Independent of rate considerations and the question of whether such changes would attract new tonnage to trucking, those factors that determine regional imbalance between producing and consuming areas would always limit the extent to which major improvements in empty backhaul levels are

---

[14] Derived from 1967 and 1972 Census of Transportation.

[15] See Drake Sheahan/Stewart Dougall, Inc., *Evaluation of Potential Changes to Federal Economic Regulations Governing Private Carriage,* report prepared for the Department of Transportation, December 6, 1974, p. F-1. Also, Interstate Commerce Commission, Petition for Declaratory Order Regarding Intercorporate Parent–Subsidiary Transportation, November 3, 1975, p. 783.

generated, regardless of market structure. Thus, the savings attributable to deregulation relative to empty backhaul would likely be insignificant and close to zero. There is even a strong chance that additional social costs would be incurred as a larger number of firms increased the possibility of service chaos as a result of deregulation.

4. Water carriers: As an estimate of the cost of regulation due to the inefficient use of water carriers, Dr. Moore specifies an amount between $270 million and $298 million. This inefficiency is attributed to the barge mixing rule which precluded use of the bulk exemption (in application of freight rates) where more than three bulk commodities were handled in the same tow of barges. Dr. Moore overlooked the fact that this rule was never enforced (pending court action and economic study). In any event, in 1973 with the enactment of Public Law 93-201, the mixing rule was eliminated. Dr. Moore has acknowledged this; nevertheless, he continues to suggest the same level of cost impact.

Since the inefficiencies these costs are reputed to measure arise from the mixing rule, Dr. Moore's estimates are clearly in error. Whatever conceivable ICC regulatory cost might impact upon water carriers can only be minimal, since the vast majority of carriers and almost all tonnage carried (estimated to be in excess of 90 percent) is exempt from ICC regulation.

Modal choice. Dr. Moore contends that the shift of long-haul traffic from motor carriers to railroads would save from $0.2 billion to $2.9 billion. He asserts that regulation prevents this modal shift, because it inhibits railroads from adjusting their rate structure downward and thus securing motor carrier traffic now handled at higher cost. The argument suggests that deregulation, per se, would effect a beneficial redistribution of traffic towards railroads. However, this rationale conflicts significantly with recent evidence concerning the competitive relationship between rail and motor carriers.

Competition encompasses not just differences in rates but also differences in the quality of service. A rate comparison alone, as Dr. Moore suggests, might show that rail service is priced at a level lower than that of motor carriers. However, in choosing between rail or truck, shippers also consider such indirect expenses as comparative loading costs, inventory financing, equipment availability, transit time, loss and damages in transit, service flexibility, convenience, and availability of service as "cost" factors. When these factors are included, the total perceived "cost" of using motor carrier service has apparently been viewed quite often as the less expensive alternative.

The bureau's observation of intermodal rate dynamics suggests that, although railroads have long had the opportunity to take advantage of a lower underlying cost/rate position in long-haul traffic, the opportunity has not been generally seized, and motor carriers have succeeded in increasing their market share over time, particularly in connection with manufactured commodities.

The supposition that railroad rates cannot be reduced to attract long-haul motor carrier traffic is also contrary to observed railroad practice in connection with general rate increase requests. It is the railroad industry itself which has sought and applied a 69.4 percent increase in the general rate level between 1969 and 1975. In every increase request the industry has, however, employed its expert judgment to readjust rates among commodities and regions through "hold-downs" and "flag-outs" before and after the increase was granted. An increase in the overall rate level of 69.4 percent would seem to have been more than sufficient to allow for the restructuring of long-haul rates selectively or generally if a competitive advantage existed or were seen as a desirable policy objective by rail management.

Contrary to Dr. Moore's perception, considerable evidence suggests that with deregulation railroad rates would in fact rise, not fall. For example, if railroads were to seek to recapture long-haul traffic, they would be obliged to improve the quality of the service. However, it has been estimated that if railroads sought to invest in the capital improvements needed to offer such improved service they would have to generate $400 million per year, probably through increased rates (as measured in real terms without the effects of inflation). It seems possible that the consequences of such an increase in rates could be self-defeating and result in additional traffic diversion to motor carriers.

Traffic not carried. The last type of loss to which Dr. Moore assigns a cost estimate is "traffic not carried"—a loss to the economy from goods not transported because freight rates were so excessive that they made shipment unprofitable. Aside from the fact that regulation is designed to ensure against such an occurrence, as was indicated above, it is unlikely that the overall rates of either rail or trucks would be significantly reduced as a whole with deregulation. The updated rail demand equation shows railroad demand to be very inelastic with respect to changes in rates; hence, the railroads are likely to face reduced profits if they reduce their rates. Truckload rates may decline, but rates on LTL traffic are more likely to increase total expenditures for truck transportation. In such an environment, deregulation would not result in bargain freight rates and a subsequent massive availability of additional freight traffic; consequently, there can be no economic loss because of "traffic not carried."

By way of testing this conclusion, if the reaction to deregulation in the United States were similar to the British experience, the weighted average of truck freight rates would increase by approximately 20 percent. The bureau's updated truck demand equation (see equation 4) indicates a price elasticity of 0.9; hence, a 20 percent increase in rates would result in about an 18 percent reduction in truck demand. This is precisely the opposite of the situation that Dr. Moore describes. Thus, using Dr. Moore's methodology, this scenario would not result in a cost for regulation but rather in a $0.2 billion static welfare gain.

Conclusion—Costs. In our evaluation of Dr. Thomas Gale Moore's estimates of the cost of ICC regulation, we have derived an updated estimate (in 1975 dollars) ranging from minus $4.8 billion (a benefit) to $1.7 billion (a cost). This compares with Dr. Moore's estimates of a $6.5 billion to $15.2 billion cost. In terms of 1968 dollars, these estimates range from a bureau-derived estimate of minus $2.8 billion (a benefit) to $1.0 billion (a cost) contrasted with Dr. Moore's cost estimates of $3.8 billion to $8.9 billion. The largest portion of this difference occurs in the category of "inefficient use of mode," as summarized in Table 2-3.

Dr. Moore's estimates are based partly on Dr. Alexander L. Morton's 1969 study of rail and truck demand functions. Dr. Morton used data from the period 1947 to 1966 to derive his relationships. Much has happened since, both to the transportation industry and to the U.S. economy as a whole, suggesting that the relationships Dr. Morton obtained are not relevant today. Using data covering the period 1955 to 1974, the Bureau of Economics was able to capture these more current trends with significantly different results.

In order to evaluate Dr. Moore's analysis of surface freight transportation regulation and his estimates of "economic loss" because of regulation, the bureau was forced to assume a comparable analytical approach. However, the bureau's examination of Dr. Moore's study shows that even if a basically similar approach is followed, the Moore cost estimates are significantly overstated (see Table 2-3).

The bureau's updated analysis of the demand equation for railroads is more relevant to 1975. Nevertheless, the methodology which Dr. Moore used and which was traced to obtain new equations leads to ambiguous results. The equations are too all-inclusive and too

Table 2-3

ESTIMATES OF ECONOMIC LOSS FROM THE REGULATION OF SURFACE FREIGHT TRANSPORTATION

(billions of dollars)

	Moore's Estimates			Bureau of Economics' Estimates	
Type of Loss	Low	Medium	High	Low	High
Inefficient use of mode					
Railroads	$1.7	$2.0	$2.4	$ 0.0	$0.0
Common carrier trucks	1.4	1.7	1.9	(2.2)	1.0
Private trucks	0.1	0.2	1.0	0.0	0.0
Water carriers	0.2	0.3	0.3	0.0	0.0
Subtotal	3.4	4.2	5.6	(2.2)	1.0
Modal choice	0.2	1.1	2.9	(0.4)	0.0
Traffic not carried	0.2	0.3	0.4	(0.2)	0.0
Total estimated loss (1968 base)	3.8	5.6	8.9	(2.8)	1.0
Total estimated loss[a] (1975 base)	6.5	9.6	15.2	(4.8)	1.7

[a] Dr. Moore's cost estimates were expressed in 1968 dollars. Since complete data are not yet available for 1975, Dr. Moore's individual cost categories were evaluated in terms of 1968 data and then inflated to a 1975 dollar base.

Note: Figures in parentheses indicate a benefit.

aggregated. Private, contract, and common carriers are treated as one mode, whereas, realistically, they are distinct competing modes offering different services. Also, the price elasticities and cross-elasticities for the different modes are observed to vary greatly among commodities, regions, types of traffic, and types of carrier.

A variable not adequately explained by these equations is the service factor. This was demonstrated dramatically during the analysis when data for various time periods were used and results compared. A variety of different elasticity coefficients resulted, depending on the time period chosen. Such results were not considered definitive. Rather it was believed that with additional, extended research it would be possible to derive more representative demand equations which would take time variables into account and would better explain the determinants of freight transportation demand.

The supply side of the freight transportation question also needs closer examination. It has been commonly assumed that, if the truck industry were deregulated, it would be composed of many highly competitive firms. There is evidence to suggest that this assumption is highly questionable, particularly with regard to LTL traffic.[16]

Although Dr. Moore attempted to assess the major costs of ICC regulation arising from the alleged inefficiencies in the transportation sector, his framework cannot be considered a complete economic analysis of ICC regulation. The entire benefit side of ICC regulation was ignored in his study. Without a review of benefits, a comprehensive assessment of the usefulness of public policy is impossible. To correct this shortcoming, the following section deals with the analysis of benefits, in terms of both their identification and their quantification.

Benefits of ICC Regulation: An Evaluation

Introduction. Even before the establishment of the Interstate Commerce Commission, drafters of what became the Act to Regulate Commerce extolled the benefits of the regulation of the transportation industry which then existed. Since its establishment the commission has been administering the act, which was developed on the basis of its perceived benefit to the public. The benefits of interstate commerce regulatory legislation, highly visible at the time of passage, were considered to far outweigh any cost involved. Discrimination, preference, excessive profits, rebating, drawbacks, and other unsavory practices were not simply a potential or theoretical danger to be guarded against, they were and had been for some time very real and unhappy facts of economic life. The capacity of big shippers to dominate and overpower small competitors simply by reason of their transportation bargaining leverage was overshadowed only by the railroads' own power over all shippers—big and small—and over waterborne competitors, who represented their only threat to total transport monopoly. There was no serious question about the benefits of effective regulation under such conditions. The public interest and the national interest clearly demanded it. The nation had made and was making, as a matter of public policy, an enormous investment in railroads, and regulation was seen as clearly in the national interest, including regulation of the railroads. It is particularly

16 See D. Daryl Wyckoff, "Factors Promoting Concentration of Motor Carriers Under Deregulation," in *Proceedings of the Fifteenth Annual Meeting, Transportation Research Forum*, vol. 15 (1974), pp. 1-6.

significant that no assumption was made then that because regulation might be beneficial to a special interest—namely, the carriers—it must be presumed detrimental to the public interest. It was not believed that public interest and vested (private) interests were automatically in conflict. Little effort, however, was or has since been made to quantify those perceived benefits into dollars.

In the previous section it was observed that most critics implicitly base their position on the belief that the economic regulation of transportation is inefficient because regulation cannot simulate the conditions of free market resource allocation. The ICC is criticized for (1) protecting carriers from competition, (2) restricting entry and thereby stifling new motor common carrier entry, (3) unnecessarily holding up the rates of carriers, (4) stifling carrier innovation, (5) allowing mergers where no economies of scale exist, and (6) permitting a host of other inefficient actions. Dr. Thomas G. Moore, as has been noted, claims that the price of such inefficiency may be as high as $15 billion annually.

Dr. Moore's study totally ignores the benefits of regulation, a side of the process which must be included in any analytical approach. This section identifies and quantifies some of the benefits of regulation.

The economic justification for regulation is inherently benefit oriented. According to accepted economic theory, regulation or partial exemption from competitive market processes may be desirable when one or more of three conditions are found within an industry:

(1) Competition cannot exist for long, and will therefore not produce optimum results;

(2) Competition can exist, but because of market imperfections will not produce all of the desirable results; and

(3) Competition can exist and produce optimum results, but because of other policy goals this is not desirable.

In each situation regulation suggests a means to make necessary corrections and, thereby, to assure public benefits that would be reduced or absent if sole reliance were placed on the competitive market system. Thus, the magnitude of benefits resulting from ICC regulation largely depends on the degree to which market imperfections would develop as a consequence of deregulation.

The process of evaluation involves *identifying* and *quantifying* areas of benefit. In this section, the major areas which tend to be affected by regulatory policy both in the transportation industry and in the rest of the economy have been examined. During the first identification phase, careful considerations were given to avoid double-counting of benefits, to distinguish between internal and external effects, and to assess both direct and indirect impacts.

The second phase involved quantifying those regulatory benefits. Here the magnitudes of various social gains were established in several important benefit areas, and annual dollar estimates were provided. But several areas—such as the value of motor carrier operating authority, the value of financial stability, national defense, and the value of the absence of rate discrimination—were not estimated. Despite the fact that benefit dollar values were assigned to significant functions of regulation, the thrust of this section lies not so much in the dollar estimates of key benefits, but in the approach that was taken to make possible a program of ICC policy assessment. Its comprehensive and pioneering effort provides the elements and outline of a cost/benefit evaluation program of regulatory functions.

Rationale for Motor Carrier Operating Authority Regulation. Some general views will be presented first, and then the legal foundations will be discussed.

General views. The provisions of the act dealing with operating authority are of benefit to the public in two broad ways. The process attempts to assure adequate service when a need is established for that service and to assure that the certificated common carriers are capable of and actually do provide adequate service.

Once "public convenience and necessity" (PC&N) has been established and grants of operating authority have been awarded, the commission has the additional ongoing responsibility of assuring that the carriers continue to satisfy both the PC&N and the fitness requirements in a way which complies totally with the provisions of the act. Rates, charges, and rules must be filed, made public, and adhered to. Failure to provide required services, conduct of operations beyond the scope of authority, failure to adhere to applicable tariffs, and willful failure to file required data with the commission will bring fines and/or suspension (possibly even revocation) of authority against the offending carrier.

A strong presumption can be made (and is made by critics of regulation) that, where the elements of PC&N exist, market forces will, given the opportunity, satisfy the need. The law of supply and demand is far more efficient than the laws administered under regulatory fiat. In an industry where the threshold costs of entry are relatively low—and certain trucking industry segments fall into that category (notably truckload traffic)—the argument has some substance, *if* one overlooks the public utility characteristics of public transportation. The argument assumes, a priori, that PC&N is to be measured exclusively in microeconomic terms, that is, the need of individual economic entities or production units. If one accepts that premise, then the only regulatory issues governing operating authority would relate to the fitness requirements of safety, financial viability, and integrity. The benefits of such fitness requirements and the concurrent cost of achieving them generally are not in serious dispute. What are in serious dispute are the benefits of adhering to the PC&N requirements of entry and operating authority regulation.

In a study submitted to the American Society of Traffic and Transportation (AST&T) for publication in the Winter 1975 issue of its *Transportation Journal,* Theodore O. Wallin, director of the Transportation Distribution Management Program at Syracuse University, has produced an excellent statement of the benefits which the economic regulation (including operating authority) of transportation strives to achieve. Wallin states:

> Economic regulation has as its traditional aim the assurance that the benefits of competition—if not de facto competition itself—will be achieved in a situation—namely, transportation in which workable competition is not a necessary eventuality. The argument, easily applied to the rail monopoly, can be expanded with minimal difficulty to the situation of overcompetition corrected by route, price, and service regulation. This perennial and highly-developed approach to the rationale of economic regulation is hardly, however, complete, despite textbook implications to the contrary. Economic regulation exists not only—or even, perhaps primarily—to achieve the benefits of competition; it provides as well a vitally important tool in the achievement of social, or non-economic goals. Transportation is imbued with public interests, one of which is efficiency; at the same time, though, regulation provides an ample and enviable tool of primarily social goals: national defense, economic development, competition (sometimes preservation of alternatives at the expense of efficiency), service (often to the degree of maintaining uneconomic operations), ecology, and special interests (such as the postal service). There would be no guarantee without regulation that a transportation system geared to achieving these goals would prevail, largely because these social goals hold no economic payoff.[17]

---

[17] Theodore O. Wallin, "Alternatives in Transport Policy: A Matrix Approach," *Transportation Journal*, vol. 15 (Winter 1975), p. 43.

Another timely discussion of regulatory benefits and objectives is a paper presented by Dr. Robert W. Harbeson of the University of Illinois at the 1975 meeting of the American Economic Association in Dallas. Dr. Harbeson said, in part:

> The transport policies of the United States and virtually all other countries have almost from the beginning reflected, explicitly or implicitly, various economic and social objectives in addition to the competitive pricing standard. In the United States these objectives have included economic growth, regional development, distribution equity, and, in recent years, environmental protection and resource conservation. It should be noted in this connection that to the extent that the competitive pricing standard has been approved as a policy objective it has been because its distributional effects have been regarded as preferable to those of unregulated monopoly or oligopoly; there is no evidence that this standard has been approved because of an understanding of, or concern for, its economic efficiency implications.[18]

It is probably necessary and certainly appropriate to define what is meant by the term "public convenience and necessity." As is true with almost all interpretations of the provisions of the act, the definition of this term has developed through case litigation and agency proceedings. The social and economic benefits of regulation largely are based upon having established, defined, and pursued these goals.

Legal foundations. The meaning of the term "public convenience and necessity" is stated in section 1(18) of Part I (Railroads) of the act: "no carrier by railroad . . . shall undertake the extension of its line . . . unless and until there shall first have been obtained from the Commission a certificate that the present or future public convenience and necessity require or will require (the) . . . operation . . ."[19] Section 207 of Part II (Motor Carriers) of the act states: "[a] certificate shall be issued . . . if it is found . . . that the proposed service . . . will be required by the present or future public convenience and necessity . . ."[20]

---

18 Robert W. Harbeson, "Social Welfare and Economic Efficiency in Transport Policy," paper presented at the annual meeting of the American Economic Association, Dallas, Texas, December 29, 1975.

19 49 U.S.C., section 1 (18).

20 Ibid., section 207.

Some of the leading decisions establishing the definition for motor carriers add further substance to the basic legislation:

> The question, in substance, is whether the new operation or service will serve a useful public purpose, responsive to a public demand or need; whether this purpose can and will be served as well by existing lines or carriers; and whether it can be served by applicant with the new operation or service proposed without endangering or impairing the operations of existing carriers contrary to the public interest.[21]

> The phrase "convenience and necessity" implies more than mere adequacy for availability of agencies by which a traveler can be conveyed from one point to another, without regard to special and distinguishing characteristics of the service afforded, just as it implies something less than an absolute and acute need.[22]

> Based upon the tripartite test of *Pan-American Bus Lines Operations, supra,* the operations and services of protesting carriers must not be ignored under any circumstances, and the effect of a grant of authority upon the total quantity and quality of service available to the public must be weighed to determine where on balance the public interest may lie.[23]

> The issue before the Commission is not whether the service of existing carriers has met some "absolute standard of performance, but whether the public convenience and necessity would be served by the entry of new carriers to the markets served . . ." by existing carriers.[24]

Finally, these decisions demonstrate and define the primary responsibility of common carriage—the obligation to provide service to the public. The magnitude of benefits attributable to this obligation depends heavily on the degree to which this is achieved.

The Benefits of Motor Carrier Regulation. Regulated carriers benefit from operating authority control through the *stability* which such

---

[21] Pan-American Bus Lines Operations, 1 M.C.C. 190, 203 (1936).

[22] All American Bus Lines, Inc., Common Carrier Application, 18 M.C.C. 755, 776 (1939).

[23] Motor Carriers of Property, Routes and Services, Ex Parte No. 55 (Sub-No. 8), 119 M.C.C. 170, 187 (1973).

[24] Bowman Transportation v. Arkansas Best Freight System, 42 L.Ed. 2d 447, 95 S. Ct. 438 (1974).

control brings to the industry itself. The value of this stability is especially apparent in two areas: the cost of capital and the financial ability to provide service to marginally profitable traffic.

Cost of capital. The financial integrity of individual firms and industries is recognized as being of paramount importance in contributing to the economic stability and steady growth in productivity of the United States.

In the June 1973 issue of the *Federal Reserve Bulletin,* Arthur Burns, chairman of the Federal Reserve Board, wrote:

> Throughout business-cycle history the major force making for economic instability has been the rather large fluctuation characteristic of business investment. At times, of course, the spending and taxing policies of government have been a source of economic trouble, especially in connection with wars and their financing. On occasion, also, large changes in the spending propensities of consumers have played their part in carrying aggregate activity to unsustainably high, or unacceptably low levels. But it is in the pronounced changes of the investment plans of business firms, with respect both to their fixed capital and inventories, that much of the cyclical instability of advanced industrial economies has originated.
>
> Business investment is, of course, vital to the growth in productivity, and the improvement in material welfare, to which all nations aspire. Over the long run, incentives to invest therefore need to be enhanced. But it would be far better if a high average level of investment could be achieved without the sizable fluctuations that have characterized the past. The general economy would benefit from a reduction of this source of instability. Business enterprises would also benefit from a more regular pace of investment, since they would thus avoid a concentration of expenditures at times when financing costs are high, when the capabilities of suppliers are strained, and when delivery and installation dates become more uncertain.

Transport Statistics in the United States for 1972 and 1973 show that long-term debt for Class I motor carriers—as a percentage of total capital structure—was 33 percent. For some carriers, of course, the debt/capital structure ratio is much higher. Carriers depend on a high cash flow in order to service this debt. To the extent that deregulation would reduce cash flow, debt servicing could be made difficult, if not impossible.

In an investment research report released in November 1975 addressing the proposed Motor Carrier Reform Act, Blyth, Eastman, Dillon and Company stated:

> The overall effect of this legislation, if passed, would be to substantially increase competition, reduce the potential market served, lower rates and revenues and culminate in lower rates of return on investment to motor carriers. Many marginal carriers would be forced under in a very short time after enactment, thereby increasing unemployment. Even the stronger carriers' returns would be reduced, so that they would be unable to attract investment capital for growth or just to renew their equipment fleets. The risk level would be increased tremendously for the industry, which already has been judged as one of the highest of any U.S. industry, regulated or not, in the "Sum of Money" study by Irving Silberman. If industry returns are currently inadequate to compensate for the added risk incurred, deregulation would hasten the flow of capital away from this industry and lead to its demise. This in classical economic theory would be an appropriate end for an industry that has nothing to offer. Unfortunately, there are no substitute means for moving the level of traffic now handled by the common carriers and numerous disruptions in the distribution cycle would occur. In the end it would be more rather than less costly to the consumer.

The regulated motor carriers survived the recent recession with relatively few bankruptcies, although there were layoffs and unused capacity. Had freedom of entry existed prior to the recession, there probably would have been many motor carrier failures. The 1975 *Financial Analysis of the Motor Carrier Industry* prepared by the First National Bank of Boston (the country's foremost lender to the motor carrier industry) stated:

> There is little doubt that some potential providers of capital have, and may continue to delay investing in motor carriers and other transport modes due to the fear of the unknown. It may appear strange, but it is a fact that an industry which has had difficulty attracting capital because it is regulated will also encounter many problems in attracting funds from equity sources in the event of deregulation. It is agreed that government must concern itself with the consumers' (voters') welfare. However, replacing a functioning system with a no controls, hands-off policy may cost the public incalculable sums to correct, if in fact the

> damage is reparable. . . . In view of the recent rapid appreciation and possible temporary peaking of motor carrier stocks, together with many blue chips still selling below book, the investor may opt to place his dollars in other than motor carrier stocks. It follows that there may be difficulty in raising equity to finance a company's acquisitions and normal growth. It is again important to point out that motor carriers realistically are not first in line when institutions are in the market to purchase debt, and if conditions are tight, the motor carrier's chances are non-existent.

With deregulation, the existence of an excess number of firms in the motor carrier industry would reduce efficiency not only by diluting equipment utilization and introducing destructive competition, but also by greatly increasing uncertainty—a word that strikes fear into the hearts of individual investors and financial institutions.

Since passage of the Motor Carrier Act, the regulated motor carrier industry has demonstrated a financial responsibility that has contributed significantly to the growth of the industry and to the industries and regions it serves. Regulation has ensured that rate increases have been cost justified, reflecting the impact of spiraling costs rather than helping to fuel the fires of inflation of the last few years.

Of critical importance to stability, growth, and efficiency in the motor carrier industry is the confidence that the investment and banking communities have in the industry. The introduction of more uncertainty to any business has at least two detrimental effects. First, because the risk is increased, equity financing becomes less attractive, forcing greater reliance on debt financing. Second, the introduction of greater risk/uncertainty inevitably increases the cost of debt financing, regardless of the debt instrument. Only a handful of carriers would be relieved from the impact of higher cost in debt financing under economic deregulation. It is estimated that marginal carriers would face increases in interstate rates of at least 1 to 2 percent above present rates, and the majority of carriers would likely be required to pay at least 1 percent more.[25] As an initial order of magnitude estimate, it is believed that the cost of capital to

[25] The financial community agrees with the premise that, as risk and uncertainty rise, pressure for higher interest yields will rise, as will the probability that loans will not be available at any interest rate. Although the financial community is reluctant to predict any precise upward movements in interest rates or in the number of rejections, we believe increases of the magnitude suggested would not be unwarranted.

regulated motor common carriers would increase under deregulation of entry and rates by at least $35 million annually: [26]

Debt Financing

1% additional interest on $1.2 billion of long-term debt	$12 million
10% of $470 million additional debt needed as result of shift from equity financing, less 5% of $470 million (dividends avoided)	23 million
Total additional cost of capital	$35 million

A conservative estimate is that deregulation would result in an eventual shift of 20 percent of $2.348 billion of equity financing to debt financing. The additional cost of debt over equity financing initially is calculated as follows: 20 percent of $2.348 billion = approximately $470 million; multiplying this by 10 percent interest rate = $47 million interest on additional debt; subtracting from this $23.5 million avoided dividends (estimated 5 percent of $470 million) = $23.5 million additional cost of debt over equity financing.

Rural areas and small business. Any scenario which scrutinizes the motor carrier industry under deregulation must consider the possible adverse impact upon small shippers and rural communities.

1. Inventory holding costs: The probable reduction in the reliability of service that is likely to result would cause shippers and receivers to react in a number of ways, one of the more observable of which would be by making less frequent but larger shipments. The consequent impact of such a reaction can be measured in terms of the resulting changes in inventory levels, in terms of the greater use of private trucking (at higher cost), or in terms of both.

Unfortunately, such a reaction would aggravate the disadvantage already encountered by small shippers (in remote areas). In a review of the overall problem of small shipments, the American University stated:

> Marketing changes today will probably increase rather than reduce the numerous problems involved in the future handling of small shipments. Continuing a trend taking

[26] According to figures taken from *Transport Statistics in the United States* for 1972 and 1973, the long-term debt for Class I carriers is $1.135 billion and the total long-term debt for both Class I and Class II carriers is $1.228 billion. The shareholders' (or proprietors') equity for Class I carriers was $2.284 billion in 1973 and the total shareholders' equity for both Class I and Class II carriers was $2.348 billion.

> form shortly after the end of the late war, the proliferation of products and the increasing tempo of competition among sellers, especially distribution outlets, will aggravate the problems of small shipments, in the absence of positive steps to consolidate, containerize, and give special attention to these shipments. . . . Currently, based on interviews, questionnaires, and other contacts, the trend apparently is to reduce both the size and weight of small shipments. Whether (because of) uncertainty as to business conditions or sharpening competition and price cutting, the present practice of many retailers is to maintain minimum inventories and to engage in "hand-to-mouth" buying. In effect, inventory is carried "in the distribution pipeline" rather than in the warehouse or on the retailer's shelves. There is very little likelihood that this trend will be reversed.[27]

It seems highly probable that deregulation would result in less reliable, slower, and less frequent truck service to small communities.[28] Small businessmen would be faced with the prospect of continuing to follow normal reorder cycles and encounter "stock out" situations. There are certain alternative options—such as catalog ordering and reducing variety. Clearly, however, ordering in larger quantities (to save on increased shipping costs) less frequently would seem a typical response to insure continuation of the normal customs of the business and expectations of customers. It would not be unreasonable to expect business to add one week's to one month's additional supply to average inventory. At such a level the cost for holding additional inventory is estimated to be: [29]

One week's supply	\$ 59 million
One month's supply	\$259 million

---

[27] American University, *Small Shipments—A Matter of National Concern,* final report prepared for the U.S. Department of Transportation, January 1974, pp. 257-58.

[28] See American Trucking Associations, *Small Town Blues* (Washington, D.C., May 1976).

[29] These amounts are based on the following figures and represent what are believed to be conservative estimates: (1) 1970 census rural area population of 53.9 million persons (26.5 percent of the United States). (2) Annual income of \$1,400 per capita. (3) Annual income spent on retail inventory items: \$1,400 × 40 percent = \$560. (4) Income spent on retail inventory transported to retail units by regulated common carrier: ½ of \$560 (est.) = \$280. (5) One month's inventory usage per capita: 280 ÷ 12 = about \$23. (6) One month's inventory usage for rural population: 53.9 million × \$23, transported by regulated common carrier = \$1,240 million. (7) At holding rate of 20 percent per year, annual cost of holding one month's additional supply of average inventory = \$258 million. (8) Annual cost for holding one week's additional average inventory = \$59 million.

The cost impact of other alternatives, such as reduced variety or the effects of less reliable transportation service for highly service-oriented businesses, have not been quantified. Undoubtedly, these would have a long-term measurable effect upon the continued viability of a merchant in a small town attempting to continue to compete in his traditional market.

2. Service of marginally profitable traffic: Motor common carriers of passengers and freight incur an obligation to provide service for all traffic tendered (with certain minor exceptions) within the scope of the granted operating authority. "Bad freight" must be handled along with the "good," the profitable along with the marginally profitable. Therefore, the ability to provide service to relatively undesirable traffic is dependent largely upon the opportunity which the carrier's operating certificates offer to handle relatively desirable traffic.

A terminal, a bus, or an over-the-road truck is classified as a "lumpy" resource, because of both its inherent capacity and the high proportion of fixed labor costs incurred in its operation. Unless available traffic is well matched to a service need, excess capacity (low load factors) will create inefficiencies and will result in relatively high operating costs. There is little chance of such a result occurring between two major traffic-producing areas or in cases in which easily and heavily loaded freight traffic generates the major portion of total revenues. But in cases where the carrier is obligated to serve sparsely populated areas or handle shipments which pose transportation problems, a way was found to accommodate both needs and still assure carrier solvency. Such a solution, known as "cross-subsidization," is not uncommon and is an accepted norm in virtually all businesses. Under transport regulation, reasonable discrimination is permissible; however, unjust discrimination is not allowed. Therefore, this principle, although controlled, serves to benefit all by providing a climate of reasonable equity. The pure theorist, however, finds such a concept inefficient and unacceptable.

Essentially the question is: do the benefits made possible by regulation, such as preserving motor common carrier services to small or out-of-the-way users or to producers of necessary but less than "ideal" traffic, outweigh its costs?

Benefits from transport regulation are often found in the form of broad, national impacts which are partially the result of ICC policy. For example, the consideration of transport service to rural areas has associated with it national policy ramifications, such as the desirability of concentrating economic activity and population in metropolitan centers and the extent to which population distribution and concentration are affected. Although these are important issues, analysis of such a broad mandate is seen to be beyond the scope of this research effort. However, future studies will consider these secondary benefits in greater detail.

A possible approach for quantifying these benefits would be the following: for a given set of national priorities, which include protection and preservation of small businesses and rural communities, those public expenditures and subsidies which are currently channeled into the preservation and promotion of these conditions can provide a useful dollar measure of the benefits to the nation of preserving rural communities and small businesses. In contrast, motor transport systems (the economic lifeline of most communities and businesses) have been preserved under regulatory guidance without the need for such direct external subsidies. The exact magnitude of internal or indirect (cross) industry-devised subsidies, however, is extremely difficult to measure. Although there is a belief that the amount is substantial, it is probably less than would be necessary under alternative government subsidy programs. A further advantage of "internal" subsidy is its tendency to assure a close linkage between those who pay for and those who benefit from the service in question.

A deregulation scenario without subsidy support would tend to insure that small businesses and rural communities would eventually be isolated from the "mainstream." This would occur by way of an almost immediate withdrawal of substantial portions of rail service, and it would be only partially abated through the substitution of limited amounts of motor carrier service at a significant increase in rates. The effects on production, inventory, marketing, and sales cost to small businesses, especially in rural areas, would likely be substantial in all cases and would generally lead to a certain termination of the various contributions of these areas to our economy and public welfare.

The logical offset to such a result would be external subsidization in some form, although the exact amount is not easily determinable. However, approximate requirements can be inferred from programs that are already in existence and committed to aid programs for small business and rural areas. On the basis of the numerous administrative considerations which underlie many of these current programs, one might logically expect that a similar bureaucracy would be necessary to insure adequate transportation service without regulation. The substitution of subsidies for regulation would require a control mechanism for assessing the need and

Table 2-4

FEDERAL GRANTS AND LOANS TO SMALL BUSINESSES AND RURAL AREAS, FISCAL YEARS 1974–1976

(billions of dollars)

	1974 (actual)	1975 (estimate)	1976 (estimate)
Grants			
Total	46.0	52.6	55.6
SMSA	32.2	36.7	39.0
Non-SMSA	13.8	15.9	16.6
Loans[a]			
Total	2.07	1.70	2.20
Non-SMSA	0.83	0.68	0.88

[a] Loans approved by the Small Business Administration. The SBA estimates that approximately 40 percent of such loans are directed to non-SMSA businesses.

Note: SMSA refers to standard metropolitan statistical area.

Sources: For grants, U.S. Bureau of the Budget, *The Budget for Fiscal Year 1976*, Special Analysis, pp. 241-45. For loans, the data was provided by the Small Business Administration.

assigning subsidies at the appropriate level. In effect, its result would consist of a new type of "control mechanism" in place of regulation. It is difficult to speculate on the appropriate level of subsidy, and the possibility that this new mechanism might well result in a higher level than the present cross-subsidy system cannot be lightly dismissed.

Even in the event that external subsidy is substituted for internal cross-subsidy, there is no guarantee that the market mechanism could wring all of the so-called excess cost attributable to cross-subsidization out of the present rate structure. It is an economic axiom that prices tend to be inflexible in the downward direction. As a point of reference, the $360 million in federal subsidy funds available for light-density lines through the Railroad Revitalization and Regulatory Reform Act of 1976 promises no reduction in rates upon application of funds to preserve the line. More likely is the possibility that various surcharge or cost-sharing plans will be advanced to ameliorate the impact on public cost.

Although no attempt is made at this time to compute the dollar value of a subsidy program which would be necessary absent regulation, an approximation of the magnitude can be inferred from the size of current public expenditures designed to preserve the viability of small businesses and rural areas (see Table 2-4). It would appear highly likely that with deregulation a substitute mechanism would be necessary to deal with the economic and social objectives which the internal cross-subsidy mechanism has satisfied, and that the total cost would surely be greater than the total cost of the present system.

3. Rate stability: The benefit of rate stability under regulation consists primarily of its effect on the level of risk. Stable rates tend to reduce risk and thus exert a positive influence on business activity. Regulation provides certain guidelines which assure general stability of rates over time; the rates can be modified only on the basis of proper justification. This tends to create a relatively stable and reliable rate climate, with rate adjustments occurring in increments which allow the economy to anticipate and adjust to change with limited difficulty. In contrast, experiences under deregulation in Australia in providing service to remote areas and those in connection with the trucking of exempt commodities in the United States suggest that this element of stability would certainly be lost should regulation be removed. Rates would fluctuate rather substantially with demand cycles, with the possible results of exerting destabilizing pressure on general business cycles as well as increasing the level of risk of conducting business. Both effects have a tendency to influence adversely total business activity. Because of the enormous task such measurement would entail, this benefit has not been quantified in this study.

The Benefits of Rail Regulation. Economic benefits result from ICC regulation of the railroads in the form of rail abandonment proceedings and impacts on rate level and rate structure.

Rail abandonment proceedings. Much of the reasoning and many of the conclusions reached in connection with the reduction of motor carrier service would apply equally to the rail mode in terms of "train-offs" and line abandonment. There are, however, some rather significant differences in the analytical approach to measuring the benefits of rail abandonments. These differences arise from three factors:

(1) Rail abandonment has a finality not found in motor-common-carrier service cessation. Removal of truck service still leaves the highways intact, while rail abandonment generally removes the infrastructure with it, including the property, the roadbed, and the track structure.

(2) The ratio of fixed to total costs for railroads is much greater than for motor carriers, especially if opportunity costs are

taken into account. "Train-offs," which eliminate operating expenses, for example, still have a large fixed asset in place upon which taxes continue to be levied, et cetera.

(3) There is no viable substitute for rail service for many shippers. Size, weight, type of product, or the economics of marketplace simply dictate the use of rail service if the shipper is to remain competitively viable.

The benefits of the regulation of abandonment proceedings can be quantified in terms of the potential cost to industry, communities, and society in the form of traffic permanently lost as a result of unfettered abandonment allowed by deregulation. Under deregulation and the consequent removal of standards requiring management to justify its decisions, it seems clear that extensive abandonment of branch lines would inevitably occur. There were 216 abandonment cases pending before the commission as of March 18, 1976, calling for the termination of 6,049.57 miles of track. By adding 5,000 miles to the mileage proposed to be abandoned, under the Regional Rail Reorganization Act of 1973, the total mileage currently proposed for abandonment exceeds 11,000 miles or 3.2 percent of the entire U.S. system. It would seem reasonable to expect, however, that abandonment under deregulation (which would ignore all factors other than carrier analysis and judgment of the line's viability in terms of its contribution to profits) would be much greater. Abandonment of so-called duplicating lines and lines considered to be marginal under a narrow profit test could result in substantial additional abandonments. Probably no single estimate of the number of lines and/or the total mileage would meet the standards necessary for a generally acceptable scenario.[30] For purposes of testing possible impacts, however, it would not be unreasonable to assume that, under tough "cost effective" management standards, mileage abandonment could quadruple, and that only 87 percent of the present total rail mileage would remain in operation following deregulation. Under such conditions, an estimated 3 to 4 percent of the total U.S. rail traffic would likely be permanently lost for various reasons. Such a loss of total rail traffic would have considerable economic impact on the nation, particularly in rural areas. An impact on gross national product (GNP) of approximately $300 million could be foreseen, not including the effects on unemployment. The different priorities and

[30] See United States Railway Association, *Final System Plan*, volumes I and II (Washington, D.C., July 1975); and U.S. Department of Transportation, *Railroad Abandonment and Alternatives: Report on Effects Outside of the Northeast Region*, May 1976.

standards which obligate the furnishing of such service under regulation have, however, prevented such an impact. Consequently, it is possible to estimate that the benefit to society of abandonment regulation is $300 million per year.[31]

Rate level. Regulation has tended to act as a brake on carrier contribution to inflation by requiring, upon challenge, that rate increases be justified as necessary and appropriate. Measurements suggest that carrier rates have generally reflected a lesser inflationary trend than the economy as a whole.

Using 1969 as a base year (1969 = 100), the wholesale price index had risen 64.2 percent through the end of 1975. During the same period (1969–1975) the regulated motor-common-carrier freight rate index rose by 41.0 percent, based upon analysis of general increases

Table 2-5
COMPARISON OF WHOLESALE PRICE INDEX WITH RAIL AND TRUCK FREIGHT RATE INDEXES, 1969–1975

Year	Wholesale Price Index	Rail	Truck
1969	100.0	100.0	100.0
1970	103.6	108.8	107.8
1971	107.0	123.4	117.2
1972	111.8	126.1	119.9
1973	126.5	129.3	120.4
1974	150.3	149.7	135.0
1975	164.2	169.4	141.0

Source: General rate increases granted by the ICC weighted by traffic volume, as compiled by the Bureau of Economics and the Department of Labor, Bureau of Labor Statistics.

[31] The analysis was based primarily on the research work in the area of inter-industry economic analysis conducted by the Bureau of Economic Analysis at the U.S. Department of Commerce. With the aid of 1963 and 1967 national input–output tables, estimates of economic impacts on levels of GNP and industry outputs were derived as a consequence of certain rail traffic assumptions. The estimate does not include expected impacts on the quality of the environment, land use, energy usage, and expected carrier savings as a result of the abandonments. See also Jack Faucett and Associates, *The Potential Economic Impact of a Sudden Termination of Operation of the Penn Central Railroad,* study prepared for the U.S. Department of Transportation, 1970 and 1973; and B. J. Allen, "The Economic Effects of Rail Abandonment on Communities: A Case Study" (Ph.D. diss., University of Illinois, 1974).

actually granted by the ICC. Had regulated motor carrier rates risen to the same level as the wholesale price index, the regulated motor carrier freight bill for 1975 would have been $26,435 million instead of the estimated actual amount of $22,700 million. (See Table 2–5.) This difference of $3,735 million would probably have been even greater absent regulation, since escalating fuel costs in 1975 had a much greater impact on motor carriers than on the general economy. Moreover, to the extent the estimate overlooks hold-downs, rollbacks, and rates negotiated between individual carriers and shippers (without reference to general increases), the truck index is somewhat inflated.

On the other hand, during the same period (1969–1975) the rail rate index rose to 169.4, while the wholesale price index had risen only to 164.2. Had the rail index risen only as fast as the wholesale price index, the 1975 rail freight bill would have been $15.3 billion, instead of $15.8 billion (preliminary), or $500 million less than actual. Even so, it is clear that the railroads have not enjoyed generous profits or overall real prosperity. Given the current rail labor and tax environment, the continuous need of the industry for additional capital, and its tendency toward a monopolistic market structure, it is reasonable to expect that the rail rate level, if permitted to react solely to market pressures, would tend to rise after deregulation.

Had the aggregate freight rate index risen as high and as fast as the wholesale price index, it is estimated that the nation's annual common carrier freight bill (rail balanced with motor) would be higher by $3.24 billion.[32]

Rate discrimination. A fundamental intent of the Interstate Commerce Act is to prevent unreasonable rates, unjust discrimination, and undue preference or prejudice. Regulation of transport rates attempts to insure that the value-of-service (cross-subsidization) element in the rate structure is directed to achieve an overall benefit

---

32 This dollar value represents the benefit attributable to ICC impact on the rate level of the transport industry as differentiated from ICC impacts on the rate structure. Rate level benefits are measured in terms of the difference in the degree of inflation in the overall private market economy (as approximated by the WPI) and the transport industry (as measured by the freight rate indexes). It is assumed here that upward pressures in the rate level are predominantly attributable to a change in the market structure of the industry. In contrast to this effect there exists the rate structure effect on the overall price level because of changes in the rate structure. Here it is assumed that upward rate pressures are the result of a change in the commodity mix as well as a change in existing supply and demand conditions, which are expected to come about immediately after deregulation.

Figure 2-1

RATE STRUCTURE WITHIN AN ENVIRONMENT OF CROSS-SUBSIDIZATION

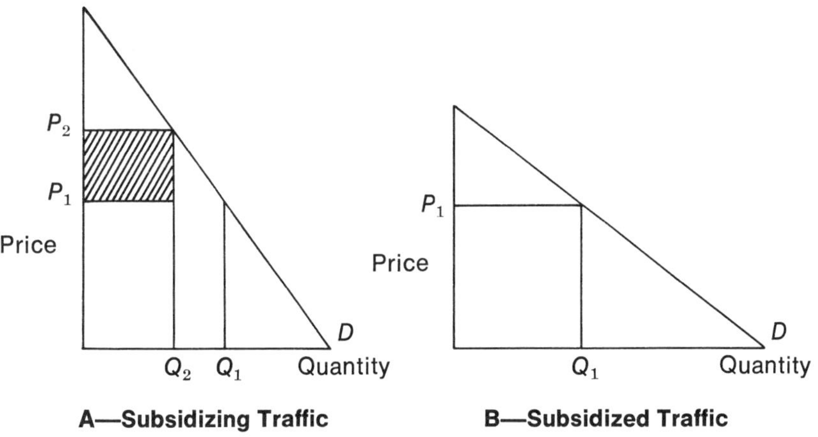

A—Subsidizing Traffic **B—Subsidized Traffic**

to the economy and society.[33] As noted, this includes benefits to rural areas and small shippers. Other benefits include: increased competition among shippers; increased choice of supplier and product, greater stability, and lower risk in location choice; maintenance of competitive viability, for example, through port relationships; and the provision of services in the public interest that might not otherwise be offered, for example, rail branch line service and motor carrier service to outlying communities. For railroads, it permits greater plant utilization and maximization of net revenue subject to limitations with respect to unjust discrimination.

A key responsibility in insuring a sound rate structure involves the judgment of a reasonable relationship among all of the elements of the structure. In this way the objective of regulation is not only to maximize the amount of total benefits, but also to insure the reasonable distribution of these benefits. This is presented graphically in Figure 2–1. Users of traffic A would be subsidizing users of traffic B, since the price of traffic A at P_2 exceeds its marginal cost so that traffic B's price at P_1 (at equal to its marginal cost) will not result in a diversion of traffic B. This form of cross-subsidization may be an

[33] Cross-subsidization exists within a given rate structure for a particular mode of transportation when certain categories of traffic make no, or a disporportionately low, contribution to overhead burden which has to be made up by higher rates on other traffic. Usually, this condition is expressed by comparing revenues to variable and fully allocated cost relationships.

acceptable policy in order to achieve a social goal; however, its desirability will depend very heavily on the extent to which the membership of each of the traffic user groups (A and B) can be clearly identified, in order to make the transfer or redistribution of income reasonable. The question of whether the general identification of various industrial shippers and commercial users of these transportation services is sufficient to justify the dilution of economically efficient pricing is central in the attempt to attach costs and benefits to alternative rate structures.

Quantification of the benefits derived from these "regulated relationships" is difficult to achieve if objectivity is to be preserved. However, one approach, used by Professors Grant Davis and Charles Sherwood, is the concept of marginal social benefits and marginal social costs. Simply stated, it emphasizes the rate of change in costs and benefits rather than changes in the totals. For example, if the ratio of marginal benefits divided by marginal costs exceeds one, the particular regulatory program is favorable. But, the difficulty is that this methodology does little to solve the problem of quantification, except to provide a means based on an incremental approach to quantification. Value judgments still have to be made regarding the quantity of what Professors Davis and Sherwood refer to as "indirect consumption benefits."[34] To measure accurately the benefits of cross-subsidization, it is first necessary to estimate the amount of such cross-subsidization and then its desired distribution. Market structures, as they have developed under regulation of rates and service, can be observed, but what adjustments the transportation industry would make to continue to accommodate those markets in the absence of regulation is open to speculation. In view of these difficulties, quantification is not possible within the scope of this study.

The Benefits of Service Regulation. In addition to those economic benefits which result from ICC regulation in the form of operating rights, abandonment proceedings, and rate level and rate structure policy impacts, regulation offers a benefit by insuring equitable and proper treatment in the area of service. These service benefits are found in the following areas:

- Car supply, service, embargoes, and reasonable dispatch;
- Loss and damage claims; and
- Movement of household goods.

---

[34] Grant M. Davis and Charles S. Sherwood, "Transportation Regulation: Another Dimension," *ICC Practitioners' Journal*, January-February 1975.

Car supply and service. In order to improve car service, regulation provides for incentives and/or imposes penalties, whichever is seen as necessary to improve the availability, utilization, and distribution of freight cars. Typical regulatory actions include the setting of requirements designed to insure that proper quantities and types of cars are made available to meet changing demands, imposing special charges when cars are in short supply, applying service rules designed to direct the distribution of certain cars to areas in which they are in short supply, setting various requirements relating to car repair, and designing regulations to insure sound coordination of equipment among railroads. Without this overview and enforcement role as exercised by the ICC, regional imbalances in equipment, the use of off-line cars, and proper coordination of traffic movements would likely result in critical problems to the carriers, the shippers, and the public.

The Section of Railroads at the Bureau of Operations conservatively estimates that a 5 percent greater rail car utilization is realized nationally because of the commission's car service efforts. This is to say, by virtue of its activities to achieve an efficient car distribution, this policy actually increases total rail capacity by 5 percent by maintaining a more timely balance between car supply and car demand. This is accomplished largely through demurrage rules and charges, interchange rules, embargoes, service orders, and other provisions stemming from service monitoring activities.

It is reasonable to believe, therefore, that the net investment in rolling stock by railroads, collectively, would be greater in the absence of regulation in order to handle current traffic volumes. Using a 1974 average freight car price index and applying a deflator to convert it to 1975 prices, the average cost per new freight car in 1975 was $23,790. There were 1,720,573 freight cars in service in 1974 (according to the Association of American Railroads as published in their annual book, *Railroad Facts*). Of that fleet, 5 percent (86,029 cars) would represent a one-time investment of $2,047 million in 1975 prices, plus financing costs. If one assumes that equipment trust certificates are normally issued to cover 80 percent of car costs extended over fifteen years and that interest rates are close to 9 percent, after making the initial down payment and allowing for amortization, the total annual benefit because of ICC car service efforts is $149 million.

Claims against carriers. Loss and damage claims to shipments carried by regulated carriers amount to about $500 million annually (approximately equally divided between motor carriers of property and railroads). The law requires, with limited exception, that carriers be responsible for the full value of any losses or damages attributable to them (unless shipments are made under released value rates approved by the commission). Carriers must be responsive to the party making the claim, both in acknowledging and in settling the claim. In addition, the commission also requires carriers to adhere to charging only the lowest applicable rates for movement of passengers and property and insists that valid claims for overcharges be settled in a timely manner.

If carriers were not required to be responsive to shippers' claims as under regulation, experience in somewhat parallel transportation environments suggests that it would be logical to expect the processing and payment of claims to be more costly. Under such conditions, as an expedient alternative, shippers would likely find it more convenient, if not necessary, to seek third-party cargo insurance (such as inland-marine insurance employed in overseas shipping) to assure prompt payment of claims and to provide relief from the increased problems connected with processing claims. Clearly, such insurance cost would increase shipping costs, which would eventually be passed on as higher consumer prices.

Domestic land carriers generally have had an excellent loss and damage record, presenting certain (perhaps substantial) distinctions from other transport situations where third-party insurance is customary. However, by way of comparison, third-party insurance paid by exporters using air and water carriers is generally fifteen cents per $100 of valuation for protection and insurance service comparable to that which might be necessary absent regulation. At such a rate, the premium cost to domestic surface shippers and receivers would total approximately $1,113 million. Since total insurance premiums generally equal the dollar value of loss and damage experienced, at such a premium level, the additional loss and damage cost in the absence of regulation could amount to as much as $613 million more than the present cost of $500 million.

Household goods. In this major area of consumer protection, the commission has taken an aggressive stand in making information available to consumers before they move, in alerting them to pertinent factors in selecting a mover, and in providing assistance when difficulties arise at moving time. Consumers are instructed about how to obtain help in handling complaints at all stages in the move and about how to satisfy possible loss and damage claims subsequent to the move. Each year the commission helps and advises thousands of people in this way, largely through the effort of field office personnel.

Without this protection, which has evolved with the experience offered by the commission, in cases of controversy, consumers would have little recourse (except the courts) to resolve problems that arise from inequitable and unfair treatment.

Although these service benefits are not readily quantifiable in the aggregate, it has been acknowledged, even by the moving industry, that the commission's persuasive power, its special attention to householders' problems, and its exacting requirements have helped relieve the source of many traditional difficulties. The commission has assured standards of service for the industry as a whole which are backed by the strength of stringent legal requirements. Clearly, deregulation would fail to provide a substitute for this type of consumer benefit.

Conclusion—Benefits. The benefits of surface transport regulation should be compared with certain costs attributable to regulation. As indicated earlier, the costs have received far more public attention than have the benefits. Generally, only a very limited effort has heretofore been attempted to provide a "balanced" comparison.

In the first part of this study, it was shown, upon review, that the costs are substantially lower than the amounts claimed by critics of regulation. Indeed, the results of the "high" alternative suggest "costs" may not even exist if Dr. Moore's methodology is followed. In this second section, the benefits of regulation have been identified and, as objectively as possible, have been reviewed and quantified with respect to one deregulation alternative. Since the weight of criticism has traditionally fallen on the regulatory control of motor carrier operating authority, the study included a substantial review of the overall objectives and foundations of motor common carrier regulation and operating authority regulation. The criteria used and methods employed to achieve those objectives were identified and discussed. In brief, the study suggested that regulation of operating authority attempts to achieve two broad objectives: first, to insure service adequate to the total needs of the public convenience and necessity (PC&N) without destructive competition and, second, to assure the fitness of those carriers granted such authority to serve. Although regulation of operating authority unquestionably benefits the motor carriers holding such authority, it does not follow that the public interest must necessarily suffer accordingly and proportionately. That is, a private interest is not automatically in conflict with the public interest.

Motor carriers benefit from entry control regulation significantly by facilitating capital formation and by virtue of certain protection from ruinous competition. Review showed the industry benefits (savings) to fall in the range of $35 million.

The economy benefits from the carrier obligation to provide adequate service and reasonable rate levels to rural areas and small shippers through transport stability and through assurance that service will be available on demand to all shippers on an equitable basis. In one effort to measure at least a portion of these benefits (particularly to rural areas), it was estimated that lower inventory levels because of regulatory assurance of service amounted to a benefit of $59 million. More significant savings were seen flowing from the fact that, with regulation, necessary service is available to less desirable or marginally profitable traffic and is beneficially handled under regulation without the need for external subsidies.

In the area of rate levels, the benefits of rate regulation resulted from containment and limitations of excessive inflationary pressures on the aggregate rate level. The value of $3.2 billion revealed a very substantial quantifiable benefit of regulation.

One other means to attempt to measure the magnitude of this effect was through comparing transport freight rate indexes with an index representative of the private market economy, in this case the wholesale price index (WPI). By such comparison it was estimated that regulation saves the public approximately $3.2 billion per year. The benefits of abandonment proceedings were also measured by way of gross national product (GNP) impacts, which equalled $300 million.

Service represents an additional area of benefits which was difficult to quantify. Potential abuses protected against by regulation were identified, and "loss and damage" benefits were quantified to equal $613 million.

Summary: ICC Costs and Benefits

Total deregulation of the surface transport industry would not necessarily solve current transportation problems, nor would it necessarily produce an optimal allocation of resources. From a social policy perspective, deregulation would have detrimental impacts on the public welfare. In fact, this study shows that the total level of ICC annual benefits could well double the level that has been estimated, since

Table 2-6
BUREAU OF ECONOMICS' ESTIMATES OF COSTS OF SURFACE TRANSPORTATION REGULATION
(billions of dollars)

Type of Loss	Cost
Inefficient use of mode	
Railroads	0.000
Common carrier trucks	(3.800)
Private trucks	0.000
Water carriers	0.000
Subtotal	(3.800)
Modal choice	(0.700)
Traffic not carried	(0.300)
Total estimated loss	(4.800)

Note: Cost figures in parentheses represent negative costs and are thus considered benefits.

several ICC benefits have not been quantified at this time. Total elimination of the ICC would likely result in the loss of billions of dollars annually in the form of resultant adverse impacts on shippers, the economy, the industry, and the public in general. These conclusions were reached as a result of this study.

The bureau's reevaluation of Dr. Thomas Gale Moore's cost figures as described in the first part of this study yielded the costs (benefits) as a result of the "low" alternative as shown in Table 2–6. These values dealt primarily with regulation impacts relative to economic efficiencies, and the total amounted to $4.8 billion (benefit).

To complement the estimates of the cost section with the benefit of regulation, this report also focused on regulatory impacts in addition to those of economic efficiency, such as the level of rates, rate discrimination, and service levels. These regulatory benefits also included impacts on other sectors of the economy in the form of GNP losses resulting from massive rail abandonment, inflation, and effects on inventory levels. For the purpose of an overview, the benefits which were quantified are shown in Table 2-7; they totaled $4.4 billion.

Table 2-7
BUREAU OF ECONOMICS' ESTIMATES OF BENEFITS OF SURFACE TRANSPORTATION REGULATION
(billions of dollars)

Type of Benefit	Value
Rate level	
Motor	3.740
Rail	(0.500)
Abandonment proceedings	0.300
Rail car utilization	0.149
Carrier financing	0.035
Inventory reductions	0.059
Loss and damage impact	0.613
Total estimated benefits	4.396

Note: Benefit figures in parentheses represent negative benefits and are thus considered costs.

Table 2-8 compares both the cost and the benefit estimates of the annual value of surface transport regulation. It can be perceived that the benefits assignable to motor carrier regulation are considerably higher than those assignable to other modes. In a number of instances factors which might have been significant to the level of benefits for another mode were at times not included nor quantified (for example, national defense might well be viewed as significant to the level of benefits in rail transportation). Therefore, the figures represent only the value of those components for which the quantification process was completed, and this did result in a disproportional distribution of benefits among modes. However, the study and its results have demonstrated a feasible methodology, and they represent a possible approach for identifying and measuring the benefits and costs of ICC regulation.

In view of the difficult problems associated with selecting the proper time horizon and the appropriate interest rate, the more "classical" cost/benefit methodology was not found to be very useful for the particular purpose at hand. Rather, the present analysis relied more heavily on the combination of separate research analyses, each uniquely designed to measure, assess, and evaluate particular areas where regulatory impacts were anticipated. Future research efforts, however, should examine more closely the feasibility of all cost/benefit techniques and their role in the regulatory process. This study represents a step in that direction.

Table 2-8

LISTING OF ICC VALUES OF BENEFITS

(billions of dollars)

Railroads	
Inefficient use of mode	0.000
Rate level	(0.500)
Rate discrimination	N/A
Abandonment proceedings	0.300
Rail car utilization	0.149
Motor carriers	
Inefficient use of mode (common)	3.800
Inefficient use of mode (private)	0.000
Rate level	3.740
Rate discrimination	N/A
Carrier financing	0.035
Inventory reduction	0.059
Water carriers	0.000
Modal choice	0.700
Traffic not carried	0.300
Loss and damages	0.613
Service stability	N/A
Excess capacity	N/A
Technology and innovation incentives	N/A
National defense	N/A
Environment and conservation	N/A

Notes: The above listings of ICC benefits represent the dollar values of the major impact areas which are affected by ICC regulation. The total value of these benefits equalled $9.2 billion. However, in view of the differences in assumptions which at times existed in the various methodologies used, aggregation of the estimates is not desirable. Instead, the $9.2 billion total should be considered as a maximum limit of attainable benefits (for the quantifiable categories) that can be attributed to ICC regulation. ICC budgetary expenditures ($45 million for FY 1975) are not included.

3

THE COSTS AND BENEFITS OF SURFACE TRANSPORT REGULATION: ANOTHER VIEW

W. Bruce Allen and Edward B. Hymson

Introduction and Summary

The Bureau of Economics of the Interstate Commerce Commission has prepared an economic analysis of the costs and benefits of economic regulation of surface transportation.[1] The bureau should be commended for undertaking such an analysis. A study of the costs and benefits associated with regulation prepared by the staff of a regulatory agency is most welcome. Unfortunately, its conclusion that society derives substantial net benefits from regulation is unsupported by the material it presents.

The first part of the bureau's study focuses on the costs of ICC regulation and consists almost entirely of an attempt to show that Professor Thomas G. Moore's well-publicized estimates of the costs of railroad and motor carrier regulation are incorrect.[2] The bureau

---

This paper is edited from a report which was originally prepared in 1976 under the auspices of the Office of Government Operations and Research of the U.S. Council on Wage and Price Stability. At that time, W. Bruce Allen was associate professor of regional science and transportation at the University of Pennsylvania; Edward B. Hymson was a senior economist with the U.S. Department of Transportation. The three appendixes in the original report have not been included here.

[1] Interstate Commerce Commission, Bureau of Economics, *A Cost and Benefit Evaluation of Surface Transport Regulation,* 1976. An edited version of the bureau's analysis is included in this volume as Chapter 2, and all references in the present paper to the bureau's analysis will be to pages in this volume.

[2] Thomas G. Moore, *Freight Transportation Regulation* (Washington, D.C.: American Enterprise Institute, 1972); idem, "Deregulating Surface Freight Transportation," in *Promoting Competition in Regulated Markets,* ed. Almarin Philips (Washington, D.C.: The Brookings Institution, 1975), pp. 55-98.

does this by questioning Moore's methodology and certain assumptions he adopts. It then chooses its own assumptions and, using Moore's basic methodology, estimates the costs of ICC regulation. The bureau's estimates turn out to be significantly lower than Moore's—ranging from an annual benefit of $4.8 billion to a cost of $1.7 billion, as opposed to Moore's cost estimates (inflated to 1975 dollars) ranging from a low of $6.5 billion to a high of $15.2 billion.

Next, the bureau tries to demonstrate that ICC regulation of railroads and motor carriers results in substantial benefits to society. The benefits alleged are increased price and service stability, lower motor carrier rates, lower motor carrier capital costs, lower firm inventory costs, better equipment utilization, lower cost of loss and damage, and a reduced rate of railroad abandonment. The bureau estimates that ICC regulation generated benefits to society of at least $4.4 billion during 1975, leading to the bureau's conclusion that regulation generates net benefits to society ranging from $2.7 billion to $9.2 billion annually.[3]

In our judgment, the bureau's study, though commendable in its objectives, adds little to our knowledge of the costs and benefits of ICC regulation. As we demonstrate in this report, the bureau has committed numerous and substantial analytical errors. We believe too that the bureau, by dwelling on the work of Moore, first presented in 1971,[4] is remiss in not analyzing more recent and, in some respects, more sophisticated cost studies such as those by Kenneth Boyer (1975), Richard Levin and Merton Peck (1976), Joseph Altonji (1976), and Theodore Keeler (1976).[5] We believe many of the

[3] Moore did not attempt to estimate the benefits to society of ICC regulation, although it is implicit in his work that he considers them to be zero. Thus, his gross cost figures should be considered his estimates of the net cost to society of ICC regulation.

[4] Moore's work is based on 1966 data and was first presented at a conference held at the Brookings Institution in October 1971. The results of the study were first published in Moore's American Enterprise Institute study (1972), whereas the entire analysis appears in his Brookings contribution (1975).

[5] See Kenneth Boyer, "The Price Sensitivity of Shippers' Mode of Transport Selection and the Intermodal Allocation of Freight Traffic" (Ph.D. diss., University of Michigan, 1975); Richard Levin and Merton Peck, "Allocation in Surface Freight Transportation: Does Rate Regulation Matter?" Department of Economics Discussion Paper no. 31, Yale University, New Haven, Connecticut, August 1976; Joseph Altonji, "Estimating Misallocation of Traffic between Rail and Truck Transport," in *Proceedings: Seventh Annual Meeting, Transportation Research Forum* (Oxford, Ind.: Richard B. Cross Co., 1976), pp. 378-87; Theodore Keeler, "On the Economic Impact of Railroad Freight Regulation," Working Paper no. SL-7601, Department of Economics, University of California, Berkeley, September 1976.

bureau's criticisms of Moore's cost estimates are valid. But we find it inexplicable why the bureau then used the same methodology, repeating the same errors, in its own analysis of the costs of regulation.

The bureau's estimates of the benefits of ICC regulation suffer from arithmetic errors and from numerous unsupported assertions. The primary shortcoming of these estimates is that they fail to distinguish between *transfers* of income from one group in society to another and *net social costs or benefits.* None of the quantitative estimates of benefits alleged by the bureau can stand up to scrutiny. Properly calculated, several of the alleged benefits actually become costs.

In the remainder of this report, we discuss in detail the bureau's analysis of Moore's work, giving our views on the latter's shortcomings. We then address the bureau's estimates of the benefits of ICC regulation, drawing a distinction between net benefits (or costs) and transfer payments, and criticizing certain of the bureau's assumptions. Finally, we place the debate over the net impact of regulation in some perspective, particularly its relevance to the issue of "deregulation" or regulatory reform.

The Bureau's Estimates of Costs

Rail Rate Regulation. Moore's estimates of the cost of rail rate regulation ($1.7 billion to $2.4 billion annually, in 1968 dollars) are based, in part, on estimates of rail demand by Professor Alexander Morton.[6] The bureau correctly points out that Morton's analysis is crude (page 49). Despite this, the bureau simply updates Morton's data base and uses the same methodology to calculate its own demand equation. Thus, its results suffer from all the problems that were criticized in the original work.

As the bureau itself observes (page 53), during the period covered by the Morton study (1947 to 1966) many events occurred that would have influenced the demand for rail services. For example, the growth of the Interstate Highway System affected the competitive relationship between motor carriers and railroads, since it improved the speed and reliability of the former. Also, private trucking made substantial inroads into traditional railroad markets, and growth in the size and weight of trucks, without corresponding increases in user

[6] Alexander Morton, "A Statistical Sketch of Intercity Freight Demand," *Highway Research Record* 296 (1969), pp. 47-65.

charges, resulted in lower costs for trucking.[7] As a result, Morton's demand equations, like the bureau's, suffer from substantial specification bias because they neglect many relevant variables.

Moreover, the approach suffers from significant "aggregation problems"—that is, trying to estimate overall "railroad demand" rather than the demand for specific rail services. Although the use of aggregated demand functions is almost universal, the bureau's demand functions are more aggregated than those currently employed by the rest of the business and economics profession. Had it chosen to, the bureau could have dealt with some of the more significant aggregation problems inherent in the time series data used. One possibility would have been to adopt a cross-sectional approach, using dummy variables to represent different regions. Such an analysis could have been applied to time periods sufficiently short that the results would not have been affected by structural changes. Also, use of cross-sectional data would have provided far more observations and thus greater reliability of the results.

The bureau was kind enough to provide us with the data set used in its 1955–1974 demand analysis.[8] We used this data to replicate the bureau's results and to undertake an expanded analysis based on the data. Specifically, we produced:

(1) A correlation matrix of the independent variables.

(2) Significance tests of the coefficients.

(3) A sensitivity analysis of the bureau's estimates with respect to:

  (a) changes in the bases of the independent variables,

  (b) "outliers" and errors in the data, and

  (c) addition or deletion of variables.

(4) Results reflecting the addition of some coefficients not presented in the bureau's results and corrections of an error in the reporting of the bureau's results.

A detailed examination of our results appeared as Appendix II of our original report. A brief summary follows.

An examination of the correlation matrix reveals that four variable pairs in equation 4 are highly collinear[9]—that is, log truck

---

[7] *Toward Rational Road User Charges* (Washington, D.C.: Urban Institute, 1976).

[8] This data set was not disaggregated by region, so we were unable to perform the cross-sectional analysis described above.

[9] Equations cited by number in this report refer to those found in the bureau's analysis (pp. 50-53 above).

rate and log gross national product, log truck rate and log time, log time and log gross national product, and log truck rate and log rail rate. When the independent variables used in a regression are highly collinear (such as in equation 4), a statistical problem, "multicollinearity," results. When some or all of the explanatory variables in a relation are so highly correlated with one another, "It becomes very difficult, if not impossible, to disentangle their separate influences and determine a reasonably precise estimate of their relative effects." [10] Since the correlation of the first three pairs mentioned above is close to perfect, the coefficient estimating procedure breaks down, and thus one should place little confidence in the *magnitude* and *signs* of the individual coefficients.

Suppose, however, that we accept (as we should not, given the above) the bureau's results. Questions then arise concerning the bureau's interpretations of equations 4 and 5, since both contain coefficient estimates which statistically are not significantly different from zero.[11] These are the log truck rate coefficient in equation 4 and the log rail rate coefficient in equation 5. The bureau's results suggest that truck demand is not related (significantly) to truck rate and that rail demand is not related (significantly) to rail rate—results which seem counterintuitive.

It should be pointed out that the log truck rate coefficient in Morton's rail demand equation (equation 1) is also not significantly different from zero. This mitigates the bureau's extended discussion concerning the counterintuitive negative relationship of truck rates and rail volumes (pages 50–51).

Next, we tested the bureau's equation 4 by changing the base year for gross national product (GNP) from 1958 to 1975, and the base used for the time trend variable from 1955 = 9, . . . , 1974 = 28 to 1955 = 1, . . . , 1974 = 20. These changes yield vastly different coefficients for the log truck rate and the log rail rate variables. Since no base is a priori superior to any other base and since the change in base so severely impacts the coefficients, little credence should be placed in the bureau's estimates of equations 4 and 5 or in its statements regarding the magnitude of the resulting coefficients.

---

[10] John Johnston, *Econometric Methods* (New York: McGraw-Hill, 1963), p. 201.

[11] The meaning of "significance" here refers to the probability that in the *true* relationship being estimated the independent variable has *no* effect on the dependent variable. Statisticians commonly say that, if there is a 5 percent probability that there is no effect, the coefficient is "insignificant." (In many cases where reference is made to "insignificance" in the report, the coefficients fail at much higher probabilities.)

Several errors were found in the bureau's data base, and the year 1974 was felt to be nontypical because of the economic downturn. We reran the bureau's equations using corrected data and then deleting the data for 1974. The coefficients change measurably with the corrected data, and they are sensitive to the time period chosen.

We also ran the bureau's equations 4 and 5 in the manner suggested by Morton—that is, with a time trend in the rail equation instead of in the truck equation as was done by the bureau. The results yield counterintuitive signs and insignificant coefficients for the truck and rail rate variables. Our runs of the bureau's equations 4 and 5 also yield the constant terms which were not reported by the bureau and a significant correction of the coefficient of determination (R^2) of equation 5 from 0.749 to 0.475. The latter point implies that equation 5 has much less explanatory power than that attributed to it by the bureau.

The major conclusion of our statistical analysis is that one should not place great reliance on the bureau's results. Thus, its conclusion that "the cost of regulation 'due to the inefficient use of railroads' is zero" (page 56) and its conclusion that "using Dr. Moore's methodology, this scenario [that is, traffic not carried] would not result in a cost for regulation but rather in a $0.2 billion static welfare gain" (page 63) cannot be substantiated.

Motor Carrier Rate Regulation. The bureau argues that Moore's estimate of a 20 percent saving resulting from deregulating truck rates and entry is incorrect. In its judgment, the sample upon which Moore bases his analysis is too limited,[12] and Professor D. Daryl Wyckoff's appraisal of the English experience yields better results.[13] It further argues that motor carrier rates have been gravitating toward marginal profitability. A 20 percent rate reduction, it asserts, would result in losses for all truck movements (pages 57–58).

We agree that Moore's extrapolation of the limited agricultural experience is not a reliable basis for estimating the precise benefits of deregulating the entire trucking industry. However, all the evidence we are familiar with suggests that truck rates would fall under deregulation, although perhaps not to the magnitudes suggested in

[12] J. C. Winter and Ivan W. Ulrey, *Supplement to Interstate Trucking of Frozen Fruits and Vegetables under the Agricultural Exemption*, U.S. Department of Agriculture, Marketing Research Division, Supplement to MRR-316, July 1961.

[13] D. Daryl Wyckoff, "Motor Carrier Deregulation—Some Unanswered Questions" (speech delivered to the Joint Meeting of the Ohio Chapter of the Transportation Research Forum and the Eastern Central Motor Carriers Association, December 17, 1974).

the agricultural case. For example, utilizing Canadian experience between regulated and unregulated provinces, Professor James Sloss estimates that deregulation would lower trucking rates in the United States by 6.73 percent.[14] Rates in the Philadelphia Commercial Zone are slightly lower than those for comparable regulated moves outside the zone.[15] Finally, in a separate study, Moore presents evidence that rates fell 40 to 50 percent when deregulated in some European markets.[16]

The fact that truck operating rights were worth 15 to 20 percent of a firm's gross annual revenue, or between $1.5 billion and $2.0 billion in 1968,[17] indicates that monopoly profits exist in this industry. Operating rights command a price only because the future stream of profits is expected to exceed the cost of capital. If normal profits were earned by the trucking industry, franchise rights would not command high prices. There would be no point paying for a certificate of public convenience and necessity if the same rate of profit could be earned elsewhere in the economy.

As the bureau notes, the question of scale economies in trucking is pertinent to the outcome under deregulation. Although the bureau cites several studies which question the existence of constant costs in the trucking industry, many other studies conclude that the motor carrier industry is characterized by constant returns to scale. Apparent economies of scale are often the result of failure to consider the effects of such factors as average shipment weight or distance. When these factors are taken into account, average cost remains constant as shipments handled increase.[18] In addition, the existence of more than 15,000 firms and between 100,000 and 200,000 owner-

---

[14] James Sloss, "Regulation of Motor Freight Transportation: A Quantitative Evaluation of Policy," *Bell Journal of Economics and Management Science*, vol. 1 (Autumn 1970), pp. 334-47.

[15] See W. Bruce Allen, Verified Statement on Behalf of the U.S. Department of Transportation before the Interstate Commerce Commission on Commercial Zones and Terminal Areas—Notice of Proposed Rulemaking, Ex Parte MC-37 (Sub-No. 26), Washington, D.C., October 1975. An edited version of this paper is included in the present volume as Chapter 10.

[16] Thomas G. Moore, *Trucking Regulation: Lessons from Europe* (Washington, D.C.: American Enterprise Institute, 1976), p. 145.

[17] American Trucking Associations, *Accounting for Motor Carrier Operating Rights*, Brief and Petition of American Trucking Associations, Inc., before the Financial Standards Board of the Financial Accounting Foundation, Washington, D.C., 1974.

[18] Richard Klem, *The Cost Structure of the Trucking Industry*, paper prepared for the U.S. Department of Transportation, Office of Transportation Regulatory Policy, 1975. An edited version of this paper is included in the present volume as Chapter 4.

operators indicates that there are no serious financial barriers to entry and no shortage of entrepreneurs.

In support of its contention that it is unreasonable to assume that deregulation would lead to a 20 percent overall reduction in trucking rates, the bureau presents data on alleged cross-subsidization of small shipments by large shipments.[19] Yet, in raising this issue, the bureau ignores it as a source of inefficiency resulting from regulation. How can one conclude that the transfer payments made by those who ship large-sized shipments to those who ship small-sized shipments improve social welfare? Pricing certain transportation services below cost leads to overconsumption of those services; pricing other services in excess of cost to generate revenues for cross-subsidy leads to underconsumption of these services. If we accept the bureau's allegation about the existence of cross-subsidy, we are forced to conclude that because of the rate distortion society demands "too much" small shipment service and "too little" large shipment service. The result is an inefficient mix between small shipments and large shipments.

As noted earlier, the bureau criticizes Moore's estimate of savings from trucking deregulation on the ground that the agricultural sample is too narrow. The bureau, however, commits the same error in adopting Wyckoff's evidence on the English experience as its basis for estimating the benefits accruing from regulation. The problem is compounded in the bureau's case, for two reasons. First, it did not adjust Wyckoff's figures for the 20 percent inflation rate occurring in England at that time. Correcting Wyckoff's data for the (one-year) British inflation results in a 30 percent decline in truckload rates and an increase of 20 percent in less-than-truckload (LTL) rates.[20] Second, Wyckoff's figures are not adjusted for differences in service quality. Moore's data (from his 1976 study), which is adjusted for changes in service quality, indicates little increase in LTL rates after deregulation.

The bureau did not provide the data to which it applied Wyckoff's report to compile its estimate of the cost of motor carrier regulation. However, we have collected the necessary data and have calculated the costs and benefits of motor carrier regulation using

---

[19] See Tables 2-1 and 2-2. Of course, the carrier estimates of the costs of handling different-sized shipments reported by the bureau may not be correct. For example, United Parcel Service and Greyhound may dispute the contention that it is unprofitable to handle small shipments.

[20] This assumes that no shipper altered the size of its shipments in response to the change in relative prices. This is unrealistic, but we make the assumption in order to be consistent with the bureau's analysis.

Table 3-1

INTERCITY MOTOR CARRIER FREIGHT REVENUES, 1968
(thousands of dollars)

Type of Carrier	Class	Truckload	Less than Truckload	Source
General common	I	2,126,180	3,783,787	ICC table 13A, p. 34
General common	II	39,841	87,471	ICC table 48A, p. 138
Other than general common	I and II	2,548,941	556,307	Assignment of all moving revenues to LTL (TRINC'S, p. S-4)
Total		4,714,962	4,427,565	

Note: Revenues of all "other than general common" carriers are treated as resulting from truckload movements, except for "household movers," whose traffic is treated as resulting from LTL operations. The Bureau of Accounts divides revenues of "other than general common" into Class I ($2,670,127; See ICC table 14, p. 36) and Class II ($435,121; ICC table 49, p. 140). The bureau does not divide these revenues into truckload and LTL. The bureau divides the revenues of Class I and Class II "general common" carriers into truckload and LTL when it collects the data.

Sources: TRINC Transportation Consultants, *TRINC's Blue Book of the Trucking Industry*, Washington, D.C., 1969 edition. Interstate Commerce Commission, Bureau of Accounts, *ICC Transport Statistics in the United States for the Year Ended December 31, 1968,* Part 7, Motor Carriers, 1969.

Wyckoff's data adjusted to account for the British inflation. The raw data are reproduced in Table 3-1.

Increasing LTL traffic revenue by 20 percent and reducing truckload traffic revenue by 30 percent yields a net *cost* of trucking regulation of $529 million annually. This contrasts with the bureau's conclusion (using Wyckoff's uncorrected data) that trucking regulation saves the economy $2.2 billion per year in 1968 dollars or $3.8 billion in 1975 dollars. This erroneous calculation is *very important,* since it represents almost 80 percent of the bureau's estimated "benefits" (or negative costs) resulting from ICC regulation.

The bureau argues that the possibility that motor carrier rates would decline 20 percent under deregulation is nil. It adjusts average revenues and costs of Middle Atlantic carriers by size of shipment to show the effect of a 20 percent decline in rates with costs held constant. It uses the data to argue that the carriers would incur losses on shipments of every size. The bureau concludes on the basis of this analysis that the maximum feasible reduction in motor carrier rates under deregulation is 10 percent (page 60).

This effort fails on several grounds. First, the cost allocation problem mentioned earlier is serious because, under regulation, carriers have an incentive to overstate costs. Small carriers can do this through a variety of means, ranging from use of leasing companies to payout of equity in the form of salary.[21] Larger, publicly held firms generally experience higher rates of return. For example, the *Business Week* survey of earnings for the twelve-month period ended September 30, 1976, indicates a weighted-average rate of return on equity of 11.5 percent for the firms surveyed. For the truck companies included in the survey the rate of return on equity was 20.9 percent.[22] Measures of profitability reported to stockholders of large, publicly held motor carriers indicate higher rates of profit than the averages the rate bureaus report to the ICC in rate cases.[23]

The variation in rate of profit from firm to firm is further evidence that the commission is protecting inefficient firms either by manipulating rates or by manipulating service opportunities on different routes so that, for a given level of efficiency, some sets of operating authority permit their owners to earn substantially higher profits than other sets of authority. This is especially true of the Middle Atlantic district, which contains some of the more profitable carriers as well as some of the industry's poorer performers. Since competition would be expected to eliminate the more inefficient carriers, the average is an overstatement of the costs that would obtain under deregulation. In addition, the increased costs resulting from regulation (because of such things as additional personnel, too much equipment due to a lack of peak-load pricing, extra legal staff, filings to comply with regulations, et cetera) are included in the bureau's figures (Tables 2-1 and 2-2). Finally, operating ratios are inflated because of the conversion of what would normally be fixed costs into variable costs through the leasing of equipment from subsidiary, capital-owning companies (for example, a carrier will lease a truck from a truck-owning subsidiary). Since these are not consolidated

---

[21] Edward B. Hymson, "An Evaluation of the Accuracy of the Interstate Commerce Commission Measures of Profitability of Motor Carriers Applying for General Rate Increases," report submitted to the National Science Foundation, Washington, D.C., 1974.

[22] *Business Week*, November 15, 1976, pp. 107-8.

[23] Irwin Silberman, *The Sum of Money* (Washington, D.C.: American Trucking Associations, 1973).

statements (at least for rate-making purposes), we suspect this latter situation is not reflected in the bureau's figures.

Private Carriage, Service Quality, and Other Cost Estimates. The bureau argues that private carriers would continue to operate at roughly the same level of empty backhauls in the absence of regulation. It argues that speed, flexibility, and special service—rather than cost—are the major reasons for the use of private trucking. It further asserts that, to the extent that private carriers reduced empty backhaul under deregulation, the empty backhaul would shift to common carriers and social costs could increase as a larger number of firms competed for a fixed amount of traffic (pages 60–61).

Undoubtedly, some private carriers would acquire backhauls if there were less restrictive regulation. To the extent that such service caused a reduction in the demand for common carrier service, however, the common carriers adversely affected would be forced to adjust their rates downward and modify their services offered or be forced to leave the market.[24] This would lower the costs of transportation.

The reason the bureau comes to the contrary conclusion is that it fails to consider the net impact on efficiency of an elimination of inefficient carriers and an elimination of an empty backhaul for a common carrier from point A to point B by having a private carrier already moving full from point B to point A take a return load. In such a case, *two* empty backhauls would be eliminated. Thus, in our judgment, there is no evidence to support the bureau's assertion that liberalization of private carriage restrictions would aggravate the empty backhaul problem and lead to service chaos.

The bureau criticizes Moore's work for not taking into account differences among modes in the quality of service. It concludes that "when these [service] factors are included, the total perceived 'cost' of using motor carrier service has apparently been viewed quite often as the less expensive alternative" (page 61).

It is true that Moore did not consider quality-of-service differences. But the service factor has been captured in other studies

---

[24] It appears clear that many firms have been inhibited from entering private carriage because of restrictions caused by regulation. (For example, there have been a number of efforts by large firms to secure the right to haul for their own subsidiaries.) But shippers have been turning increasingly to private carriage, despite restrictions imposed by regulation which put private carriage at an inherent cost disadvantage. This indicates that the regulated marketplace is either failing or being prevented from providing the kind of carriage desired by a growing number of shippers.

Table 3-2

RECENT ESTIMATES OF THE ANNUAL COSTS OF ICC REGULATION

Source of Cost	Author	Annual Cost Estimate
Distortions between truck and rail transportation	Boyer (1975)	$125 million (for 16 manufactured commodities)
	Levin and Peck (1976)	$17 million (for 45 manufactured commodities)
	Keeler (1976)	$500 million (upper bound)
	Altonji (1976)	$ $\approx$ 0
Distortions because of excess rail capacity	Keeler (1976)	$3.5 billion

Note: The methodologies employed in these studies are briefly described in Appendix II of the original version of this report.

Sources: Kenneth Boyer, "The Price Sensitivity of Shippers' Mode of Transport Selection and the Intermodal Allocation of Freight Traffic" (Ph.D. diss., University of Michigan, 1975); Richard Levin and Merton Peck, "Allocation in Surface Freight Transportation: Does Rate Regulation Matter?" Department of Economics Discussion Paper no. 31, Yale University, New Haven, Connecticut, August 1976; Joseph Altonji, "Estimating Misallocation of Traffic between Rail and Truck Transport," in *Proceedings: Seventeenth Annual Meeting, Transportation Research Forum* (Oxford, Indiana: Richard B. Cross Co., 1976), pp. 378-87; Theodore Keeler, "On the Economic Impact of Railroad Freight Regulation," Working Paper no. SL-7601, Department of Economics, University of California, Berkeley, September 1976.

ignored by the bureau. For example, recent studies by Boyer, Levin and Peck, Keeler, and Altonji, among others, have all included service factors in making their estimates of the costs of ICC regulation.[25]

The study of the costs of regulation by the commission is certainly incomplete. Although the Moore methodology may be subject to criticism, the bureau does not provide anything better on this issue, contrary to its claims. Also, the bureau ignores other, newer studies which are available and should have been examined. A summary of the estimates of the costs of ICC regulation prepared by the researchers mentioned above is found in Table 3-2.

[25] See Boyer, "The Price Sensitivity of Shippers' Mode of Transport Selection"; Levin and Peck, "Allocation in Surface Freight Transportation"; Keeler, "On the Economic Impact of Railroad Freight Regulation"; and Altonji, "Estimating Misallocation of Traffic."

The Bureau's Estimates of Benefits

General Remarks. The bureau's estimates of the benefits of regulation are not well grounded either in economic theory or in empirical verification. The bureau argues that without ICC regulation, transportation costs would be much higher and that "socially desirable" income redistribution would not take place. Too often, however, the bureau calculates the benefits accruing to one group from a given commission action but neglects to deduct the costs that same action imposes on other groups.

The bureau quotes Professor Theodore Wallin as arguing: "Economic regulation exists not only—or even, perhaps primarily—to achieve the benefits of competition; it provides as well a vitally important tool in the achievement of social, or noneconomic goals." [26] Wallin goes on to include maintenance of uneconomic operations and economic development among the goals to be considered at the expense of efficiency. The bureau's estimate of the benefits of regulation, therefore, rests on an assessment not only of whether the costs of transportation would be lower without regulation but also of whether regulation provides "noneconomic" benefits. A major problem with this approach is that neither Wallin nor the bureau draws a distinction between: (1) net benefits to society, and (2) income transfers from one group to another.

The bureau repeatedly refers to the benefits of redistributing income through cross-subsidy, but it fails to point out that some pay for what others receive. That such income redistribution is a "benefit" to society is no more than a subjective judgment. Moreover, if it were considered socially desirable to subsidize certain groups, there are more efficient and, arguably, more equitable means available.

In general, economists have argued that it is more efficient to accomplish social goals directly via taxation and government subsidy rather than indirectly through cross-subsidization of one group by another. To the extent that a noneconomic branch line is maintained by commission policy, the equity holders of the railroads must be subsidizing those on the branch line by accepting lower profits and/or non-branch line shippers must be subsidizing branch line shippers by paying rates higher than they would have otherwise. If it is public policy to subsidize branch lines, one may ask why it should be the rail equity holders and non-branch line shippers (and, ulti-

[26] Theodore O. Wallin, "Alternatives in Transport Policy: A Matrix Approach," *Transportation Journal*, vol. 15 (Winter 1975), pp. 43-53, quoted in the bureau report on p. 68 above.

mately, their customers) who bear the cost, rather than the public at large. Under direct subsidy, the program is more "public" and, presumably, under constant review. However, where subsidy is hidden, there is less public scrutiny of the program.[27]

The bureau's contention that cross-subsidization "is an accepted norm in virtually all businesses" (page 76) is incorrect. An entrepreneur would not likely provide a service or a product unless such an activity contributed to profit. But this is not what "bad freight" does. "Loss leaders" do exist but only because loss leaders are felt to contribute to the overall profit of the firm by bringing in customers who then purchase more profitable goods or services. Since regulated firms petition to exit from unprofitable markets or are reported to provide poor service on such "bad freight," it is unlikely that these are loss leaders.

We now turn to the specific areas identified by the bureau where regulation allegedly generates net benefits. In several of these the bureau has attempted to quantify the alleged benefits in dollar terms. These are: (1) motor carrier rate regulation; (2) lower cargo insurance costs to shippers; (3) lower costs because of reduced rail abandonments; (4) lower car costs for railroads resulting from improved utilization; (5) lower costs to firms because of inventory reductions; and (6) lower costs of motor carrier capital. In other cases the bureau simply alleges that there are important benefits resulting from regulation but makes no attempt to quantify them.[28] Here, we will comment on only the quantified benefits, although we have serious reservations about the allegations that these nonquantified items are also a source of benefits.[29]

The reduced level of motor carrier rates alleged to result from rate and service regulation accounts for 85 percent of the net benefits estimated by the bureau. The bureau notes that the wholesale price index (WPI) increased by 64.2 percent between 1969 and 1975, while the regulated motor-common-carrier freight rate index increased

[27] The bureau asserts that the costs of supporting small businesses and rural communities through cross-subsidy "is probably less than would be necessary under alternative government subsidy programs" (p. 77). Yet, it gives no basis for drawing this conclusion.

[28] These other, unquantified cases are: (1) prevention of "undue" rail and motor carrier rate discrimination; (2) inefficient use of private carriage; (3) maintenance of service and rate stability; (4) maintenance of excess capacity; (5) technology and innovation incentives; (6) ensuring transport facilities for national defense; (7) improvement of the environment; (8) service standards for household goods movement; and (9) maintenance of service to unprofitable traffic.

[29] Many of our criticisms of the quantified benefits also apply to the unquantified benefits.

by only 41.0 percent during the same period (page 81). The bureau concludes that, if motor carrier rates had increased as much as the WPI, motor carrier revenue would have been raised $3.735 billion in 1975. On the other hand, the rail rate index increased over the same period more rapidly than the WPI—implying a $500 million difference in the total (1975) rail bill. The bureau then subtracts the "excessive" rail bill from the motor carrier savings to arrive at a $3.24 billion saving resulting from ICC regulation during 1975.

The consumer price index (CPI) rose 46.8 percent during the same period, whereas the GNP deflator rose 46.7 percent. Yet the bureau does not say why the WPI was used instead of the CPI or the GNP deflator. If the GNP deflator were used, for example, the "benefit" from motor carrier regulation would be $0.758 billion, whereas the rail negative benefit (or cost) would be $2.126 billion, turning a net benefit of $3.24 billion into a net cost of $1.37 billion. The point here is that the choice of an index is critical to the bureau's methodology.

The bureau's analysis is incorrect on more substantive grounds. First, comparisons of price indexes reveal nothing about either levels of profit or levels of competition, but only about price changes. Second, during the period under review, the trucking industry experienced below-average cost increases and substantial increases in productivity. The cost of truck equipment increased by 43.5 percent, labor costs increased by 60.0 percent, and output per employee increased by 12.1 percent. Reducing the average rate of increase in labor cost by the rate of increase in productivity gives a *net* cost increase of 48.0 percent. The slight difference between this figure and the index may be explained by the fact that 1975 was a "bad" year. As economic conditions improved in 1976, productivity presumably rose sharply.

A competitive industry which experiences increased costs will increase the price it charges for its output. A monopolist experiencing no change in costs and no shift in demand for its product will not raise its price. Different industries experience different changes in input costs, productivity, and demand, and they change their prices accordingly. Simply observing that a price increases does not mean that the firm is a monopolist. It is not the rate of change in prices that characterizes a monopolist but the level of prices relative to costs. Price index comparisons reveal nothing about the price-cost relationship.

Loss and Damage. The bureau alleges that regulation results in a reduction in the cost of loss and damage claims associated with the transportation of goods. The bureau applies the insurance rates paid by exporters on international shipments to the value of domestic service shipments and concludes that the total cost of loss and damage claims under deregulation would be $1,113 million, or $613 million more than the current level of damage claims (page 86). The bureau's assumption of shipper-financed cargo insurance is based on the questionable theory that, if there were no ICC regulation, carriers would not be liable for loss and damage claims, or at least that it would be impossible for shippers to collect from carriers. Such reasoning runs counter to the experience in the unregulated sector, where failure to deliver products according to contract specifications is reason for court action.

The bureau's analysis, however, suffers from even more fundamental errors. First, it is highly unlikely that the cost of insuring domestic shipments is anywhere near as high as the cost of insuring international shipments. The dissimilarity of conditions in domestic commerce relative to international commerce makes such insurance rate comparisons all but meaningless. Second, even if one accepts the incorrect assumption that carriers would not be liable for damages in the absence of regulation, the study completely ignores the current cost of insurance to carriers. There is no more reason to assume that all carriers would self-insure than to assume all shippers would self-insure. If either party self-insured, the cost would be about the same. If carriers were released from liability, their costs, and therefore their rates, would decline. Shippers would save the portion of rates that formerly went to cover insurance costs (whether the carrier self-insured or contracted with an insurance company). Shippers would be able to use these savings to buy insurance on their shipments. The argument that deregulation would increase insurance costs fails because liability would not be transferred in the manner suggested by the bureau. Even if liability could be shifted, however, in a competitive market the cost of a shipper's insuring its shipment should not be materially different from the cost of a carrier's insuring the same shipment.

Railroad Abandonments. The bureau asserts that, by preventing "wholesale" railroad abandonments, regulation has a $300 million positive impact on GNP (pages 79–81). Unfortunately, the bureau does not explain the basis for this calculation other than to indicate that national input-output tables were used. The bureau cites studies by Jack Faucett and B. J. Allen.[30] The first deals with the transitional problems associated with a sudden (and, presumably, unexpected) termination of service of an entire railroad, rather than of a branch line. Allen concludes with respect to abandonments that "the short-run and long-run adverse economic effects [are not] significant." [31] Furthermore, he concludes that few firms actually had to close down and that the major effect encountered was somewhat higher transportation costs. Other studies not cited by the bureau also suggest that the impact of rail abandonment is not severe. Industries that said they would be driven from business were found to exist after abandonment. Businesses exiting were largely marginal firms with a low probability of survival even with rail service or businesses which were destined to expire and only expired sooner because of abandonment.[32]

Preventing abandonment of uneconomic lines necessitates subsidy from some source. Since the federal government has now begun large-scale subsidy programs of branch line operations, the transfer payment is becoming one from general taxpayers rather than from rail stockholders or rail shippers in other areas.[33] But in either case, the effect is one of transferring income from one group to another; whether this per se is a net benefit to society is a matter of subjective judgment.

The size of the impact attributed to abandonment has been overstated by the bureau. There is no doubt that more rail abandon-

---

[30] Jack Faucett and Associates, *The Potential Economic Impact of a Sudden Termination of Operation of the Penn Central Railroad,* study prepared for the U.S. Department of Transportation, 1970 and 1973; B. J. Allen, "The Economic Effects of Railroad Abandonment on Communities: A Case Study" (Ph.D. diss., University of Illinois, 1974); an article by Allen with the same title appeared in *Transportation Journal,* Fall 1975, pp. 52-61.

[31] Allen, "The Economic Effects of Railroad Abandonment on Communities," *Transportation Journal,* p. 60.

[32] See, for example, Simat, Helliesen and Eichner, *Retrospective Rail Line Abandonment Study,* report prepared for the U.S. Department of Transportation, Office of the Secretary, 1973; Boston University, Bureau of Business Research, *Studies of the Economic Impact of Railway Abandonment and Service Discontinuance: An Economic Impact of the Discontinuance of the Rutland Railway,* 1967; Public Interest Economic Center, *Community Impacts of Abandonments of Railroad Service* (Washington, D.C., December 1974).

[33] There is ample reason to believe that cross-subsidy is less efficient than direct subsidy. To the extent that the failure to allow abandonments has resulted in railroad failures or inability to upgrade the system, the vast majority of shippers who are located on major lines suffer. A railroad has every incentive to continue to operate any line as long as the line proves to be profitable. There is little economic incentive to discontinue service unless the service being provided does not bring in revenues sufficient to cover its costs.

ment would occur if exit from rail service were not constrained by regulation. The Penn Central trustees at one time proposed abandoning 9,000 miles of their 20,000-mile system. Studies by the Department of Transportation and its Federal Railroad Administration have shown that 1 percent of the nation's rail traffic travels on 33 percent of the nation's rail network.[34] Thus, substantial abandonment of branch lines would not seriously affect traffic volume since, presumably, only the lines with the lightest density would be abandoned. This does not square with the bureau's estimate that 13 percent of the trackage carries between 3 percent and 4 percent of the traffic.

Car Utilization. The bureau asserts that by virtue of the commission's car service efforts, rail cars are utilized 5 percent more efficiently than they would be in the absence of regulation. It argues that this provides a $149 million annual benefit in the form of a reduced car supply requirement.

It is important to understand, however, that car service and demurrage rules were developed primarily by the railroads, not by the commission. Moreover, available evidence does not support the view that regulation improves the utilization of rail equipment. Two recent studies on car utilization indicate that rail car utilization has been inhibited by regulation and could be increased substantially.[35] The commission does adjudicate disputes between carriers over car service rules. Although such adjudication services may have some value, it would be hard to impute to them a dollar value of the magnitude the commission ascribes.

Inventory Costs. The bureau asserts that firms carry smaller inventories today than they would if there were no regulation. The reason is that the commission compels carriers to provide small shipment service at rates which, the bureau believes, are lower than costs. The bureau argues that in the absence of regulation rates for small shipments would rise or small shipment service would disappear. In either case, the bureau asserts, the firms would be required to carry larger inventories, and it estimates this would cost society an additional $59 million per year (pages 74–75).

---

[34] See U.S. Department of Transportation, Federal Railroad Administration, *Preliminary Standards, Classification and Designation of Lines of Class I Railroads in the United States*, 1976.

[35] ADD Systems, *The Extent that Car Service Rules Restrict Freight Car Utilization* (Washington, D.C., May 1972); Association of American Railroads and Federal Rail Administration, *Freight Car Clearing House Experiment—An Interim Evaluation* (Washington, D.C., 1975).

This argument fails on numerous grounds. First, the bureau neglects to subtract the savings resulting from the reduced rate on larger shipments from the increased inventory cost. The bureau's own data, properly adjusted, suggest that truckload rates would decline 30 percent under deregulation. Those shippers who substituted truckload shipments at 30 percent below current rates for small shipments at current rates and who experienced higher inventory costs would still be likely, in many instances, to reduce their total cost of transportation and inventory.

If small shipments move at below cost, this means that those who ship in larger sizes must pay rates in excess of costs to make up the difference. Under deregulation, small-package shippers would experience a rise in rates, but larger shippers would experience a reduction in rates as the requirement for cross-subsidy was removed. The result would, if anything, be a net *saving* to society, not a cost. Although one class of shippers would end up better off and another would end up worse off, the *net* effect would be a reduction in the total costs of transportation and distribution.[36] Today, many choose to utilize small shipments rather than carry larger inventories, largely because small shipments are subsidized. If shippers could take advantage of lower rates on large shipments, it would become profitable for them to carry larger inventories. If the bureau had adjusted the data to take into account the lower costs of moving large shipments, on balance the cost of inventories would be cancelled out by the benefits to society of the lower rates.

Moreover, we take issue with the bureau's assertion that "deregulation would result in less reliable, slower and less frequent truck service to small communities" (page 75). Several studies show that some carriers now specialize in such service and tend to do well.[37] There is no reason to believe that such carriers would terminate service after deregulation; indeed, the market presumably would grow. It is not clear that the commission is improving the quality of service to small shippers. The independent General Accounting Office recently reported to Congress that service to small

[36] As long as the cross-elasticity of demand between the two services is not zero, the total transportation bill must fall since the proportion of LTL shipments would decline.

[37] See, for example, R. L. Banks and Associates, *Economic Analysis and Regulatory Implications of Motor Common Carrier Service to Predominantly Small Communities*, report prepared for the U.S. Department of Transportation, Office of the Secretary, June 24, 1976. An edited version of the analysis is included in the present volume as Chapter 5.

shippers was substandard and that the ICC was not taking adequate corrective action.[38]

Motor Carrier Financing. The bureau asserts that deregulation would make the motor carrier industry riskier than it is now (pages 71–74). This would, according to the bureau, result in a shift toward more debt financing. The bureau further asserts that debt financing is more costly than equity financing. The bureau estimates that deregulation would require a shift of 10 percent of the industry's capital from equity to debt, and this would result in an increase in capital costs of $23 million per year. An additional $12 million per year in costs is identified as resulting from a higher interest cost on debt, for a total of $35 million per year increased cost of capital.

As a number of authors have shown, this reasoning is in error.[39] First, as risk increases it becomes harder to secure debt financing, so firms are forced to shift to a greater percentage of equity financing. Second, equity financing is more costly than debt financing, which is why, everything else being equal, firms prefer to use a higher percentage of debt financing. Third, the chattel mortgages which are utilized by most truckers use specific real assets as collateral. These assets can be repossessed in case of default. As a result of debt financing based largely on chattel mortgages, the riskiness of a firm has little effect on the amount of debt a firm can secure or on the interest expense associated with that debt. Finally, contrary to the Irving Silberman study referred to by the bureau (page 72),[40] the motor carrier industry is among the least risky in the economy. The extremely small number of bankruptcies relative to any other industry of comparable firm composition is evidence of this.[41] To the extent that reduced risk results from regulation, the commission is giving motor carriers an artificial advantage over the unregulated

---

[38] General Accounting Office, *Improved Service to the Small Shipper Is Needed*, report prepared for the U.S. Congress, 1976.

[39] See Franco Modigliani and Merton Miller, "The Cost of Capital, Corporation, Finance, and the Theory of Investment," *American Economic Review*, June 1958, pp. 263-97; Modigliani and Miller, "Some Estimates of the Cost of Capital to the Electric Utility Industry, 1954-1957," *American Economic Review*, June 1966, pp. 333-39; John Lintner, "The Cost of Capital and Optimal Financing of Corporate Growth," *Journal of Finance*, May 1963, pp. 292-310; and Richard Norgaard, "An Examination of the Yields of Corporate Bonds and Stocks," *Journal of Finance*, September 1974, pp. 1275-86.

[40] Silberman, *The Sum of Money*.

[41] See Hymson, "Accuracy of the Interstate Commerce Commission Measures of Profitability."

sector of the economy when it comes to competing in the capital market. This is a source of *cost* to the economy (in terms of an inefficient allocation of capital resources), not a benefit as the bureau alleges.

If we accept the commission's assumption that risk would increase under deregulation, then the literature on finance indicates that firms would be forced to shift to a higher proportion of equity financing. Equity is held by owners and debt is held by lenders. If a company fails, the smaller the proportion of debt to total capitalization, the higher the likelihood that debt holders will recover their investment. Under current bankruptcy law, all debt claims must be paid off in full before any return is made to equity holders. The bureau is thus incorrect when it assumes that higher risks would result in increased debt financing. As a practical matter, risk is less important in the motor carrier industry than in almost any other industry. The reason (as mentioned earlier) is that almost all motor carrier assets can be secured by chattel mortgages. The loading dock and lot facilities can be secured by a normal real estate mortgage. The tractors and trailers can be secured by loans in which the equipment is pledged as security. Since there is a very good market for used equipment (and for real estate), financiers are willing to lend a large proportion of asset value since they could repossess it and get their money back.

The bureau's assertion that debt is more expensive than equity is incorrect. The commission erroneously states that the only cost of equity is dividends paid out. This totally ignores retained earnings. Few would settle for a 5 percent dividend return when they can get a 7 percent return in a savings and loan association at less risk. It also neglects the existence of the corporate income tax. Under the tax laws, a firm must pay corporation taxes on earnings prior to paying them out in dividends. Assuming a marginal tax rate of 48 percent, this means that a firm must earn 9.61 percent to pay a 5 percent dividend. Again, this ignores the retained earnings and consequent capital appreciation an equity purchaser expects when he buys a stock.

The bureau also fails to account for the tax law relating to interest expense. Interest expense is deducted prior to paying income tax. Thus, a profitable firm that pays 10 percent interest expense reduces its tax liability by 48 percent times the interest expense. If the firm shifts the debt into equity, to pay the same 10 percent it must earn 19.23 percent. If we followed the bureau's reasoning, increased risk would result in a $45.19 million saving from reduced dividend payments, rather than the $23.5 million asserted by the bureau (that is, 5 percent of $470 million).

The studies cited by the bureau in support of its contention that regulation is beneficial because it lowers motor carriers' cost of capital are also subject to criticism. For example, the Blyth, Eastman, Dillon and Company report cited by the bureau (page 72) implies that deregulation would be costly for society, even though it concedes that this would lead to more competition and lower rates.[42] The Silberman report, a study sponsored by the American Trucking Associations, comes to the inexplicable conclusion that, where competition is suppressed and bankruptcy is minimal, the trucking industry is more risky than U.S. industry generally.[43] The First National Bank of Boston report cited by the bureau (pages 72–73) is also unsubstantiated.[44] Moreover, investment bankers tend to be oriented toward the status quo, and it is in their self-interest to make statements such as these in order to protect their collateral.

Conclusions

The bureau correctly identifies several problems associated with Moore's analysis of the costs of current regulatory policy. This is not surprising since Moore's was an early work. The bureau's analysis of the cost of railroad regulation suffers from so many statistical shortcomings that one should place little confidence in the results. Its analysis of the costs of motor carrier regulation is dependent on data which are unadjusted for inflation, making the results incorrect. Adjusting for inflation turns the bureau's $2.2 billion yearly gain resulting from motor carrier regulation into a $529 million yearly loss. The bureau's estimates of the benefits of regulation cannot be supported. Of the total benefits resulting from regulation, 85 percent are derived by showing that an index of motor carrier rate increases went up by less than the WPI. Had the GNP deflator been used instead of the WPI (and the bureau gives no reason why one index is more appropriate than another), this benefit would have turned into a loss. Of course, as we show, this whole approach makes little sense, and it is easy to explain the rate of increase in motor carrier rates on grounds other than regulation.

42 Blyth, Eastman, Dillon and Company, *The Trucking Regulatory Reform Act* (New York, 1975).

43 Silberman, *The Sum of Money.*

44 First National Bank of Boston, *Financial Analysis of the Motor Carrier Industry* (Boston, 1975).

The allegation that in the absence of regulation the cost of cargo insurance would rise was shown to be unfounded, on grounds both that legal liability remains with the carrier and that the cost of insurance is likely to remain relatively constant regardless of who pays the premiums. The bureau's analysis of the benefit of reduced rail abandonments was shown to be in error since the effect is one of cross-subsidy, where the gains are offset by the losses of those who pay. The alleged benefit resulting from better utilization of railroad cars was shown not to have occurred. Available evidence supports the view that, if anything, regulation has inhibited equipment utilization. The assertion that cross-subsidy of small shipments by large shipments results in a saving because firms carry lower inventories is incorrect because there is no evidence that service to small shippers would deteriorate under deregulation and, further, the lower costs of larger-sized shipments (not considered by the bureau) would, on balance, offset increases in inventory costs. Finally, the assertion that regulation reduces motor carrier capital costs is based on the erroneous assumptions that under deregulation firms would shift to more debt financing and that equity financing is cheaper.

The bureau's assertion that more work needs to be accomplished on the costs and benefits of regulation is correct. However, we wish to emphasize that current disagreements among economists over *precise* estimates of the costs and benefits of regulation should not be interpreted as evidence that no problem exists. After all, the vast majority of economists who have looked at this issue have concluded that the net social cost of ICC regulation is truly substantial.

According to the bureau report, "Total deregulation of the surface transport industry would not necessarily solve current transportation problems, nor would it necessarily produce an optimal allocation of resources" (page 88). The statement is a straw man. The issue currently debated is not whether to abolish the ICC but whether to make substantial reforms in ICC regulation. In our judgment, the current system of regulation creates enormous inefficiencies and inequities, and these can and should be addressed.

PART THREE

SOME EFFECTS OF REGULATORY REFORM

Much of the debate over the Ford administration's trucking reform proposal turned on differing perceptions of the likely effects of the bill. Three major areas of dispute—market structure, service for small communities, and certificate values—are treated in this section.

Some critics of the administration's reform proposals contended that deregulation would lead to predatory pricing and eventual monopolization. The validity of these views was closely tied to the question of whether trucking is a decreasing-cost industry. If it is, then the risk of predatory pricing and monopolization has to be given heavier weight and the case for maintaining price regulation is, of course, strengthened. If trucking is not a decreasing-cost industry, then these risks can be heavily discounted, and a basic justification for regulation vanishes. Thus, the nature of costs became a critical issue in the debate over motor carrier regulatory reform. The paper by Richard Klem presents the results of studies by the U.S. Department of Transportation on the cost question. Dr. Klem, an economist with the Office of the Secretary, was responsible for the DOT research in this area. His analysis did not reveal any economies of scale in the trucking industry.

Critics of the administration's motor carrier reform proposals often made the argument that deregulation would cause a serious reduction in service to small communities. According to this view, service to many small towns and rural areas is inherently unprofitable, and carriers can provide such service only if they are able to earn sufficient profits elsewhere to offset these losses. Deregulation would eliminate these profits so that carriers would be forced to withdraw service to many small towns and rural areas. This question of cross-subsidy and service to small towns assumed a central role in congressional consideration of the motor carrier reform proposals. The paper by R. L. Banks and Associates reports the findings of a study prepared for DOT reviewing the experience of a group of carriers who specialized in providing service to small communities. The study found that these carriers, without the benefit of dense traffic markets, were able to operate profitably serving smaller communities.

A third major issue centered on the effect of the reform proposals on the value of operating authorities and what, if anything, could or should be done to protect those certificate values. The paper by John W. Snow and Stephen Sobotka treats these issues. It analyzes the relationship between certificate values and regulation, examines the likely effect of deregulation on certificate values, and reviews some options for compensating certificate holders for any loss of value. The paper concludes that maintaining certificate values is not compatible with deregulation and that compensating certificate holders would not be sound public policy.

4
MARKET STRUCTURE AND CONDUCT

Richard Klem

Changes in the economic regulation of the trucking industry are being considered. Many of the changes being considered involve the relaxation of some aspects of regulation in order to allow market forces to have greater influence on the allocation of resources in the industry. If such changes are to be considered properly, it is necessary to ascertain the probable reaction by the industry to greater freedom in such areas as rate making and market entry.

The Empirical Investigations

Two different pictures of the motor carrier industry have been put forward. In the first scenario, described by those advocating greater reliance on market forces, the industry is thought of as one which would be stable and healthy if regulations were relaxed. Proponents of this view argue that rate wars would not occur, profits would be adequate, and bankruptcy rates would be acceptable. In the second scenario, described by those advocating retention of present regulatory controls, a deregulated industry is believed likely to become chaotic. Proponents of this view argue that relaxing controls on entry and rate making would allow the large firms to drive the smaller firms out of business. It is further argued that prices would then be raised to high levels.

This paper is edited from a study entitled *The Cost Structure of the Regulated Trucking Industry,* prepared in 1975 by Richard Klem, an economist with the Office of Transportation Regulatory Policy of the U.S. Department of Transportation. A slightly revised version of the original study was presented by Dr. Klem in March 1977 at a conference on trucking regulation sponsored jointly by the National Academy of Sciences and the Transportation Center at Northwestern University, Evanston, Illinois.

The first scenario implies that the industry would be competitive (though it need not be perfectly competitive). The second scenario is basically that of a natural monopoly. Undoubtedly, a firm would like to be in the position of a natural monopolist and, undoubtedly, some firms would be willing to undertake a rate war if the final result would be a monopoly position. However, their ability to achieve that result depends heavily on the cost structure of the industry, and knowledge of the cost structure is needed in order to determine which scenario is accurate.

If the stable scenario is accurate, then the cost structure will be found to be such that the largest firms would have little, if any, cost advantage over the others. Since the preconditions for natural monopoly would not be present, a rate war would not give one firm a monopoly position. Therefore, a rate war strategy will not be chosen by an intelligent firm. A firm could act foolishly in starting a rate war, but with this cost structure such a rate war would be mild, and the results would be detrimental to the firm starting the rate war.

If the chaos scenario is accurate, then the cost structure must exhibit economies of scale, or, in other words, the largest firms must be able to produce a given level of service quality at a lower average cost. This cost structure would provide the conditions for monopoly:

(1) The large firms would have a competitive advantage which would allow them to drive the small firms out of business.

(2) Higher costs experienced by all but the largest firms would act as a barrier to entry of new firms when prices are later raised to monopoly levels.

The importance of understanding the cost structure in order to predict the likely market structure of the industry under a different regulatory environment has long been recognized. In the early work done in the 1950s, the conclusion drawn was that the industry exhibits nearly constant average cost.[1] More recently, several authors have argued that economies of scale and the concomitant tendency

---

[1] See, for example, John R. Meyer, Merton J. Peck, John Stenason, and Charles Zwick, *The Economics of Competition in the Transportation Industries* (Cambridge: Harvard University Press, 1960); and Robert A. Nelson, *Motor Freight Transport in New England, A Report to the New England Governor's Council* (Boston, 1956).

towards concentration do occur in the trucking industry. These arguments are often accompanied by the contention that the long-run average cost curve is an inverted U, that is, with no economies of scale for small firms but with economies of scale for large firms.[2] The unusual shape for the long-run cost curve was generally believed to result from certain management considerations within trucking firms. D. Daryl Wyckoff, for example, argued that firms with revenues between $1 million and $5 million are of an awkward size; they are too large for informal management and too small for formal management. Some of the sources of the apparent economies of scale would seem to have been explained earlier by Robert A. Nelson, John R. Meyer and his colleagues, and Stanley I. Warner, who traced them to longer average lengths of haul for larger firms.[3] However, a variety of interesting new questions have been raised. For example, it is argued that concentration is most likely to occur in the sector of the industry which specializes in the carriage of less-than-truckload (LTL) shipments.

Because the intention here is to determine the relative abilities of different sizes of carriers in competing for shipments, it is essential to insure that any cost advantage results from carrier characteristics rather than shipment characteristics. For that reason, an econometric specification which allows important shipment characteristics to be included is required. Important characteristics would seem to be commodity, shipment size, and length of haul. The average shipment size and length of haul for a carrier is easily calculated. The commodity can be standardized to a degree by dealing only with general freight carriers. It could be argued that, since all firms dealt with are common carriers which, by law, are required to accept any freight offered to them, all general freight carriers should have similar com-

---

[2] See, for example, Gary N. Dicer, "Economies of Scale and Motor Carrier Optimum Size," *Quarterly Review of Economics and Business*, Spring 1971, pp. 31-37; Mark A. Ladeson and Alan J. Stoga, "Returns to Scale in the U.S. Trucking Industry," *Southern Economic Journal*, January 1974, pp. 390-96; D. Daryl Wyckoff, "Factors Promoting Concentration of Motor Carriers under Deregulation," *Transportation Research Forum*, 1974, pp. 1-6; and Michael L. Lawrence, "Economies of Scale in the General Freight Motor Common Carrier Industry: Additional Evidence," *Transportation Research Forum*, 1976, pp. 169-76.

[3] See Nelson, *Motor Freight Transport in New England*; Meyer et al., *The Economics of Competition*; and Stanley I. Warner, "Cost Models, Measurement Errors, and Economies of Scale in Trucking," in *The Cost of Trucking: Econometric Analysis* (Dubuque, Iowa: William C. Brown Co., 1965), pp. 1-46.

modity mixes.[4] This paper takes as a starting point the analysis by Stanley Warner, in which cost is described as a function of a measure of output as well as a variety of shipment characteristics. The output measure is the only independent variable which is related to a scale of the firm. The other independent variables are measures, such as length of haul, which need not vary with the scale of the firm. Thus,

$$C = f(O,S) \tag{1}$$

where

C = total cost
O = total output
S = a vector of shipment characteristics.

With this formulation, the measure of output chosen is relatively unimportant, provided that the shipment characteristics adequately describe the features which both affect cost and are correlated with the output measure. Any shipment characteristic which did not affect cost would clearly be irrelevant, and one which did affect cost but was not correlated with the output measure would not affect the estimate of economies of scale, though its exclusion would lower the explanatory power of the model.[5] Thus,

$$C = aS^{b_1}L^{b_2}W^{b_3}e^{\Sigma Dc_i} \tag{2}$$

where

C = total cost for the firm for one year (1971)
S = number of shipments carried in the year
L = the average length of haul for the firm in the year
W = the average weight of a shipment
$e^{\Sigma Dc_i}$ = a set of dummy variables for geographic area.

The log linear form was chosen so that the coefficient b_1 would

---

[4] Presumably, there are geographic differences in commodity mix but, to a certain extent, these may be taken into account by the inclusion of dummy variables for geographic area. In fact, however, carriers can and do solicit more desirable freight and discourage freight which is less desirable. This remains an area for further research; in particular, it would be desirable to know the bulkiness and fragility of the shipments. Another unknown is the quality of service offered by the individual firm. Although there is no known correlation between quality of service and size of firm, such a relation has been postulated by Lawrence and has the potential to affect any conclusion in regards to economies of scale.

[5] To verify that the results are independent of the choice of output measure, regressions were run with ton-miles as the measure of output. These gave identical estimates of the elasticity of cost with respect to output.

be the elasticity of cost with respect to changes in output.[6] Thus, in this model a constant elasticity is assumed. This is appropriate if the level of economies of scale is the same at all firm sizes but inappropriate otherwise. Later the elasticity will be allowed to vary with firm size, making it possible to examine the possibility that the long-run average cost curve is U-shaped.

The data used in this study are from the Interstate Commerce Commission's Motor Carrier Annual Report forms for Class I carriers of general freight. Selected data from the annual reports are recorded on magnetic tape by the ICC. Copies of these tapes have been obtained by the Department of Transportation. Initially, all the firms which reported all necessary data and which had at least 75 percent of their revenue from intercity general freight were examined. This resulted in 518 observations being available. A variety of subsamples were examined in which the carriers specialized more in intercity general freight or more in less-than-truckload shipments. Particular attention was paid to determining the shape of the long-run average cost curve. This was done not only by allowing the elasticity to vary with firm size but also by portioning the sample by size and by inserting a dummy variable which allowed the constant term in the regression to be different for firms which had revenues between $1 million and $5 million. The considerable variance in firm size, from $1 million to hundreds of millions of dollars in revenue, combined with the large number of observations available, makes it possible to address this question in some detail.[7]

One variable was sometimes included in the cost function despite the fact that it is not, strictly speaking, a shipment characteristic. This variable measured the extent of interlining.[8] Based on

---

[6] The coefficient b_1 shows the percentage change in the dependent variable associated with a unit percentage change in shipments, that is, $(\partial C/\partial S)(S/C)$, provided that none of the other independent variables change. Hence, it shows what happens to cost if additional shipments are carried which have the same characteristics as the old ones. It is also the ratio of marginal cost to average cost $(\partial C/\partial S) \div (C/S)$. If it is less than one, the average curve is downward sloping and shows economies of scale.

[7] The possibility of heteroscedasticity has been raised by Lawrence. Although it is presumably true that the variance of total cost is greater for larger firms than for smaller ones, this is not necessarily true for the variance of the log of total cost. Any given amount of error in equation 2 implies a certain percentage error in total cost. Homoscedasticity would occur if percentage errors were equally large for the different size levels. There appears to be no reason to expect heteroscedasticity.

[8] A shipment is interlined when one carrier moves it part of the way and then turns it over to another carrier who continues the movement. In some cases, as many as three or more carriers would be involved. Interlining generally occurs when the first carrier does not have legal authority to carry the shipment the entire distance.

the assumption that all shipments must be picked up from a shipper and eventually delivered to a consignee, the variable gives the number of pickups and deliveries per shipment. There were about 1.6 pickups and deliveries per shipment, with the remaining 0.4 being transfers to other carriers. Thus,

$$C = aS^{b_1}L^{b_2}W^{b_3}P\&D^{b_4}C^{D_{c_i}}. \tag{3}$$

Because this variable is not truly a shipment characteristic, the assumptions necessary in order to interpret the coefficient on shipments as the economies-of-scale parameter may not hold. In other words, it may not be realistic to assume that as the firm increases size the extent of interlining remains unchanged. For this reason, results from regressions which contain this variable must be interpreted cautiously. Two factors led to the conclusion that it should be included. First, better understanding of the interlining question would be a desirable side benefit and, second, excluding the variable could also distort the conclusion about the level of economies of scale. This comes about because the cost of an interlined shipment is reported by two (or more) carriers, and in this data such a shipment would be counted by each of the carriers involved. Firms which interline more could save on apparent cost advantage (because of fewer pickups and deliveries) which would not reflect a lower cost for the entire movement.

Results of the Empirical Investigations

The empirical results presented here are divided into four parts. In the first part it is assumed that the elasticity of cost with respect to output is fixed (in other words, that economies or diseconomies of scale, if they occur, will occur at all levels of output). In the second part, the assumption of constant elasticity is removed. This is done in three ways: first, by partitioning the sample into size categories; then, by inserting a second order scale term into the regression; and finally by inserting a dummy variable which allows firms with revenues of from $1 million to $5 million (Wyckoff's awkward size) to have higher or lower costs. In the third part, firms which are more specialized in small shipments are examined. This is done in response to the assertion that the less-than-truckload sector of the industry has a natural tendency toward concentration. In the final part, the profitability of the firms is examined. This is done in response to the allegation that the higher profitability of large firms is evidence of economies of scale.

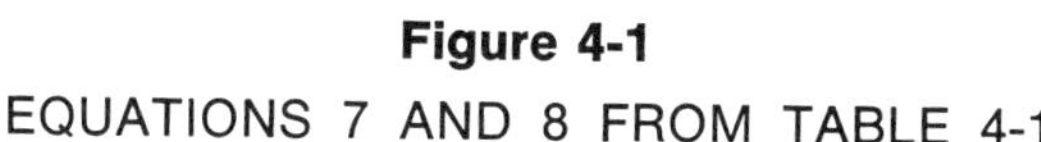

Figure 4-1
EQUATIONS 7 AND 8 FROM TABLE 4-1

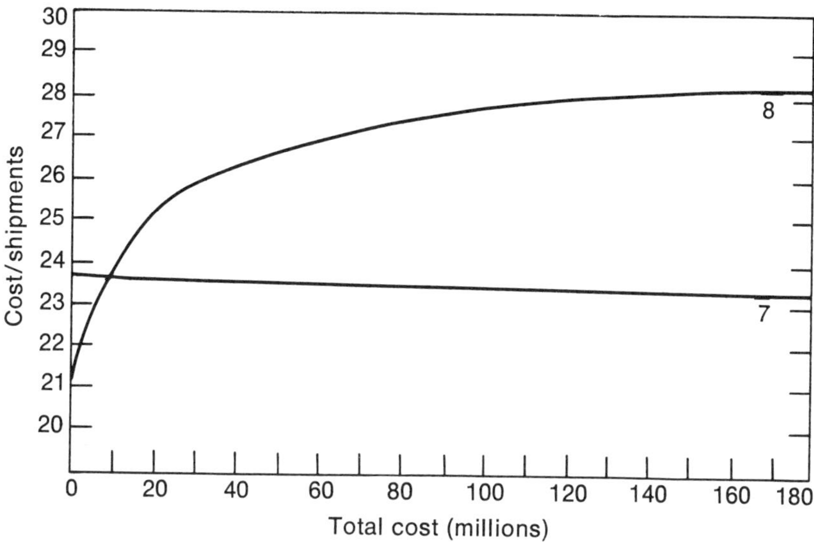

Results from the Constant Elasticity Model. Results from this model are shown in Table 4-1, and the curves are graphed in Figure 4-1. Equation 1 in Table 4-1 is drawn from the work of Warner. Differences stem presumably from the differences in the data base. In this case, all Class I general freight carriers which had in excess of 75 percent of their revenue from intercity general freight and reported all necessary data are included. In addition, the data had been through the full ICC verification process. The coefficient on shipments, b_1, is the elasticity of cost with respect to output. If it were exactly 1, the situation would be one of constant cost. In equation 1, it is 0.991, giving the appearance of some small amount of economies of scale. However, the standard error on the coefficient is 0.011, so the hypothesis of constant cost cannot be rejected. In other words, the coefficient is not significantly different from one. This is far from a definitive result. A 95 percent confidence interval on the elasticity would be from 0.969 to 1.013, or, in other words, from economically significant economies of scale on the one hand to diseconomies of scale on the other.

The first step that was taken to clarify this situation involved an examination of the significance of measurement errors, an issue raised

Table 4-1
RESULTS FROM THE CONSTANT ELASTICITY MODEL

No.	Description	Dependent Variable	Constant	Scale Variable	Length of Haul	Size of Shipment	Others
1.	518 cases $R^2 = 0.962$	$LnC =$	-3.573 (0.195)	+ 0.991 LnS (0.0108)	+ 0.323 LnL (0.015)	+ 0.689 LnW (0.015)	
2.	518 cases $R^2 = 0.965$	$LnS =$	4.268 (0.158)	+ 0.951 LnC (0.0103)	− 0.274 LnL (0.016)	− 0.699 LnW (0.012)	
3.	359 cases $R^2 = 0.967$	$LnC =$	-3.934 (0.226)	+ 0.999 LnS (0.0127)	+ 0.345 LnL (0.019)	+ 0.706 LnW (0.018)	
4.	359 cases $R^2 = 0.965$	$LnS =$	4.489 (0.181)	+ 0.946 LnC (0.0120)	− 0.288 LnL (0.021)	− 0.708 LnW (0.015)	
5.	359 cases $R^2 = 0.975$	$LnC =$	-4.034 (0.213)	+ 1.012 LnS (0.0115)	+ 0.370 LnL (0.018)	+ 0.691 LnW (0.017)	+ ΣDc_i
6.	359 cases $R^2 = 0.974$	$LnS =$	-4.433 (0.172)	+ 0.946 LnC (0.0107)	− 0.320 LnL (0.019)	− 0.683 LnW (0.015)	+ ΣDc_i
7.	359 cases $R^2 = 0.977$	$LnC =$	-5.859 (0.377)	+ 0.996 LnS (0.0113)	+ 0.361 LnL (0.017)	+ 0.647 LnW (0.018)	+ 0.464 $LnP\&D$ (0.081) + ΣDc_i
8.	359 cases $R^2 = 0.975$	$LnS =$	5.922 (0.363)	+ 0.961 LnC (0.0109)	− 0.321 LnL (0.019)	− 0.658 LnW (0.016)	− 0.372 $LnP\&D$ (0.080) + ΣDc_i

Note: Definitions of the variables used in Tables 4-1 through 4-4:

LnC = the log of total cost for one year (1971).
LnS = the log of the total number of shipments carried in that year.
LnW = the log of the average weight of the shipments carried.
LnL = the log of the total distance a shipment is carried.
Dc_i = a set of dummy variables, with coefficients, which denote geographic area.
$LnP\&D = Ln\,(2a+b)$ where: a is the percentage of shipments which are originated and terminated by the carrier and b is the percentage of shipments which are either originated by the carrier and delivered to a connecting carrier or received from a connecting carrier and terminated by the carrier.
$SqLnC = (Ln\ C)^2$
$SqLnS = (Ln\ S)^2$
Revdum = one if revenue is between $1 million and $9 million. Otherwise it is zero.

by Warner. This was done by making shipments the dependent variable and using cost as an independent variable. In this case, b_1 is the elasticity of output with respect to changes in cost. In equation 2 in Table 4-1, b_1 is more than four standard errors less than 1, indicating economies of scale which are both economically and statistically significant. When equations 1 and 2 are examined together, it is clear that errors of measurement, the so-called regression fallacy, present substantial problems in estimating the elasticity with the accuracy which is required.

Since most general freight carriers receive at least some income from sources other than intercity general freight, it is desirable on a priori grounds to exclude those which have significant amounts of other types of revenue. This was done by excluding from the sample any carrier which had more than 1 percent of its revenue from the other sources. This left 359 firms. Equations 3 and 4 in Table 4-1 are identical to equations 1 and 2 other than for the change in the data base. Unfortunately, there is no indication that this helped the problem of measurement error since the spread between the coefficients is as large as before. To calculate this spread between them, it is necessary to invert one of the coefficients so that all measure the same elasticity. For example, if the coefficients in equations 2 and 4 are inverted, the spread, which originally was 6.1 percent, becomes 5.8 percent. Nevertheless, because of the a priori soundness of dealing only with firms which carry only intercity general freight, the new data base is retained for later regressions, though similar regressions were actually performed on the other data base as well.

The next attempt to reduce the problem of errors of measurement was somewhat more successful. This involved the use of eight dummy variables to allow costs to vary over the nine ICC regions. This was done primarily to allow for the possibility that physical conditions, such as congestion, in a different region would have an effect on costs. Another possibility is that a freight mix in one region may be different from that in another region. Inclusion of the dummies reduced the spread in the elasticities to 4.6 percent. In addition, the R^2 for the regression was raised significantly, and the confidence intervals for both regressions were almost entirely in the diseconomies-of-scale range, so the policy implications were somewhat clearer.

In the final pair of regressions in Table 4-1, an additional variable was included which reflects the amount of interlining done by the firm. It is the average number of pickups and deliveries per shipment multiplied by 100. This variable, unlike the other shipment characteristics, describes not only the market but also the method of providing service. Although interpretation of the economies-of-scale question is somewhat less certain, it appears acceptable to continue to regard b_1 as an appropriate measure of economies of scale. The variable was included since it reduced the spread between the two estimates, had a highly significant coefficient, and provided insight into an important policy question, that is, the impact of interlining cost. Analysis of the coefficient on this variable indicates that carriers which interline more have lower cost. This may be surprising until it is recalled that carriers which interline report only their portion of the cost. A hypothetical example was constructed in which a firm which did no interlining was contrasted with two firms which were assumed to interline with each other on every shipment. This resulted in the two firms which interlined having the same number of shipments and the same average shipment size as the firm which did not interline, but average lengths of haul and average numbers of pickups and deliveries only one-half as large. The parameters from equation 7 implied that the total combined cost of the firms which interline would be 14 percent higher than the total cost for the firm which did not interline. If the parameters from equation 8 were used, the combined cost of the firms which interline would be only about 1 percent higher than the single firm. These results appear to contradict the conventional assumption that interlined shipments are substantially more costly than noninterlined shipments.

Results from the Variable Elasticity Model. One way of allowing the extent of economies or diseconomies of scale to be different for different firm sizes is to partition the sample by firm size. This is usually done by examining firms of a particular revenue category. This was done, and the results are presented in Table 4-2. The first four regressions represent the sort which have been presented elsewhere.[9] At first glance, they would seem to offer strong support for the hypothesis that economies of scale exist in the industry. In all four regressions the estimate of the elasticity of cost with respect to output is less than one by a statistically significant amount. However, various curious features of these results, such as the close correlation between the R_2 and b_1, indicate the need for further analysis. Curves

[9] See, for example, Lawrence, "Economies of Scale."

Table 4-2

RESULTS FROM THE VARIABLE ELASTICITY MODELS

No.	Description	Dependent Variable	Constant	Scale Variable	Length of Haul	Size of Shipment	Others
1.	Revenue < $2.5 M 85 cases $R^2 = 0.689$	$LnC =$	1.294 (1.430)	+ 0.685 LnS (0.065)	+ 0.193 LnL (0.040)	+ 0.478 LnW (0.050)	+ 0.157 $LnP\&D + \Sigma Dc_i$ (0.142)
2.	Revenue < $5 M 169 cases $R^2 = 0.818$	$LnC =$	−2.869 (0.832)	+ 0.842 LnS (0.034)	+ 0.266 LnL (0.027)	+ 0.504 LnW (0.030)	+ 0.516 $LnP\&D + \Sigma Dc_i$ (0.112)
3.	$5 M < Revenue < $20 M 119 cases $R^2 = 0.860$	$LnC =$	−3.031 (0.955)	+ 0.883 LnS (0.039)	+ 0.294 LnL (0.028)	+ 0.664 LnW (0.040)	+ 0.249 $LnP\&D + \Sigma Dc_i$ (0.135)
4.	Revenue < $50 M 328 cases $R^2 = 0.965$	$LnC =$	−5.437 (0.405)	+ 0.977 LnS (0.013)	+ 0.335 LnL (0.018)	+ 0.637 LnW (0.019)	+ 0.469 $LnP\&D + \Sigma Dc_i$ (0.082)
5.	Revenue < $2.5 M 85 cases $R^2 = 0.927$	$LnS =$	6.603 (1.433)	+ 0.882 LnC (0.084)	− 0.261 LnL (0.042)	− 0.660 LnW (0.035)	− 0.381 $LnP\&D + \Sigma Dc_i$ (0.157)
6.	Revenue < $5 M 169 cases $R^2 = 0.926$	$LnS =$	6.507 (0.752)	+ 0.945 LnC (0.038)	− 0.286 LnL (0.029)	− 0.601 LnW (0.023)	− 0.552 $LnP\&D + \Sigma Dc_i$ (0.118)

Table 4-2 (Continued)

No.	Description	Dependent Variable	Constant	Scale Variable	Length of Haul	Size of Shipment	Others
7.	Shipments < 162,755 124 cases $R^2 = 0.883$	$LnC =$	−4.554 (0.994)	+ 0.927 LnS (0.043)	+ 0.333 LnL (0.035)	+ 0.635 LnW (0.031)	+ 0.401 $LnP\&D + \Sigma Dc_i$ (0.147)
8.	Shipments < 109,098 81 cases $R^2 = 0.883$	$LnC =$	−5.226 (1.367)	+ 0.980 LnS (0.062)	+ 0.323 LnL (0.044)	+ 0.679 LnW (0.038)	+ 0.399 $LnP\&D + \Sigma Dc_i$ (0.204)
9.	Cost < 3,269,017 133 cases $R^2 = 0.920$	$LnS =$	5.879 (0.905)	+ 0.949 LnC (0.051)	− 0.299 LnL (0.033)	− 0.596 LnW (0.028)	− 0.438 $LnP\&D + \Sigma Dc_i$ (0.131)
10.	Cost < 2,191,288 82 cases $R^2 = 0.924$	$LnS =$	5.746 (1.554)	+ 0.934 LnC (0.092)	− 0.249 LnL (0.042)	− 0.670 LnW (0.037)	− 0.354 $LnP\&D + \Sigma Dc_i$ (0.156)
11.	359 cases $R^2 = 0.968$	$LnC =$	−0.915 (1.190)	+ 0.546 LnS (0.176)	+ 0.336 LnL (0.019)	+ 0.686 LnW (0.020)	+ 0.018 $SqLnS$ (0.007)
12.	359 cases $R^2 = 0.965$	$LnS =$	2.620 (1.730)	+ 1.182 LnC (0.217)	− 0.285 LnL (0.021)	− 0.709 LnW (0.016)	− 0.007 $SqLnC$ (0.006)
13.	359 cases $R^2 = 0.977$	$LnC =$	−3.278 (1.124)	+ 0.623 LnS (0.154)	+ 0.355 LnL (0.017)	+ 0.631 LnW (0.019)	+ 0.015 $SqLnS$ + 0.438 $LnP\&D + \Sigma Dc_i$ (0.006) (0.081)
14.	359 cases $R^2 = 0.976$	$LnS =$	3.796 (1.511)	+ 1.233 LnC (0.188)	− 0.318 LnL (0.019)	− 0.659 LnW (0.016)	− 0.009 $SqLnC$ − 0.377 $LnP\&D + \Sigma Dc_i$ (0.006) (0.080)

Table 4-2 (Continued)

No.	Description	Dependent Variable	Constant	Scale Variable	Length of Haul	Size of Shipment	Others
15.	359 cases $R^2 = 0.977$	$LnC =$	-5.257 (0.473)	$+ 0.972\ LnS$ (0.016)	$+ 0.356\ LnL$ (0.017)	$+ 0.630\ LnW$ (0.020)	$+ 0.445\ LnP\&D$ (0.081) $- 0.071\ LnRevdum$ (0.034) $+ \Sigma Dc_i$
16.	359 cases $R^2 = 0.976$	$LnS =$	6.343 (0.420)	$+ 0.939\ LnC$ (0.016)	$- 0.319\ LnL$ (0.019)	$- 0.659\ LnW$ (0.016)	$- 0.065\ LnRevdum$ (0.033) $- 0.380\ LnP\&D$ (0.080) $+ \Sigma Dc_i$
17.	359 cases $R^2 = 0.978$	$LnC =$	-1.081 (1.306)	$+ 0.405\ LnS$ (0.166)	$+ 0.343\ LnL$ (0.017)	$+ 0.596\ LnW$ (0.022)	$+ 0.395\ LnP\&D$ (0.081) $- 0.113\ LnRevdum$ (0.036) $+ 0.022\ SqLnS$ (0.006) $+ \Sigma Dc_i$
18.	359 cases $R^2 = 0.976$	$LnS =$	5.361 (1.871)	$+ 1.060\ LnC$ (0.224)	$- 0.318\ LnL$ (0.019)	$- 0.659\ LnW$ (0.016)	$- 0.055\ LnRevdum$ (0.039) $- 0.381\ LnP\&D$ (0.080) $- 0.004\ SqLnC$ (0.007) $+ \Sigma Dc_i$

Note: For definitions of variables, see Table 4-1.

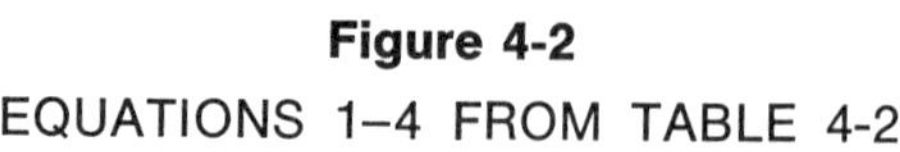
Figure 4-2
EQUATIONS 1–4 FROM TABLE 4-2

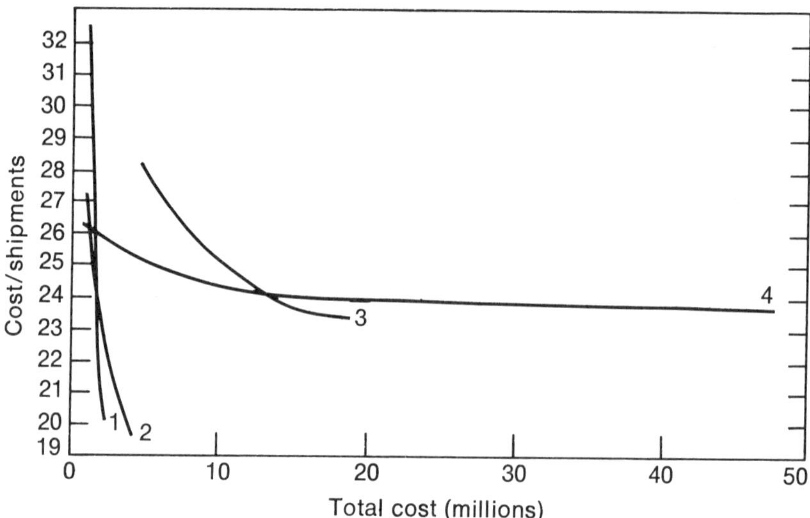

drawn from these equations are shown in Figure 4-2. As can be seen from the sawtooth nature of these curves, regressions of this type do not properly describe the cost function. This is a result of the criterion for selecting the sample. Revenue is very closely correlated with cost, the dependent variable. This can be seen from the correlation between the log of revenue and a log of cost which is 0.998. Partitioning by what in effect is the dependent variable results in a situation where the error term in the regression is no longer uncorrelated with the regressors. Recalling that the definition of a Class I carrier at that time required that the firm have revenues in excess of $1 million, it becomes apparent that at each end of the size range the criterion for inclusion is basically the dependent variable of the regression.

One way to overcome the difficulties described above is to use the reversed formulation where shipments is the dependent variable. This is less than perfect, however, since shipments is also correlated with revenue, though less strongly so, that is, the correlation between the log of revenue and the log of shipments is 0.857. Two regressions of this sort are also presented in Table 4-2 as numbers 5 and 6. In those regressions, diseconomies of scale are found, providing further evidence of the severity of the problem when the sample is partitioned narrowly. The independent variable in the regression (that

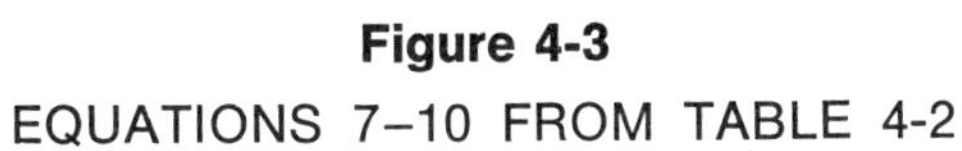
Figure 4-3
EQUATIONS 7–10 FROM TABLE 4-2

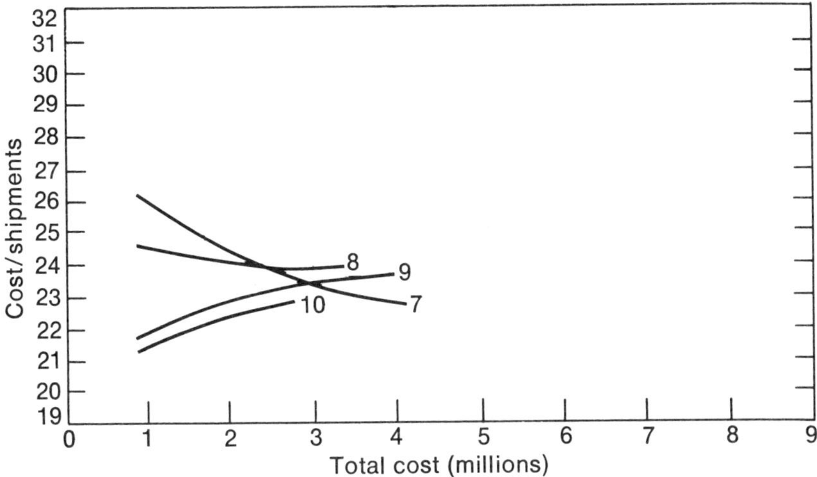

is, number of shipments in the original formulation or total cost in the reversed formulation) makes a better criterion for partitioning. This was done, and results are presented in Table 4-2 as numbers 7 through 10; curves are graphed in Figure 4-3. This only partially solves the problem, since the criterion for inclusion at the low end of the size range is still revenue, and it is difficult to determine an appropriate minimum level based on the other criterion.

Examination of regressions 7 and 8, in which the method of selection is the number of shipments (the appropriate method for the original formulation), reveals that there are apparent economies of scale in one case but not in the other. Regressions 9 and 10 show the result from the reversed formulation with the sample partitioned by total cost. The R^2 is somewhat higher than in 7 and 8 since with this formulation the definition of Class I is a more appropriate criterion for inclusion. The apparent diseconomies of scale are not statistically significant. It is worth comparing regressions 9 and 10 with their counterparts for the full sample regression 8 in Table 4-1. Except for the larger standard errors caused by the smaller number of observations, the results are virtually identical. This contrasts sharply with the noticeable differences between regressions 7 and 8 and between 7 and its counterpart for the full sample, that is, regression 7 in Table 4-1. The inappropriate criterion for the lower bound and chance are possible causes.

Figure 4-4

EQUATIONS 13 AND 14 FROM TABLE 4-2

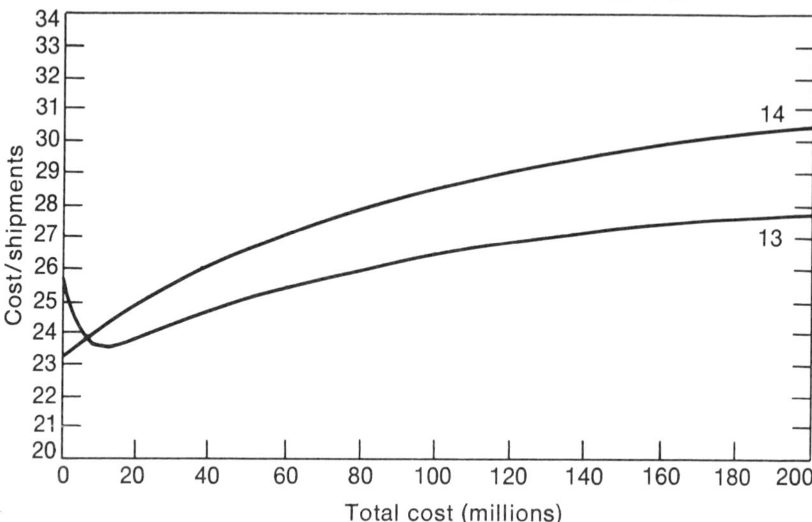

A better way to allow economies of scale to vary with the size of firm is to use the full sample but to include a second order term so that the elasticity of cost with respect to output can change as the scale of operation changes. Results in these regressions are shown in Table 4-2 regressions 11 through 14, and the curves are graphed in Figure 4-4. In regressions 11 and 13, those with the original formulation, the coefficient on the second order term is positive and statistically significant (at the 99 percent level in number 11 and at the 98.5 percent level in number 13). Thus, it would appear that the long-run average cost curve is U-shaped in the conventional fashion, rather than being an inverted U.

Regressions 12 and 14 have a somewhat different result. In these, the coefficient on the second order term is negative, as would be expected from regressions 11 and 13, but not significantly different from zero. Thus, although there is still reason to believe that the long-run average cost curve is U-shaped, it may well be that the significance of the second order term is a result of the use of the revenue criterion for determining the lower end of the sample.

The most significant formulation of the hypothesis that small Class I carriers have higher cost than carriers which are either larger or smaller was made by Wyckoff. He said that firms with $1 million to $5 million in revenue have a more difficult time controlling cost because they are too large and complex for the informal management techniques used by smaller firms and at the same time not large enough for the formalized techniques used successfully by larger firms. This hypothesis was tested by inserting a dummy variable which would take the value of one if the firm had revenues between $1 million and $5 million and would take the value of zero otherwise. The results of this insertion are shown in regressions 15 through 18 in Table 4-2. In regression 15, the original formulation with constant elasticity, the coefficient on the dummy variable is negative and statistically significant, indicating that these firms have lower costs than larger firms. In regressions 16 and 18, the reversed formulation, the coefficient is not statistically significant. Regression 17 is perhaps the most interesting, since the revenue dummy and the second order term seem to be working in opposite directions. Further research will include the insertion of a third order term and a new partition for the lower bound of the sample.

Arguments that the motor carrier industry is subject to economies of scale have centered around the less-than-truckload (LTL) segment of the industry, that is, those firms which specialize in hauling LTL shipments. Although the general freight industry is dominated by the LTL sector (only forty-three firms had more than 10 percent of their shipments as truckload shipments),[10] efforts were made to select as a subsample those firms which were the most specialized in LTL shipments. Table 4-3 shows the results of that effort. Results are basically similar to those for the full sample.

One final investigation was into the question of the effect of scale on firm profits. The elasticity of profit with respect to changes in output, shown in Table 4-4, was found to be approximately 1.8. This indicates that large Class I firms are much more profitable than small ones. However, since the R^2 in this regression is only 0.22, it is clear that the determinants of profit are largely unknown. These unknowns will have more to do with determining the actual profit of a firm than will the size of the firm.

Lawrence has argued that this result implies the existence of economies of scale. Actually, there are a variety of circumstances which would bring about this result. The American Trucking Asso-

[10] The ICC's definition of a truckload shipment is any shipment which weighs more than 10,000 pounds. So, some portion of the so-called truckload shipments are actually carried on a truck with a number of other shipments, and they have the characteristics of a large less-than-truckload shipment. Although shipments which are defined as truckload often are used by carriers for "nose load," when these firms take a serious interest in truckload freight, they generally form a separate division for that purpose.

Table 4-3

RESULTS FROM LESS-THAN-TRUCKLOAD SPECIALISTS

No.	Description	Dependent Variable	Constant	Scale Variable	Length of Haul	Size of Shipment	Others
1.	98% of shipments are LTL 107 cases $R^2 = 0.951$	LnC =	−1.949 (0.753)	+ 0.969 LnS (0.027)	+ 0.292 LnL (0.038)	+ 0.513 LnW (0.102)	
2.	98% of shipments are LTL 107 cases $R^2 = 0.940$	LnS =	2.502 (0.732)	+ 0.956 LnC (0.027)	− 0.234 LnL (0.041)	− 0.481 LnW (0.103)	
3.	99% of shipments are LTL 23 cases $R^2 = 0.887$	LnC =	−1.588 (2.585)	+ 0.989 LnS (0.082)	+ 6.146 LnL (0.099)	+ 0.607 LnW (0.371)	
4.	99% of shipments are LTL 23 cases $R^2 = 0.884$	LnS =	2.766 (2.399)	+ 0.893 LnC (0.074)	− 4.317 LnL (0.095)	− 0.538 LnW (0.347)	
5.	50% of tons are LTL 140 cases $R^2 = 0.949$	LnC =	−2.351 (0.585)	+ 0.974 LnS (0.023)	+ 0.316 LnL (0.035)	+ 0.546 LnW (0.073)	
6.	50% of tons are LTL 140 cases $R^2 = 0.939$	LnS =	3.066 (0.552)	+ 0.952 LnC (0.023)	− 0.258 LnL (0.037)	− 0.538 LnW (0.072)	

Note: For definitions of variables, see Table 4-1.

Table 4-4

RESULTS FROM THE PROFITS MODEL

No.	Description	Dependent Variable	Constant	Scale Variable	Length of Haul	Size of Shipment	Others
1.	359 cases $R^2 = 0.220$	*Ln* Profits (total) =	13.386 (4.069)	+ 1.825 LnS (0.220)	− 0.811 LnL (0.339)	+ 0.870 LnW (0.333)	+ ΣDc_i

Note: For definitions of variables, see Table 4-1.

ciations has argued that smaller trucking firms make worse profits as a result of limited operating authorities. This will be examined more closely in the following section.

Policy Implications

It appears that the cost structure of the trucking industry exhibits economies of scale only at the size range which corresponds to the smallest Class I carriers, and even in that size range the observed economies of scale may well be the result of a statistical problem. Diseconomies of scale are evident for firms with revenues more than approximately $10 million. This finding has a variety of policy implications relating to the appropriate way of regulating the industry. The cost structure is important not only in determining the likely impact of regulatory changes on concentration but also in interpreting the current situation.

It is generally accepted that shippers prefer single-line service to interline service, though the magnitude of this preference is not clear. This, along with the usual managerial incentives to expand the firm, makes the creation of a large route network desirable to motor carriers. When this situation is combined with the current restrictions on entry into the general freight industry, carriers have strong incentives to acquire operating authorities by purchase or merger rather than by applying for entry at the ICC.[11] In the absence of economies of scale in the cost structure, it would seem that these incentives are the causes of the current merger wave.

If entry restrictions were relaxed, pressures for mergers would be reduced. Carriers desiring to improve their route networks would have the option of seeking entry rather than merger. In the absence of economies of scale, the entrance of a new carrier into a route would not require the exit of any other carrier. On routes where new entry occurred, market shares would tend to fall and the number of carriers would increase. Although it is not clear what the impact on the total number of carriers would be, the type of concentration which is of particular importance is the concentration on each route, and it would likely be reduced.

Some have argued that, although the initial effect of freer entry would be to increase the number of competitors, the final effect following a period of adjustment would be to reduce the number. They anticipate that the adjustment period would resemble the second

[11] See, for example, American Trucking Associations, *Accounting for Motor Carrier Operating Rights*, Brief and Petition before the Financial Standards Board of the Financial Accounting Foundation, Washington, D.C., 1974.

Figure 4-5

EQUATIONS 13 AND 14 FROM TABLE 4-2 AND EQUATION 1 FROM TABLE 4-4

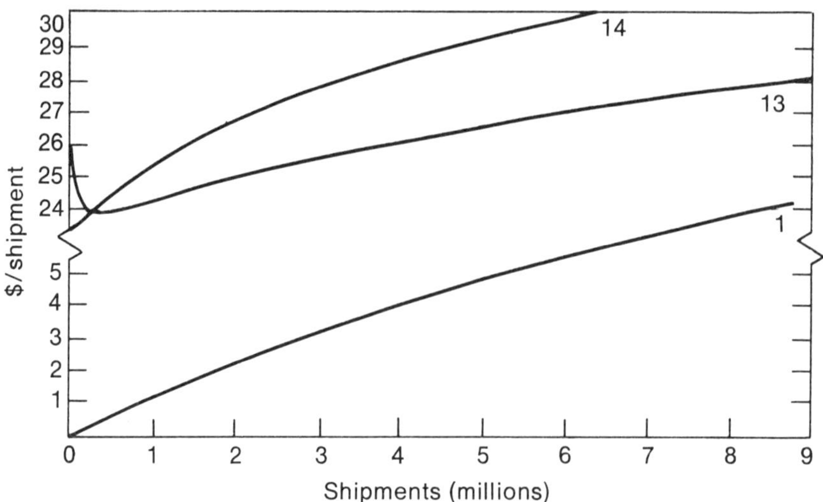

scenario described at the beginning of this paper: cutthroat competition leading to concentration. The cost structure of the industry argues against such a hypothesis, and marketing aspects are not sufficient by themselves to support it.

The impact of greater rate-making flexibility is also affected by the cost structure. If there were economies of scale or large fixed costs, rate wars would be a real possibility. However, since actual long-run marginal cost is likely to be at least equal to long-run average cost, and since the trucking industry is one which can adjust capacity rapidly, rate wars do not seem to be a realistic problem. No class of carrier would have the substantial cost advantages necessary to carry out a successful rate war. This does not mean that no firm would suffer as a result of rate flexibility. Marginal firms could be hurt by lower prices resulting from greater price competition.

An important remaining question is: Why do larger firms tend to make better profits (in relation to revenue) than smaller firms? The current situation, as can be seen from Figure 4-5, is one in which the low-cost firms also make the lowest profits. This may turn out to be nothing more significant than the small firms reducing their corporate income (and tax) by paying owners excessive salaries. However, it certainly appears to be a perverse situation which deserves attention in the form of further research and perhaps regulatory change to remove any regulatory disadvantages suffered by small firms.

5

SERVICE TO SMALL COMMUNITIES

R. L. Banks and Associates, Inc.

Introduction and Conclusions

Since the passage of the Motor Carrier Act of 1935, the United States has followed an essentially unchanged design of motor carrier regulation. With its basic elements now bottomed upon the National Transportation Policy, which constitutes the preamble to the Interstate Commerce Act, the motor carrier regulatory scheme has been amended several times in its particulars but not in its fundamental philosophy. Public policy toward motor carriers has been based on the premise that public interest is best served by formal governmental surveillance of entry, rates, service, and finance. Implicit in current regulation is the view that only by such a method will economically viable motor carriers of intercity freight provide a comprehensive national service that is responsive to shipper and community requirements, free of discrimination, abundantly competitive, and at prices calculated to encourage economic growth.

Study Objective. In recent years, and especially since the beginning of the present decade, a number of influences have combined to bring into question the established regulatory patterns for both motor carriers and other modes of transportation. Among the foremost forces in this process are the geographic dispersion of the nation's industry, an unstable economy, an awakening awareness of the finite nature of the country's resources reinforced by the energy crisis, a growing

This paper is edited from a report entitled *Economic Analysis and Regulatory Implications of Motor Common Carrier Service to Predominantly Small Communities,* prepared for the U.S. Department of Transportation, Office of the Secretary, June 24, 1976.

concern for the environment, and the crumbling structure of the railroad industry. All of this strongly suggests that the time may be approaching when a searching reexamination of national goals and means relating to transportation regulatory policy may be undertaken. Within the broad scope of federal regulation of motor common carriers, this study was structured by the Department of Transportation as an initial and limited attempt to examine economic characteristics of motor carrier service to small communities. Economic inferences drawn from this study should serve as an impetus for further, more refined research, potentially leading to improvements in motor carrier regulation. The overall approach of the study was to select a sample of profitable motor carriers serving predominantly small areas, to compare their operating characteristics with large Class I carriers, and to identify policies of operating rights which could adversely affect service to small areas.

Conclusions. Nine motor common carriers of general freight, all located in different sections of the country and all experiencing increased profits between 1969 and 1974, were chosen for the study sample. These carriers (selected from both Class I and Class II) serve predominantly small communities in several ways: as peddlers which operate out of one or two large cities and serve surrounding rural territory, as operators in states of relatively low population, and as carriers which generally serve the less densely populated areas of relatively high-population states. The average sample carrier is about one-third the size of the average Class I carrier, as measured by vehicle-miles, ton-miles, and operating revenue. Furthermore, the small-market specialist handles lighter loads over shorter distances than the larger carriers.

Although the sample was selected in a somewhat random manner, it is biased by choice; that is, all nine carriers are profitable, and thus their returns on equity and investment are higher than for the average Class I carrier. The profitability extends to the balance sheet, which shows that the sample carrier has less debt, higher coverage, and a higher turnover ratio than the larger, average Class I carrier.

Analysis of comparative statistics, supported by personal interviews with the selected carriers, indicates several possible explanations for the relative success of the small-market specialist. There was consensus, however, in one area of explanation. Some carriers may be financially stable largely because of the structure of rates, the lack of unionized employees, favorable rate divisions for interline traffic, little competition, and/or innovative management. However, the overwhelming impression after interviews with the managements of the selected carriers, as somewhat supported by comparative data, is that small carriers succeed because they are specialists in serving markets requiring the kind of attention which appears to be uneconomical for large carriers to offer. In essence, small carriers appear to be better equipped to handle shipments in small markets because their pickup and delivery service, as well as their terminal operations, are geared for small less-than-truckload (LTL) shipments. Their managements maintain close relations with customers and tight control over their organizations, and they pay close attention to changing market conditions.

One example of small market specialization is revealed in a recent Interstate Commerce Commission case where a large motor carrier (TIME-DC, Inc.) was authorized to serve sixty-four points in five states through pooling agreements with forty-four local carriers.[1] Although not all of the local carriers were small intercity specialists (some provided service solely within commercial zones), the case emphasized the special ability of small carriers to aggregate and distribute freight in small markets. This ability is supported by statistical evidence which shows the nine sample carriers selected for this analysis to be far more productive than larger Class I carriers as a whole in pickup and delivery and in platform (terminal) handling. Whether the relative cost savings in these areas outweigh the small carriers' economic disadvantage in line-haul, billing and collecting, and equipment maintenance remains unanswered. Yet, from evidence in this study, there is reason to believe that small carriers are at least as efficient as large carriers in serving small communities, and that the special needs of such markets result in superior service by small carriers and corresponding apathy on the part of some large carriers.

Identification and Profiles of Selected Carriers

Identifying motor carriers which are serving predominantly small areas is a task requiring time and definitional interpretation. For instance, about 15,000 for-hire carriers, with constantly changing route structures and operating authorities,[2] serve hundreds of thousands of cities, towns, and rural areas in this country. Furthermore, just what constitutes a small community is uncertain, and no available published document identifies motor carriers as oriented toward large

1 For a discussion of this case, see *Transport Topics*, August 11, 1975, p. 1.

2 There are usually between 5,000 and 6,000 annual applications before the ICC for motor carrier route and service changes.

Table 5-1

OPERATING STATISTICS OF 524 COMMON CARRIERS OF GENERAL FREIGHT COMPARED WITH SAMPLE OF 35 SELECTED CARRIERS, 1974

	Average of 524 Carriers[a]	Average of 35 Carriers
Vehicle-miles	12.4	4.3
Ton-miles (millions)	173.2	57.4
Operating revenue (millions)	$18.6	$7.4
Average load (tons)	13.7	10.7
Average haul (miles)	435	213
Average weight/shipment (pounds)	2,007	1,532
Revenue/ton-mile	$0.11	$0.22
Revenue/vehicle-mile	$1.50	$1.75
Operating ratio	94.2%	95.6%

[a] Class I and Class II common carriers of general freight comprising the carriers used by the ten major motor carrier traffic bureaus to study continuous traffic. These carriers are also known as Instruction 27 carriers, that is, they derive at lease 75 percent of their revenue from intercity, general commodity hauling.

Source: American Trucking Associations, Inc., *Financial and Operating Statistics*, 1973-1974.

or small markets. In a technical sense, it is unlikely that more than a few, if any, common carriers serve only small communities (defined in this study as towns and cities of less than 50,000 population). Thus, value judgments have to be made as to what constitutes predominantly small-market service. Superimposed on the definitional problems is the identification of motor carrier service areas—a time-consuming chore in view of the large number of carriers and the extensive descriptions of service in each carrier's operating certificate. Fortunately, because of previous research undertaken by the American Trucking Associations (ATA), only the definitional questions had to be addressed. Using ATA data, a review of carrier route structures was made, and a cross-section of thirty-five carriers that were judged to serve predominantly small-market areas was selected for initial economic characterization (see Table 5-1).

After the data developed for the thirty-five rural carriers were reviewed, nine carriers were selected for further analysis. Criteria employed in the selection of each of the nine carriers were:

Table 5-2

NINE SELECTED MOTOR COMMON CARRIERS OF GENERAL FREIGHT FOR ANALYSIS OF SMALL COMMUNITY SERVICE

Region	Carrier/Headquarters	Service Class	Operating Revenue (millions of dollars) 1969	Operating Revenue (millions of dollars) 1973–74	Net Profit (thousands of dollars) 1969	Net Profit (thousands of dollars) 1973–74
1	Coles Express Bangor, Maine	I	3.7	8.1	145	271
2	Evans Delivery Co., Inc. Pottsville, Pennsylvania	II	1.7	2.9	20	96
3	Liberty Trucking Co. Chicago, Illinois	I	6.4	8.3	(26)	203
4	Merchant's Truck Line, Inc. New Albany, Mississippi	I	2.3	8.2	171	405
5	Allard Express, Inc. Watertown, Wisconsin	II	2.5	3.4	39	64
6	Dodds Truck Line, Inc. West Plains, Missouri	II	1.7	4.4	13	83
7	B&B Lines, Inc. Tulsa, Oklahoma	II	1.7	2.7	49	51
8	Salt Creek Freightways Casper, Wyoming	I	5.8	14.1	189	829
9	McCracken Bros. Motor Freight Eugene, Oregon	II	1.8	2.8	58	94

Source: Table 1 of the original report.

(1) It was a motor common carrier of general freight.

(2) It operated at a profit.

(3) Its profits increased from 1969 to 1974.

(4) Its service centered on an ICC region other than that central to any of the remaining eight carriers.

Table 5-2 identifies the nine selected carriers with accompanying operating and financial characteristics, which in all cases meet the adopted selection criteria. The average size of the nine selected carriers was substantially smaller than the average size of common car-

Table 5-3
COMPARISON OF AVERAGE SIZE OF
614 COMMON CARRIERS OF GENERAL FREIGHT
WITH AVERAGE SIZE OF 9 SELECTED CARRIERS

	Average of 614 Carriers 1973	Clarification	Average of 9 Selected Carriers 1974
Operating revenue	$18,050,800		$6,085,600
Vehicle-miles	12,296,100	Common + contract	2,863,300
Ton-miles	167,321,300	Common + contract	29,567,800
LTL tons	141,857	10,000 lbs. and under	85,025
TL tons	279,153	Over 10,000 lbs.	87,211
Tons carried	421,010		172,236
LTL shipments	398,209	10,000 lbs. and under	268,551
TL shipments	18,567	Over 10,000 lbs.	6,671
Number of shipments	416,776		275,222

Sources: For 614 carriers, Interstate Commerce Commission, *Transport Statistics in the United States*, 1973; for 9 selected carriers, the carriers' annual reports to the ICC for 1974.

riers of general freight.[3] As shown in Table 5-3, the average annual operating revenue of the nine carriers is about 34 percent of the average of 614 common carriers of general freight. Vehicle-mile and ton-mile comparisons reflect an even smaller size for the nine carriers, as the composite averages (as a percentage of the 614 carriers' averages) are only 23 percent and 18 percent, respectively.

It is interesting to note from Table 5-3 that the small carriers have about an equal split of truckload (TL) and less-than-truckload (LTL) tonnage compared to a relative dominance of TL tonnage for the larger carriers. The fact that only about 2 percent of the sample carriers' shipments are TL, compared with about 50 percent of their tonnage, emphasizes the nature of their operations as small shipment specialists. They are capable of providing TL shipments, but they earn profits transporting small shipments to and from relatively small communities.

[3] The group of 524 carriers used in Table 5-1 for comparative analysis was not adopted for this more specific analysis because of data deficiencies, particularly in regard to truckload versus less-than-truckload traffic. Instead, a listing of 614 carriers, as compiled by the ICC, was adopted, as shown in Table 5-3.

Besides the comparison of the average size of the selected carriers and the other 614 carriers, a comparative analysis was also undertaken regarding financial and other operating and productivity characteristics. The original report contained three appendixes which presented these analyses in detail; here, Table 5-4 presents a summary comparison of the two groups of carriers.

Consistent with the previous comparison, Table 5-4 shows the selected small carriers to be more profitable than the other carriers. It should be remembered, however, that profitability was one of the selection criteria for the small carriers. In terms of other financial ratios, no major difference occurs, with one notable exception. The small carriers are less debt financed and better able to cover their debt with cash flow than are the other carriers, but the big difference appears in the turnover ratio comparison. The ability of the small carriers to turn over their capital at a 6.08 rate, compared with a 4.75 rate for the other carriers, could mean (for the small carriers) relatively lower capital investment or relatively higher revenue (because of specialization in higher rated traffic, favorable divisions for interline traffic, and/or a sharp taper in the rate structure for weight and/or distance).

Table 5-4 also shows some interesting comparisons in regard to productivity. The small carriers appear to be significantly more productive in pickup and delivery and at the terminal than the larger average carrier. However, just the opposite holds true for line-haul, billing and collecting, maintenance, and equipment utilization. For instance, for each driver-hour in pickup and delivery service, small carriers handled 1.61 LTL shipments and 0.51 LTL tons, compared with 0.95 LTL shipments and 0.34 LTL tons, respectively, for the average carrier. Likewise, on the platform (that is, in the terminal), for every employee-hour, the small carriers handled 2.46 LTL shipments and 0.78 LTL tons, compared with 1.38 shipments and 0.49 LTL tons, respectively, for the average carrier. The efficiency at the terminal and in pickup and delivery for small carriers cannot be explained merely by the relative magnitude of LTL shipments. As was shown in Table 5-3, although LTL shipments comprise almost 98 percent of small carrier service, they comprise about 96 percent of average carrier service—an overwhelming preponderance in both cases. However, since LTL tonnage is almost one-half of the small carriers' traffic, but only about one-third of the average carriers' traffic, small carriers (considering small shipments more important to their existence than large carriers) may gear their service to small shipments. The small carriers

Table 5-4

COMPARISON OF OPERATING AND FINANCIAL CHARACTERISTICS OF NINE SELECTED CARRIERS WITH INDUSTRY-WIDE SAMPLE

Measure	Industry-wide Sample[a]	Nine Selected Carriers[b]
Profitability		
Operating ratio	94.7%	94.8%
Return of equity	13.5%	16.6%
Return on investment	25.0%	31.8%
Other financial data		
Debt-capital ratio	30.2%	25.4%
Debt coverage	59.0%	82.1%
Current ratio	1.35	1.08
Acid test	88.0%	85.0%
Turnover ratio	4.75 times	6.08 times
Payout ratio	24.5%	—
Leasing		
Lease-investment ratio	39.8%	31.3%
Vehicle-miles leased/total vehicle-miles	27.8%	12.8%
Productivity		
Pickup & delivery:		
LTL shipments/local driver-hour	0.95	1.61
LTL tons/local driver-hour	0.34	0.51
Platform:		
LTL shipments/platform employee-hour	1.38	2.46
LTL tons/platform employee-hour	0.49	0.78
Line-haul:		
Ton-miles/driver-hour	215.6	150.6
Miles/driver-hour	15.8	14.6
Billing & collecting:		
Shipments B&C/employee-hour	7.07	6.05
Maintenance:		
Miles/employee-hour	140.1	110.8

Table 5-4 (Continued)

Measure	Industry-wide Sample[a]	Nine Selected Carriers[b]
Productivity (continued)		
Equipment:		
Average load/haul	13.61 tons	10.24 tons
Average miles/haul	397	170
Average weight/shipment	0.36 tons (LTL)	0.32 tons (LTL)
Revenue/ton-mile	10.8 cents	20.6 cents
Revenue/ton	$42.88	$35.33

[a] Common carriers of general freight with annual operating revenue exceeding $1 million in 1973; data taken from Interstate Commerce Commission, *Transport Statistics in the United States*, 1973.

[b] Data taken from the carriers' annual reports to the ICC, 1974. Data for the nine selected carriers are for 1974, as compared with industry-wide data for 1973. This variance resulting from the use of the latest statistically available data for the nine selected carriers should not have any significant impact on comparative analyses.

are thus more efficient in the areas of pickup and delivery and platform handling.

Moving to the line-haul and other functions, the larger carriers appear to be more productive than the small carriers, but such speculation needs further clarification. For example, the average carrier accounts for more ton-miles (216 compared with 151) and more miles (16 compared with 15) per driver-hour than the small carriers. This advantage is obviously because of heavier average loadings and longer hauls for the average carriers. But the miles per driver-hour comparison may be misleading because the smaller equipment used by the small carriers is more efficient per mile than the larger equipment of the average carrier. Cost analysis was not within the scope of this study; so, conclusions regarding relative efficiency cannot be reached. Thus, at this point, it appears that the only advantage larger carriers have over the small carrier sample is in heavier average loadings over longer distances, resulting in more ton-miles per driver-hour.

Two other areas where economies appear to exist for the larger average carrier are in billing and collecting (seven shipments per billing and collecting employee-hour compared with six for small carriers) and in maintenance. The relatively long time spent in pickup and delivery, as well as short-haul service, apparently takes a toll on maintenance, since small carriers achieve only 111 miles per maintenance employee-hour compared to 140 miles for the average carrier.

Personal Interviews

A number of issues were identified from comparative statistical analysis. These issues were dealt with during personal interviews with the nine sample carriers. In a general sense, the objective of the interviews was to determine the rationale for the relative success of the small carriers and to ascertain the carriers' views on how regulation does, and could, affect their service to small cities. More specific issues were: Does productivity at the terminal and in pickup and delivery outweigh diseconomies in line-haul, billing and collecting, and maintenance? What are the instrumental characteristics of successful operations in rural areas—lack of union, employees, high divisions, specialized service, management effectiveness, government regulation, et cetera? How do the carriers view ICC policy in regard to all phases of operating rights? Does the rate structure have any effect on service to small cities? The unstructured nature of the interviews also resulted in some statements which touched on important and related aspects of the rural service question, but which were beyond the scope of this study. Although the interviews were informal and unstructured, the interviewer did fill in a questionnaire to insure some degree of conformity.[4]

Certain contributory and detrimental inferences can be drawn regarding the economic viability of the nine selected carriers from the statistical profiles and the personal discussions. Carrier managements appear to be well versed in planning, organizing, and controlling their companies, and they take pride in knowing their markets and service requirements. Interviewees affirmed the rationale of terminal efficiency and espoused the special nature and efficiency of providing small shipment service to predominantly small cities. They talked of responsiveness, closeness to their customers, the competitiveness of small enterprises, and completely centralized management control over operations. Specific factors mentioned, including some of the factors mentioned above, are as follows:

(1) These carriers have become specialists in handling traffic in small cities, where LTL traffic amounts to approximately 50 percent of their total tonnage, of which a high percentage is interlined with other carriers. As specialists, they are "set up" to handle small shipments with respect to scheduling, handling at the terminal, and customer relations.

[4] The questionnaire was included as Appendix D of the original report.

(2) Over the past few years, large carriers have increasingly neglected the short-haul, small market, particularly on LTL traffic, and they have concentrated more on the long-haul market. However, this trend has reversed recently because large carriers are trying to attract additional volume to offset losses in volume incurred in the long-haul market during the economic recession.

(3) More new industry has been locating in rural areas (including small cities) in recent years.

(4) The small carriers maintain a closer relationship with shippers in rural areas than the large carriers. This allows them to be more aware of and more responsive to shippers' needs.

(5) Pay scales for motor carrier labor are generally higher than for other industries in small cities, and job opportunities are more restrictive. This allows motor carriers serving such areas to maintain a stable and experienced labor force.

(6) Small carriers have greater operating flexibility, allowing them to be more responsive to special service requirements of shippers.

(7) Costs for union drivers are generally lower for short-haul carriers, and one of the nine selected carriers (Merchant's Truck Line, New Albany, Mississippi) has no union labor.

(8) Pooling arrangements made with large carriers to perform their pickup and delivery and transfer to their terminals reduces competition. This additional traffic handled by small carriers is of the same nature as their other traffic, and it requires no costly special services to handle.

(9) On the basis of relative ton-miles, rates (and thus revenue) are higher for LTL traffic than for TL shipments. Furthermore, as consolidators and distributors of freight, the small carriers have operating revenue of $2.13 per vehicle-mile compared with $1.47 for the average carrier.

On the other hand, according to the small carriers, there was evidence that they were at a disadvantage vis-à-vis larger carriers in the following areas:

(1) Large carriers can be more selective in the traffic they handle.

(2) Small carriers generally handle more intrastate traffic than large carriers, usually at lower rate levels.

(3) Large carriers can often convince shippers that one-carrier service is faster on long-haul movements; in reality, however, it is no faster than two-carrier service on many movements. In many instances, this contention allows the large carriers to "skim off the cream" of the traffic.

(4) Line-haul cost per mile is higher for small carriers.

(5) Small carriers have less purchasing power, resulting in higher cost of purchased equipment and supplies.

(6) Small carriers cannot afford to advertise as much as large carriers.

In essence, it appears that the large carriers do not exercise a number of their potential service advantages because of their involvement and commitment to larger markets. However, they concentrate on large markets not only because of profit opportunities, but also because of the inherent characteristics of small-city service. These characteristics include the following:

(1) Many customers are infrequent users of transportation service; they are not versed in traffic matters and thus require more assistance on rates, routing, claims, et cetera; and they often expect unrealistic service.

(2) A post office box number is sometimes the only address shown on the freight bill for the consignee, which results in excessive time for locating the consignee and making delivery.

(3) Consignees are not always prepared to pay for shipments that are sent cash on delivery (COD), which requires a second delivery.

(4) Since inbound volume is higher than outbound volume in most rural communities, opportunities to balance movements and get good equipment utilization are limited.

(5) Private haulers handling shipments illegally for close friends or associates are more prevalent in rural areas.

(6) Scheduling and dispatching are more difficult in rural areas because the market is widely scattered and an agent cannot be justified at every location.

(7) The markets are scattered, which results in higher mileage per ton for freight handled in small cities and rural areas.

Interestingly, many of the nine carriers interviewed felt that they are presently operating in a somewhat deregulated atmosphere because of liberal entry policy, and that more effective regulation of entry was needed to preserve small-city service in the long run. In short, many of the carriers felt that they were realizing the disadvantages of regulation with few, if any, of the advantages. As small carriers serving small areas, they could hardly be expected to gain ICC approval for service expansion into major markets. At the same time, however, their markets were being inundated with new carriers. The alleged liberal entry policy in small markets has, according to the consensus of the sample carriers, diluted a number of markets. In fact, a carrier stated that, in one case, a certificate was granted even though only one supporting witness appeared at the hearing. Another stated that thirty-nine certificates were granted to carriers to serve one plant.

The sample carriers further contended that competition would be even more excessive at many locations if all carriers holding certificates were actually offering service. Performance of service is not policed by the ICC nor by any state commission on its own initiative. Investigations take place only when complaints are received from shippers. If other carriers serve a location, a carrier can generally terminate service to that location, and the shippers will use the services of other carriers rather than file a service complaint with the state commission or the ICC. Under such conditions, the carrier terminating the service may hold a dormant certificate for several years and then start serving the location if the market becomes more attractive. When a carrier holding dormant rights reenters a market that has become attractive, the market is again diluted for carriers that continued to serve the market during the previous period. The majority of the nine selected carriers strongly advocated the revocation of certificates if service was not performed in accordance with the authorization over a specified period of time.

The burden of the certificate application procedure has discouraged some of the carriers from applying for new certificates to serve markets that are not particularly attractive. Potential new markets are thoroughly analyzed before a commitment is made to spend time and money in a certificate application procedure. Moreover, it is often difficult to get twenty-five witnesses (the number normally needed to develop convincing supporting evidence) to appear at the hearings. The modified procedure adopted by the ICC to reduce the time generally required has been an improvement, but the majority of the selected carriers felt that the application procedure should be further revised.

In summary, these nine selected carriers have become specialists in handling small shipments in rural and small-city areas. Through management control of operations and costs, close relationship with customers, performance of good service, and responsiveness to changes in the market, these nine selected carriers have shown that it is possible for small carriers to be successful in serving small markets, even though they apparently are not overly protected by regulatory policies. They have focused on customer needs, and they control their service in an efficient manner to meet such needs.

6
CERTIFICATE VALUES

John W. Snow and Stephen Sobotka

The Nature of Certificate Values. Most businesses in the United States can be freely entered by those who are willing to bear the commercial risks involved. Governmental approval is not required. Such is not the case in industries like trucking or aviation where approval from a governmental agency is necessary. A prospective entrant into the regulated motor carrier business must convince the Interstate Commerce Commission (ICC) in a proceeding, at which potential competitors have a right to appear, that he should be allowed to provide motor carrier service. Significant legal barriers to entry into the trucking industry exist.

Because the ICC has constrained entry into the motor carrier industry, the right to serve has become valuable, and the certificate of public convenience and necessity, which is issued by the ICC, has become an asset that can be purchased and sold for a large sum of money. Through 1970 about $300 million worth of certificates had been transacted. By January 1977 the number may have reached $600 million. Certificates are worth on the order of 15 to 20 percent of the annual sales of trucking firms. The total value of all certificates may be on the general order of $3 billion to $4 billion. This includes both values that have and values that have not been explicitly put on the accounting statements of motor carriers. (Most have probably not been put on the books.) Assuming a 10 percent after-tax rate of return, something on the order of 3 to 5 percent of the transportation rates go towards paying for certificates on a nonamortized basis.

This paper is edited from various memoranda that were prepared by the authors for the Department of Transportation and from a paper entitled "A Discussion of the Relationship between Entry Liberalization and the Value of Operating Certificates" that was issued by the Office of the Secretary of Transportation, January 19, 1977.

It is inevitable that meaningful regulatory reform will erode to zero that portion of the certificate values which result from certificate scarcity. That portion which in other businesses would be "good will" should, at worst, be unaffected by regulatory reform. Good will of motor carriers would increase because they would become more dependent on it and presumably would go to greater lengths to achieve customer loyalties.

If regulatory reform has been given some possibility of enactment, then current certificate values should be below their otherwise expected value. Under these circumstances, persons engaging in transactions now will either make windfall profits or incur substantial losses, depending on whether regulatory reform is enacted.

Arguments for the Retention of Certificate Values. There are two main arguments against regulatory reform revolving around certificate values. One is that the owners of certificates would be deprived of "property" as a result of regulatory reform. But, when governmental tax or regulatory policies are altered, the values of capital assets often change. In the past, the government has not required a payment when capital values increased (as, for example, when the ICC limits on entry became effective), nor has it provided compensation when these values decreased. Moreover, debate about regulatory reform has now gone on for several years. Certificate values, no doubt, reflect uncertainty about their longevity. Persons who have purchased or sold certificates in the last several years have done so knowing that there was prospect for regulatory reform, and they took that into account when entering into such transactions.

The second argument against regulatory reform relating to certificate values is that some certificate owners have borrowed by using their certificates as collateral. These loans could go into default and, consequently, trucking services could be impaired. The first part of the argument is factually correct; certificates have been used as collateral for loans. But, it does not follow that trucking services will worsen if there is default.

Some loans were made to motor carriers to enable them to purchase certificates, or to diversify out of the motor carrier business, or to pay out partners or heirs. Other loans were made to motor carriers to enable them to purchase equipment or facilities such as terminals which are used in the basic business of providing trucking services. But, default of these loans will not impair the basic motor carrier business even if the borrowers suffer financial reverses because the certificates decline in value.

Regulatory reform will tend to increase the demand for services by common carriers. So, there is no reason to expect that trucks, terminals, or other equipment used in the industry will decrease in value. Consequently, efficient firms will be able to earn adequate returns on their physical assets and to prosper even though their certificates will decline in value. Existing firms, because they are established, will be at a competitive advantage with respect to new carriers that may wish to compete with them.

Means of Maintaining Certificate Values. Certificate values can be maintained at their scarcity value only if there is no regulatory reform. One can avoid precipitous declines of certificate values by phasing the introduction of reforms over a period of years. The Motor Carrier Reform Act provides for a reasonable phase-in period. But, the longer reform is postponed, the longer will be the delay in realizing its benefits.

A delay in a decision regarding regulatory reform may not result in the maintenance of certificate values. As long as there is uncertainty about regulatory reform, the values of certificates will be adversely affected. This kind of uncertainty also is harmful to shippers because they are denied the benefits of improved efficiency and lower rates. Thus, a delay in a decision regarding regulatory reform benefits neither the certificate owner nor the shipper.

Means of Compensating Certificate Holders for Loss in Value. There are several ways in which certificate holders could be compensated for the decrease in values of their certificates. The government might purchase certificates directly. Such action would be viewed by many as an extreme step which is inherently inequitable and which sets a very bad precedent. The inequity results from the fact that those who have been the beneficiaries of restricted entry would receive compensation, whereas those who have been injured by restricted entry would not. In addition, many would receive compensation who had not made any payment for the certificate. Alternatively, the government could allow a tax write-off. Neither system would improve motor carrier service because no part of the payment or tax reduction would be tied to services provided. Thus, this form of compensation must be justified on the grounds that the government should compensate for the losses caused by a change in policy. But government frequently takes actions which affect the value of assets, and the case of motor carriers is indistinguishable from many other instances where people gain or lose as a result of changes in tax or regulatory policies. A system of certificate value compensation is also questionable on basic equity grounds. It helps certificate owners but not others—for example, ICC practitioners, who may lose some part of their business when regulatory reform is enacted.

Means for Facilitating the Transition to a Less Regulated Motor Carrier Industry. As a consequence of regulatory reform, some new firms will wish to enter the motor carrier industry and some existing but inefficient firms may have difficulties adjusting to the intensified competitive conditions. The Motor Carrier Reform Act's provisions are phased over a period of years in order to avoid disruptions in services. It is also possible to assist both new entrants and existing firms during the transition by providing one of the following forms of financial assistance.

The government could provide loan guarantees to lenders who provide funds used for the purchase of equipment or facilities required by motor carriers. Although some existing carriers and new carriers might find such a program useful, it suffers from a serious defect: loan guarantees would encourage new entry and thus provide competition to existing firms beyond the levels that would otherwise exist.

Motor carriers might be allowed tax relief in the form of accelerated write-offs not available to industry in general. This form of assistance would provide little relief because the bulk of fixed assets (trucks and trailers) owned by motor carriers have a rather short life. Nevertheless, this form of assistance would facilitate capital investment for expansion and replacement by both new and existing firms. But this alternative would also contribute to excess capacity.

Motor carriers might, for a period of years, be allowed to deduct a portion of net revenues from their federal income tax. This form of tax relief would facilitate investments by both existing and new firms. But by basing the tax deduction on their current volume of business it would preferentially assist existing firms whose certificates would decline in value as a result of regulatory reform.

PART FOUR
IMPLICATIONS OF REFORM FOR TRAFFIC DIVERSION AND ENERGY USE

Advocates of motor carrier deregulation argued that it would make the motor carrier industry more efficient. The question naturally arose whether deregulation of trucking would shift traffic from other modes, primarily rail, to trucks. Railroads are generally regarded as the more energy efficient mode and thus, if major traffic diversion from rail to truck occurred, it could be argued that trucking deregulation would adversely affect energy consumption. Two economists from the Massachusetts Institute of Technology, Paul O. Roberts and James T. Kneafsey, prepared a paper for the Federal Energy Administration addressing this question of traffic diversion under trucking deregulation. Roberts and Kneafsey found that truck deregulation would shift a moderate amount of freight from rail to truck with a net adverse effect in fuel usage.

Two economic consultants, Stephen Sobotka and Thomas Domencich, then prepared an assessment for the Department of Transportation on the traffic diversion issue. They concluded that there would not be any significant diversion from rail to truck. In fact, Sobotka and Domencich projected a net diversion from truck to rail. Moreover, they found that the efficiency gains within the trucking industry because of truck deregulation (fewer trucks and truck-miles) would result in fuel savings which would more than offset any increased fuel usage associated with the Roberts-Kneafsey estimate of diversion from rail to truck. In other words, the Sobotka-Domencich study found that the fuel savings resulting from efficiency improvements in trucking exceeded the Roberts-Kneafsey projection of the fuel effects of traffic diversion. Thus, even assuming the most pessimistic traffic diversion estimates, the trucking reform proposals would result in net fuel savings.

Both the Roberts-Kneafsey paper and the Sobotka-Domencich paper are presented here.

7

TRAFFIC DIVERSION AND ENERGY USE IMPLICATIONS OF SURFACE TRANSPORT REFORM

Paul O. Roberts and James T. Kneafsey

The Proposed Legislation

Two major bills concerning deregulation of the surface transportation industries were proposed by the Ford administration: the Railroad Transportation Improvement Act of 1975 and the Motor Carrier Improvement Act of 1975. These two bills would have major impacts on the structure and operations of the surface transportation system of the United States. These impacts would have energy use implications. Changes in energy use would most likely follow primarily from two consequences of the bills. The first consequence is that there will be shifts in the choice of mode for moving commodities. The second is that there will be changes in load factors on each mode which result from these shifts. Other consequences of the bills will be long-term changes in total freight transportation purchases and changes in location of production for various markets. These latter consequences should be of lesser magnitude and they are more difficult to quantify. Therefore, our concern here will be primarily to analyze the energy

This paper is edited from a study entitled *Energy Use Implications of Proposed Changes in the Regulation of the Railroad and Motor Trucking Industries,* prepared for the Federal Energy Administration, Office of Transportation Research. Paul O. Roberts and James T. Kneafsey are economists with the Center for Transportation Studies, Massachusetts Institute of Technology. The paper, which is dated October 1975, was written prior to the passage of the Rail Revitalization and Regulatory Reform Act of 1976. The Ford administration's rail reform proposal is referred to in this paper as the Railroad Transportation Improvement Act of 1975.

use implications of the bill which result from changes in mode preferences and from the resulting load factors of the modes.

The basic provisions of the truck and rail deregulation bills are well known. Basically, the bills deal with rate bureaus, rate suspension powers of the Interstate Commerce Commission, rate regulation, entry and certification requirements for different classes of motor carriers, competition between modes in rate making, and various problems unique to the modes involved.

Of principal concern to the analysis of energy use implications are the provisions dealing with entry for the motor carriers and competition between modes in their rate setting. In the future, the ICC must issue a certificate of entry to any common carrier by motor vehicle that applies and meets the simple requirements of being fit, willing, and able to provide the service at a cost that is compensatory and not discriminatory. The ICC is prohibited from ruling against rates of one mode to protect the traffic of another mode.

Another major provision of the bills is the flexibility accorded the carriers with respect to rate changes. Both rail and common carrier truck bills provide that changes of plus or minus 7 percent during the first year, 12 percent in the second year, and up to 15 percent in the third year from the date of passage of the bill may not be suspended by the ICC.

The principal concern of this analysis is the extent to which traffic currently moving by one mode will be diverted to a mode that is, perhaps, more energy intensive. The analysis is also concerned with the resulting load factors of the various segments of the surface transportation industries. It is useful, therefore, to focus upon those components of the larger transportation industries which are competitive and within which the potential for diversion exists.

Competitive Components of the Transportation Industry

The modes commonly associated with the freight transportation industry are truck, rail, barge, pipeline, and air. Although these are clearly the principal modes involved, to restrict our analysis to such broad categories is very misleading. The trucking industry, for example, can be broken into regulated trucking and private trucking. Within the regulated trucking category, there are both contract and common carriers. Private trucking can be broken into owner-operator and private fleet operations. Each of these segments operates differently, has different competitors, and has different energy use characteristics.

Within the rail industry it is useful to distinguish among normal carload operations, trailer-on-flatcar operations (TOFC, or piggyback), and unit train operations. Freight shipments by inland waterway barges, pipeline, or air do not need to be further disaggregated for our purposes here. One can also distinguish small parcel movements such as those performed by the United Parcel Service, the U.S. Postal Service, and many of the freight forwarders currently in existence. It will not be necessary to elaborate upon these latter categories. We must distinguish between intracity and intercity movements, since the bills specifically address the intercity portion of the freight movement industry.

In order to compare competitive segments of the industry, it is useful to identify three major aspects of a freight shipment. These three dimensions are: size of shipment, length of haul, and type of commodity.

Freight transportation is characterized by very large economies of scale in shipment size. Transportation rates for less-than-truckload lots are several times more than those for truckload or carload shipments. It is therefore useful to distinguish four general classes: (1) bulk shipments, (2) truckload or carload shipments (TL/CL), (3) less-than-truckload shipments (LTL), and (4) minimum charge shipments (min).

Length of haul is also important in intercity freight movement, since some of the modes, particularly rail and barge, have advantages in long-haul movement. We therefore distinguish: (1) shipments more than 600 miles, (2) shipments less than 600 miles, and (3) intracity shipments of less than 50 miles.

Obviously, the type of commodity, its ease of handling, its perishability, and its other attributes greatly influence transport tariffs. For example, it is useful to distinguish the following: (1) manufacturing; (2) livestock; (3) agriculture; (4) coal; (5) iron ore, nonferrous, and miscellaneous mining; (6) lumber and products; (7) petroleum and products; (8) stone, clay, glass products; (9) chemicals; and (10) other. In fact, it is useful to look at commodities in somewhat more detail even than this major classification scheme, as we will subsequently demonstrate.

Table 7-1 compares the movement of goods in terms of each of the three dimensions for each of the major modes. Even though this characterization is rough, it quickly shows the more competitive segments of the industry and those that are not so competitive. For example, carload railroad operations are not particularly competitive with regulated common carrier truck operations. Common carrier

Table 7-1

MARKET CHARACTERISTICS OF THE MODES OF FREIGHT TRANSPORTATION

						Total Truck (412)				
						Regulated truck (170)		Private truck (242)		
	Pipe (431)	**Inland Waterway Barge** (596)	**Rail** (768) Unit train	Carload	TOFC	Contract	Common	Owner-operator	Private fleet	**Air** (3)
Size of shipment	bulk	bulk	bulk	CL & bulk	TL	TL	LTL	TL	LTL	LTL
Length of haul	all distances	all distances	all distances	>600	>600	<600	<600	>600	<600	>600
Commodities[a]	petroleum	mining coal	mining coal grains	agri. lumber food mfgrs. chemicals	agri. food mfgrs.	agri. food mfgrs. petroleum chemicals	mfgrs. food other	livestock agri. food metals mfgrs.	mfgrs. food metals other	mfgrs. food other

[a] The competitive commodities are: manufacturing (mfgrs.), livestock, agriculture (agri.; including grains), coal, mining, lumber, petroleum, glass, chemicals, other.

Note: The number in parentheses under each mode is ton-miles in millions for 1970.

truck is characterized primarily by LTL shipments, whereas railroad carloads are characterized by much larger shipment sizes. Carload shipments typically travel more than 600 miles, whereas common carrier truck shipments travel all distances, but predominantly less than 600 miles. Finally, the types of goods moving by common carrier truck include emergency and high-value shipments along with manufactured articles. By contrast, carload shipments include a considerable portion of agricultural exempt commodities and food in addition to manufactured articles. Thus, common carrier truck and rail carload shipments are not as competitive as is normally believed.[1]

On the other hand, owner-operator freight shipments appear to be quite competitive with both contract truck and rail TOFC and carload movements, particularly with respect to perishables and agricultural exempt movements.[2] Contract truck movements of liquids and specialty products also appear to be highly competitive with rail carloads and TOFC. Another competitive area appears to be common carrier trucking, private fleet trucking, and air shipments. Here the commodity makeup of the movements appears to be roughly equivalent. In the long run, air might prove to be more competitive if its rates were substantially lowered.[3] However, it will not figure as a major competitor in this larger market until specially designed freight aircraft have been demonstrated which can substantially reduce costs. In the large shipment sizes, bulk movements by barge and pipeline are competitive. For some types of commodities, particularly for coal and iron ore movements, unit train and barge operations are competitive.

In order to get a handle on the overall size of each of these competitive segments of the freight transportation industry, it is useful to determine the ton-miles of carriage transported by each mode. This information is shown in Table 7-1 in parentheses under each mode in millions of ton-miles for the year 1970.[4] It is difficult to break the modal segments into more detail than is shown here since published statistics are not available in this form. There is even considerable

---

1 Alexander L. Morton, *Competition in the Intercity Freight Market: A Waybill Study of the Motor Carrier Industry*, U.S. Department of Transportation, Office of Systems Analysis, February 1971.

2 David H. Maister and D. Daryl Wyckoff, *The Owner-Operator: Independent Trucker* (Lexington, Mass.: D.C. Heath and Co., 1975).

3 L. M. Schneider, *The Future of the U.S. Domestic Air Freight Industry: An Analysis of Management Strategies* (Cambridge, Mass.: Harvard University Press, 1973).

4 U.S. Department of Transportation, *Summary of National Transportation Statistics*, November 1973.

speculation about how many owner-operators there are, partially because they tend to work for common and contract carriers on short-term leases. Greater detail can be obtained only by using published statistics on basic commodity movements by mode.

Major Commodity Flows by Mode in the United States

Aggregate and comprehensive statistics on the flows of commodities by shipment size, length of haul, and commodity for each of the modes is unavailable. Estimates of ton-miles by mode and type of commodity have been made, however. These estimates, prepared by Jack Faucett and Associates for the U.S. Department of Transportation, are based on 1965 figures. The study uses input/output methodology to project the flows forward to 1970 and 1980. For our purposes it is most useful to look at the 1965 estimates from this study. These are shown in Table 7-2.

From this set of figures it is quickly seen that the major ton-mile movements occur as a result of the movement of fuels, principally petroleum and coal. These movements are, however, impossible to project into the future. The U.S. energy policies are likely to have an overwhelming influence on fuel transportation patterns relative to any change in transportation regulation. Our concern therefore will be principally with other commodity movements.

The total tons generated on *intercity* domestic freight shipments in 1965 were 4.89 billion. This figure includes the intercity portions of the rail, motor trucking (common, contract, and private), water, air carrier, and pipeline modes. The corresponding aggregate figures for the ton-miles generated by the same modes was 1.817 trillion ton-miles. When the local portions of domestic freight movements are included, the totals become 9.779 billion tons and 1.888 trillion ton-miles, respectively. A more detailed distribution of these figures for the individual modes of transportation and for a series of commodity sectors is presented in Table 7-2. Note that the grand totals include small amounts of unidentified freight as well as governmental and personal consumption expenditures. Otherwise, the table contains a thorough distribution of ton-miles for the major commodity-producing industries in 1965.

Implications of the Proposed Legislation on Modal Competition

If we assume that the origin to destination flows of major commodities in U.S. markets will remain proportional as they grow over the next ten years and that only modal preferences will shift, then a comprehensive overview of these flows can be developed. The key assumptions are that markets will remain the same, that modes will shift in response to the proposed legislation, and that changes in industry structure will lead to increased efficiency within the modes. We also believe that pervasive long-run shifts in the cost structure of the various modes will be a factor which must be considered.

It is impossible to view the proposed legislation as the sum of the consequences of independent sections of the individual bills. Rather, the two bills must be viewed together and interdependently, and their impacts on the various modes must be viewed comprehensively. It will be useful to review the basic impacts of the bills upon each of the modes before attempting to draw overall conclusions.

The bills' basic thrust is to establish a pattern of deregulation. Entry for the motor carriers is eased and the individual firms are encouraged to act independently. The powers of the rate bureaus are greatly diminished, and railroads are given more freedom to set rates individually. On the whole, the picture is one of greatly increased competition; however, before jumping to this as a final conclusion, it is useful to look at the individual segments of the industry.

We will first examine those aspects of the bills that apply to common motor carriers. There are a number of provisions in the bills that eliminate features of the truck industry structure which make it function like a cartel, namely, coordinated rate setting by rate bureaus and the restrictions on entry into the industry. Rate bureaus have been accused of setting rates so as to protect high-cost operators. In the future, they will no longer be able to do this, and the prices that prevail in any given market should lean toward the marginal cost of the carrier needed to furnish the last increment of supply. The freedom to enter should help to protect these lower rates, since a large carrier with a portion of a given market will be afraid to raise his rates and thus invite entry.

Entering into the regulated common carrier LTL truck market is neither a simple nor an easy thing to do. It requires setting up large terminals with tremendous capital costs and an organizational structure to handle the complex day-to-day solicitation of freight and management of operations. In spite of the argument that there are no economies of scale in trucking, there clearly are advantages that accrue to large carriers by virtue of comprehensive service to many areas. For example, it appears that large carriers can consistently maintain higher load factors than small ones. Therefore, we believe that entry into the

Table 7-2
DOMESTIC FREIGHT TON-MILES BY PRODUCING SECTOR, 1965
(millions of ton-miles)

Sector Number	Title	Railroads	Domestic Water
1	Agriculture	65,367.915	23,362.857
2	Iron ore mining	17,951.580	57,193.033
3	Nonferrous mining	8,596.187	69.898
4	Coal mining	130,427.852	28,456.395
5	Miscellaneous mining	35,827.260	36,397.880
6	Construction	0.000	0.000
7	Ordnance	2,409.889	107.663
8	Food and drugs	79,505.836	8,088.057
9	Textiles and apparel	2,025.277	23.067
10	Lumber and products	61,366.976	17,516.538
11	Furniture	2,819.996	360.042
12	Paper and products	41,316.987	1,413.541
13	Printing	518.460	138.805
14	Chemicals	45,087.098	11,271.458
15	Plastic-paint-rubber	8,570.204	1,101.733
16	Petroleum and products	14,458.431	278,539.852
17	Stone-clay-glass products	29,425.959	540.048
18	Iron and steel	34,449.234	8,506.151
19	Nonferrous metals	14,463.533	695.227
20	Fabricated metal products	5,974.079	135.262
21	Farm-construction machinery	3,431.415	618.968
22	Industrial machinery	2,830.405	563.549
23	Electrical machinery	3,123.603	1,178.008
24	Motor vehicles	15,564.653	225.886
25	Aircraft	83.804	1.714
26	Other transportation equipment	1,548.333	80.250
27	Scientific-optical instruments	70.735	7.081
28	Communications	0.000	0.000
29	Utilities	0.000	0.000
30	Services	0.000	0.000
31	Auto repairs	0.000	0.000
32	Government enterprises	20,522.099	172.386
33	Gross imports	4,623.421	1,982.088
34	Business travel-gifts	2,682.571	1,161.687
35	Miscellaneous manufacturing	2,937.580	1,350.957
36	Scrap purchases	0.000	0.000
37	Scrap sales	31,775.455	5,025.622
	Other freight (unidentified by industry of origin)	6,133.686	10,711.030
	Personal consumption expenditures	1,231.000	4,800.000
	Federal government expenditures	7,386.000	4,200.000
	State and local government expenditures	0.000	300.000
	Total	704,507.513	506,296.733

Source: Jack Faucett Associates, Inc., *Transportation Projections 1970 and 1980* (Silver Spring, Md., October 1970).

For-Hire Truck		Private Truck		Domestic		
Local	Intercity	Local	Intercity	Air	Pipeline	Total
2,995.679	13,127.941	10,945.000	6,534.368	233.502	0.000	122,567.262
0.000	45.241	144.216	312.354	0.000	0.000	75,646.424
0.000	400.193	271.271	589.808	0.000	0.000	9,927.357
0.000	3,347.909	519.283	1,131.095	0.000	0.000	163,882.534
1,272.731	14,170.724	2,364.819	5,150.466	0.000	0.000	95,183.880
0.000	0.000	0.000	0.000	0.000	0.000	0.000
6.024	982.542	24.979	86.838	0.000	0.000	3,617.935
1,304.858	24,665.404	1,706.879	9,250.625	26.814	0.000	124,648.473
9.404	6,261.704	51.332	1,155.708	91.990	0.000	9,618.482
43.990	3,400.666	284.943	2,957.811	0.950	0.000	85,571.874
19.856	1,849.627	47.600	851.676	6.173	0.000	5,954.970
106.300	4,810.123	158.385	746.715	7.895	0.000	48,559.946
85.265	1,048.346	296.516	1,038.057	0.991	0.000	3,126.440
426.151	5,915.417	725.907	2,929.203	67.321	0.000	66,422.555
74.206	7,464.604	127.012	902.755	42.611	0.000	18,283.125
361.766	6,010.280	5,665.449	10,166.496	0.000	308,861.636	624,063.910
210.436	10,091.647	1,862.551	4,288.686	16.136	0.000	46,435.463
226.660	11,022.616	972.491	820.337	13.579	0.000	56,011.068
56.358	2,862.456	91.788	561.704	23.963	0.000	18,755.029
159.468	5,939.276	221.964	1,683.001	76.693	0.000	14,189.743
5.540	2,282.767	8.396	232.021	25.731	0.000	6,604.838
50.923	5,252.007	74.737	387.643	102.438	0.000	9,261.702
10.612	4,330.685	30.495	587.925	291.769	0.000	9,553.097
83.375	5,493.782	140.193	505.946	35.775	0.000	22,049.610
0.152	113.809	1.039	1.035	24.937	0.000	226.490
3.309	610,726	11.710	352.342	13.627	0.000	2,620.297
0.205	710.675	5.724	40.658	32.504	0.000	867.582
0.000	0.000	0.000	0.000	0.000	0.000	0.000
0.000	0.000	0.000	0.000	0.000	0.000	0.000
0.000	0.000	32,717.094	57,361.143	0.000	0.000	90,078.237
0.000	0.000	0.000	0.000	0.000	0.000	0.000
0.000	402.235	0.000	0.000	218.341	0.000	21,315.061
0.000	1,022.991	0.000	0.000	0.000	0.000	7,628.500
0.000	827.370	0.000	0.000	0.000	0.000	4,671.628
0.709	1,501.182	7.537	160.684	39.532	0.000	5,998.181
0.000	0.000	0.000	0.000	0.000	0.000	0.000
0.000	427.510	0.000	0.000	0.000	0.000	37,228.587
205.237	2,041.072	4,440.322	0.000	244.788	30,165.579	53,941.714
168.000	3,332.000	0.000	0.000	86.000	0.000	9,617.000
0.000	2,200.000	0.000	0.000	281.000	0.000	14,067.000
0.000	80.000	0.000	0.000	6.000	0.000	386.000
7,887.214	154,045.527	63,919.632	110,787.100	2,011.060	339,027.215	1,888,481.994

common carrier LTL trucking business will only be by existing, financially strong carriers against smaller carriers in highly lucrative markets. To some extent, this can already happen because the financially stronger carriers can purchase the smaller carriers and their operating rights. Since there are many Class I carriers, the market warfare could be a protracted affair which takes years to sort out. However, we believe that the final results will be a consolidation of the smaller carriers into a relatively few large carriers that will blanket the United States, offering service to all regions which are profitable. There will continue to be a large network of ancillary common carriers that serve the smaller and less profitable markets.

The provisions of the proposed legislation also have several implications for contract haulers. Currently these haulers are constrained by ICC procedures to a small number of contracts (approximately seven) and to offering service only where they can provide both specialized service and dedicated equipment. In the future, these restrictions will be removed and the contract carrier will be able to function as a portion of the same firm which is performing common carrier LTL service. We expect this portion of the industry to grow consistently and to be extremely competitive with carload rail shipments and piggyback operations. It should also be easier for these contract carriers to avail themselves of the use of owner-operators. Also, because there is no necessity to set up terminal operations, entry into this portion of the industry will be more vigorous than in the common carrier areas. It is difficult to determine whether common carriers will be affiliated with contract carriers or whether they will grow largely independently.

Private fleet operations are impacted by the provisions of the bill that deal with the hauling of goods for corporate affiliates. New rules redefining a corporate affiliate are proposed and intercorporate hauling can be expanded. At the same time, it is clear that both the common carrier and the contract carrier operations will be more competitive with private fleet operations. In the past, private fleets have tended to "skim the cream" off of the LTL common carrier market by carrying those commodities in short-haul markets for which they have clearly defined backhauls. The intercorporate hauling class of the proposed legislation liberalizes this. If private fleets can find suitable backhauls among corporate affiliates, they will now be able to expand their operations. It is anticipated that for industries which function like conglomerates it will be possible to expand private truck operations. For those industries which are located in out-of-the-way spots, the service level by common carriers may actually drop as a result of infighting between major common carriers and their concentration on heavy trade routes. Therefore, private trucking may become more prevalent in these places.

Owner-operators are addressed specifically in the legislation, though not by name. The specific provisions that apply to them are those concerning the solicitation of regulated commodity backhaul after carrying an exempt commodity. This applies only to carriers with fewer than three trucks in their fleet and only under the condition that revenues will be collected at the common carrier rate and will amount to less than 50 percent of total revenue. This provision would appear virtually impossible to enforce.

The provision regarding "trip leasing" is also important to owner-operators, since it permits certain short-term collaboration between the owner-operator and various other types of haulers. For example, an exempt agricultural commodity could be hauled on the forehaul and the owner-operator could trip lease to a common carrier on the backhaul. In fact, some common carriers have set up special commodity divisions or owner-operator divisions to brokerage full truckloads for carriage by owner-operators. This practice could grow in the future. It is already widespread among common carriers on irregular routes and among household movers and haulers of special commodities such as steel, refrigerated meats, et cetera. However, the practice could also catch on in the common carriage of LTL freight. For example, there exist a few regular route common carriers of motor freight which operate with nonunionized terminals and owner-operators on contracts. The low-cost operations of an owner-operator make this an attractive possibility for some situations. However, there is some union opposition to such moves, and it is not clear that it will become a widespread practice.

There is probably as much impact upon the railroad industry from the trucking deregulation provisions as there is from the provisions contained in the rail deregulation act. However, there are some important aspects of the rail bill that are worth mentioning. The ability to raise or lower rates without suspension by the ICC and the time limits imposed upon the filing and hearing of cases regarding rates are important. In the past, railroads have frequently operated as a unified industry on rate requests. In the future, they may be able to operate more independently as individual firms. This should provide the pricing flexibility which the railroads have long argued that they need to have. Another provision that appears to be important provides that the ICC must expedite its proceedings regarding the legality of a rate which is filed in conjunction with an investment that is larger than $1 million. Thus, a railroad may feel freer to invest in a new facility (for example, a new TOFC marshalling yard) than it has in the past. The existence of federal loans in conjunction with this provision also appears to be significant.

A major question, however, is the extent to which the railroads will effectively be able to use the new rate flexibility they will be given. It can be argued rather persuasively that railroad costs for many commodities are not significantly lower than those for owner-operators in the full truckload quantities at which these commodities regularly move. Alternatively, the contract or common carrier trucker who employs an owner-operator can operate at significantly better service levels than rail and, if costs are at all competitive, traffic will be diverted to the owner-operator's service. Table 7-3 shows a comparison of typical costs for a railroad and for an owner-operator operating under lease to another carrier. The assumptions made are not dramatically out of line with recorded performance in this industry.

The question of the cost competitiveness between owner-operator trucking firms and rail will be more closely examined below under the description of the movements of individual commodities. However, it is clear that this issue is at the heart of the question of whether rails will be able to hold their market shares by pricing their service on competitive traffic at a level approaching variable cost and making up the difference by higher rates on noncompetitive traffic, or whether rails will face further diversions to trucking.

The competition between railroads and barges is not addressed by the legislation as proposed. Unit train movements in competition with barge operations are an area of railroad competitiveness that must be understood before the full rail picture can be grasped. Clearly, however, the fuel implications of this competition are less important to the energy use implications of the two bills than the matter of truck-rail competition.

The proposed legislation addresses air freight operations by increasing the size of the service zone within urban areas from a radius of 25 miles to a radius of 100 miles. This could be a significant factor to the trucking industry if air freight rates were lower. With the present generation of aircraft, it is anticipated that the air freight industry will not be able to make a serious encroachment on the major ton-mileage carried by trucks. Also, a new airframe designed specifically for freight is likely to be more than ten years into the future.

Shipments by United Parcel Service, the U.S. Postal Service, and various freight forwarders and consolidators amount to only a small

Table 7-3

COMPARISON OF OWNER-OPERATOR AND RAILROAD COSTS PER TON-MILE

(cents per ton-mile)

	Owner-Operator[a]		Railroad
1. Fuel	0.28	1. Fuel and power	0.09
Transportation labor[b]	0.46	Transportation labor	0.58
Depreciation	0.18	Equipment and joint facilities, rents, and depreciation	0.22
Total	0.92	Total	0.89
2. Maintenance	0.20	2. Maintenance of equipment[c]	0.23
Tires	0.05		
Total	0.25	Total	0.23
3. Licenses	0.06	3. Maintenance of way[c]	0.22
Fuel tax	0.11	Total	0.22
Total	0.17		
4. Overhead	0.27	4. Traffic	0.04
Insurance	0.06	Miscellaneous and general	0.09
Total	0.33	Payroll and other taxes	0.15
		Total	0.28
5. Interest	0.07	5. Interest	0.07
Net income after interest[b]	0.04	Net income after interest	0.04
Total	0.11	Total	0.11
Grand total	1.78	Grand total	1.73

[a] Based on an owner-operator operating under lease to another carrier. This assumption adds approximately 0.21 cents per revenue ton-mile to the owner-operator account. Also assumes 150,000 miles per year, no empty miles, and an average payload of 20 tons.

[b] Assumes a 0.50-cent payment to the driver less approximately 0.04 cents as a 10 percent return on cash invested in equipment and working capital. It is only coincidental that 0.04 cents is the net income after interest for both the owner-operator and the railroad figures.

[c] Does not include depreciation.

Source: David H. Maister and D. Daryl Wyckoff, *The Owner-Operator in the Motor Carrier Industry* (Lexington, Mass.: D. C. Heath and Co., 1975).

proportion of total intercity ton-miles (less than 14 percent). Revenues, however, amount to considerably more. Within this group are some of the most efficient carriers in operation today. For example, the United Parcel Service is the largest single trucking common carrier in operation today. The mechanization of its operations is well known. One of the keys to its success has been its concentration on a single segment of the market.

In summary, then, the proposed legislation would make trucking in all of its elements much more competitive than it is today. Assuming that there is rate flexibility, carriers should respond by reducing their rates. The one place where many carriers may be able to reduce them is in the use of owner-operators for their line-haul operations. Since there has always been freedom of entry in this segment of the industry, it is not clear that additional entries will play a significant role that is not already being felt in the industry. For common carriers, by contrast, there should not be much entry because of the large cost of acquiring terminals and marketing operations.

On the railroad side a variety of responses to the legislation can be expected. The more progressive and better managed carriers may be able to respond selectively with rate reductions in markets that are particularly important to them. However, railroads are faced with a variety of management crises, including the response to the Conrail (Consolidated Rail Corporation) plan, the reorganization of the railroad industry generally, the restoration of track and rolling stock to precrisis conditions, and the abandonment of excess trackage. All of these will absorb management attention, and it may be very difficult to do the marketing analysis necessary to identify and attack markets selectively. In some cases it is likely that management will raise rail rates where they should be lowering them. This will place them in a directly competitive position with long-haul, truckload trucking.

There is also some question of whether the cost per ton-mile for railroads can be substantially lowered from present levels. Already, the rates of return are lower than industry generally, and at these rates investment capital is becoming difficult to secure. Tables 7-3, 7-4, and 7-5 give an indication of the costs for owner-operators, Class I and II motor carriers, and Class I railroads. It can be seen that an average owner-operator traveling 150,000 miles per year can break even with a gross revenue of about 2.47 cents per ton-mile. This contrasts dramatically with a Class I and II motor carrier cost of 9.10 cents per ton-mile and with a railroad cost of 1.73 cents per ton-mile.

Table 7-4

CLASS I AND II MOTOR CARRIER COSTS PER TON-MILE

	Cents per Ton-Mile	Percentage of Total Expenses
Traffic	0.26	3
Equipment maintenance	0.78	9
Insurance and safety	0.35	4
Transportation	4.47	52
Depreciation	0.30	3
Terminal	1.29	15
Operating taxes and licenses	0.54	6
General and administrative	0.58	7
Total expenses	8.58	
Net revenue	0.52	
Gross revenue	9.10	

Source: American Trucking Associations, *Trucking Trends*, 1973, p. 23.

In order to identify those commodities in which owner-operators are competitive with railroads, it is interesting to look at Table 7-6, which shows average U.S. railway rates by commodity class for those commodities in which rail is already competing heavily with trucks. In the areas of great competition, the rates are in the range of the cost figures for owner-operators.

Before proceeding with a final accounting of the energy use implications, it will be useful to examine the implications of the proposed bills regarding the load factors of the various modes. We anticipate that some modes will experience improvements in their average load factors as a result of being able to increase the load on the vehicle during backhauls. Other modes will necessarily have a reduction in load factor, unless a net improvement in efficiency can be effected by structural changes. This may exist in the hauling of agricultural exempt commodities.

An indication of the modal load factors which currently exist is given in Table 7-7, which is based upon empty backhaul statistics reported by industry sources. The empty backhaul ratios must be adjusted to reflect the load factors when the vehicle is moving loaded to give average load factors for the mode as a whole. New estimates

Table 7-5

OWNER-OPERATOR COSTS PER TON-MILE

(cents per ton-mile)

Cost Category	Average Operator: 100,000 miles per year	Average Operator: Percentage of gross revenue	Average Operator: 150,000 miles per year	Average Operator: Percentage of gross revenue	Low-Cost Operator: 100,000 miles per year	Low-Cost Operator: Percentage of gross revenue	Low-Cost Operator: 150,000 miles per year	Low-Cost Operator: Percentage of gross revenue
Fuel (pre-tax)	0.47	15	0.47	19	0.28	12	0.28	16
Maintenance	0.25	8	0.25	10	0.20	9	0.20	11
Tires	0.08	3	0.05	2	0.05	2	0.05	3
Depreciation	0.30	10	0.19	8	0.27	12	0.18	10
Insurance	0.10	3	0.06	2	0.09	4	0.06	3
Licenses	0.10	3	0.07	3	0.09	4	0.06	3
Fuel tax	0.14	4	0.14	6	0.11	5	0.11	6
Labor	0.95	30	0.65	26	0.75	33	0.50	28
Overhead and traffic	0.61	20	0.48	19	0.34	15	0.27	15
Interest	0.12	4	0.08	3	0.10	4	0.07	4
Gross revenue	3.12	100	2.47	100	2.28	100	1.78	100

Source: David H. Maister and D. Daryl Wyckoff, *The Owner-Operator.*

Table 7-6
AVERAGE U.S. RAIL RATES, BY STCC COMMODITY CLASS

STCC[a]	Commodity	Cents per Ton-Mile	Percentage of Total Revenue
01	Farm products	1.7	8.78
08	Forest products	2.4	0.12
09	Fresh fish	1.5	0.02
10	Metallic ores	1.5	2.57
11	Coal	1.2	10.59
13	Crude petroleum	1.3	0.07
14	Nonmetallic mineral	1.5	3.50
19	Ordnance	3.6	0.82
20	Food and kindred	1.9	11.40
21	Tobacco	2.9	0.16
22	Textiles	3.3	0.34
23	Apparel	3.8	0.07
24	Lumber and wood	1.6	8.58
25	Furniture and fixtures	6.2	0.90
26	Pulp, paper, and allied	2.1	6.51
27	Printed matter	2.3	0.13
28	Chemicals	2.0	10.21
29	Petroleum products	1.9	3.27
30	Rubber and plastic	4.1	1.05
31	Leather	4.1	0.02
32	Clay, concrete, and glass	1.9	4.65
33	Primary metal products	2.4	5.66
34	Fabricated metal products	3.5	1.53
35	Machinery	4.2	1.17
36	Electrical machinery	4.9	1.50
37	Transportation equipment	4.8	8.64
38	Instruments	3.4	0.03
39	Miscellaneous manufacturing products	4.2	0.25
40	Waste and scrap metals	2.9	2.06
41	Miscellaneous freight shipments	4.3	0.15
42	Empty containers	2.7	0.13
44	Freight forwarders	2.5	1.15
45	Shipper associations	2.5	1.51
46	Mixed shipments	2.4	2.26

[a] Standard Transportation Commodity Code.
Source: U.S. Department of Transportation, *1972 Carload Waybill Statistics.*

Table 7-7
ESTIMATED FUTURE LOAD FACTORS
(percent)

	EBH Ratio[a]	Full Load Factor	Average Load Factor	Assumed Load Factor after Legislation
Regular route common carriers	5	80	76	78
Irregular route common carriers	10	90	81	85
Unregulated for-hire (agriculture exempt)	25	90	67	70
Private carriers	30	80	56	65
Railroads	44	85	47	46
Barges	45	95	52	52

[a] Estimates reported by industry sources.

Notes: EBH ratio = Ratio of empty miles to total miles. Full load factor = Percentage of full capacity utilized when loaded—weight or volume measure used, whichever is more binding. Average load factor = Percentage of full capacity utilized over all movements. Assumed load factor after legislation = Assumed impact on average load factor after legislation.

of the load factors that will prevail after the legislation are then estimated. Improvements in all of the truck modes are experienced. Common carrier trucks should continue operations more or less as normal. Private trucks should improve their backhauls as a result of the intercorporate hauling provisions, and owner-operators will experience improvements in their load factors as a result of the ability to haul regulated commodities. The only mode which will experience declines will be the railroads, in both carload quantity shipments and TOFC. Barges are assumed to continue the same load factors after the bill as before.

Because of the paucity of data on empty truck movements, it is misleading to attempt to provide a precise estimate of the impact of improved load factors on fuel consumption. It appears, however, that some fuel might be saved in the truck mode.

Possible Implications of the Deregulation Bills

The bills are notably silent about encouraging the use of piggyback services by rail. Although a variety of piggyback services are offered, the most successful are those involving the railroad directly. Those involving substituted transportation services by motor carriage have not been particularly successful. In fact, the TOFC growth has tended to stagnate in recent years. Nevertheless, many rail advocates argue that TOFC operations are efficient, economical services which should be encouraged. Several things could be done to promote the use of TOFC. One provision which would help TOFC would be to increase the radius of service which is allowed in an urban commercial zone. As in the administration's proposed airline industry legislation, the radius could be increased to 100 miles. A second provision which might improve TOFC services would be to allow railroads to own trucking companies. Alternatively, railroads could be allowed to enter into long-term service contracts with common carriers. There are, of course, several railroad companies in the United States which do own trucking companies as subsidiaries under the grandfather clause. Those companies in the East, however, have never used their operating rights.

A basic problem with TOFC service at the present time appears to be the lack of a realistic price-service trade-off. This may be in part because railroads have trouble offering "through" trains beyond their individual territories. There is the very real possibility that TOFC costs are not enough lower than those for line-haul full-load trucking (particularly where owner-operators are used) to make the exercise worth the effort.

Effects of Canadian Railroad Deregulation

With the enactment of the National Transportation Act on February 9, 1967, the Dominion of Canada instituted a major change in its policies and practices regarding economic regulation of Canadian railroads. By that act, most of the traditional functions of regulation, especially in the matter of freight rates, were discarded, and managements were given substantial latitude in the establishment of rates and charges, free from possible governmental intervention. According to J. W. Pickerogill, the former president of the Canadian Transport Commission: "In the field of railway rate regulation, the National Transportation Act stripped away many of the powers of the Board of Transport Commissioners to fix rates with respect to railway service." [5]

Experience under the 1967 act has demonstrated the fact that the Canadian railways have taken advantage of their new status vis-à-vis

[5] J. W. Pickerogill, "Evolving a New Policy in Canadian Transportation," *ICC Practitioners Journal*, September-October 1969.

the regulatory authorities by reducing their average rate levels or by maintaining a relative brake on inflation-fueled increases. A comparison between Canadian and U.S. railroad revenues per ton-mile for the year 1967 (when the new act took effect) and three subsequent years is presented below: [6]

Average Revenue in Cents per Ton-Mile

	1967	1971	1972	1973
Canada (domestic carloads excluding statutory grain traffic)	1.95	1.69	1.80	1.75
United States	1.27	1.59	1.62	1.62

It will be observed that, during a period when the average revenue per ton-mile for U.S. railroads increased 27.5 percent, the comparable change for Canadian lines was a 10 percent reduction.

Commodity Flow Projections

In order to ascertain the implications of these bills on modal competition and on energy usage, projections of the more important intercity commodity flows are required. The best approach to provide a solid foundation for these projections involves the use of a two-stage analysis: (1) a macroeconomic analysis that projects the aggregate traffic and ton-mile flows by mode regardless of commodity mix; and (2) a detailed commodity shipment analysis that examines the most consistently disaggregate commodity flows for each mode of transportation. These two stages are linked by imputing individual modal growth rates, derived from the aggregate analysis, to specific commodity flows in the detailed analysis.

The principal advantage of using the two-stage analysis is that one can select the level of detail appropriate to different purposes, such as aggregate fuel consumption by mode, or detailed diversions by commodity shipment size, length of haul, and mode. Also, if there is any subsequent disagreement on the expected modal diversion of a particular commodity, then adjustments can be made easily.

[6] The figures for Canada are taken from *Waybill Analysis, Carload All-Rail Traffic*, published annually by the Canadian Transport Commission, Ottawa. The figures for the United States are taken from Association of American Railroads, *Yearbook of Railroad Facts* (Washington, D.C., 1975), p. 33.

The methodology incorporated in the study can be outlined in the following way: relationships between traditional macroeconomic variables and transportation measures are estimated; reputed forecasts of economic variables are inserted into this series of aggregate transport equations; growth rates for the modal tonnages are calculated and are applied in some cases to individual commodity groups; forecasts of these commodities for 1985 are generated; an analysis of the features of the truck and rail bills is then conducted to estimate the likely modal diversions for twenty-four manufacturing commodities, fourteen agricultural commodities, coal, mining and minerals (except fuels), crude petroleum, and other major commodities; and finally the energy differentials resulting from these diversions are estimated. A flow chart of this sequence appears in Figure 7-1; a discussion of the two stages of analysis follows.

Macroeconomic Analysis

Several papers in recent years in the economics literature have related a series of macroeconomic variables with transportation data like ton-miles and carloadings. Although some of these studies in retrospect have provided reasonably accurate forecasts, the methodologies underlying these forecasts often contained serious statistical errors that conceivably might render their applications to our current needs invalid. Consequently, our macroeconomic analysis extracted the better statistical models from the literature and extended their results by specifying our own equations.

Our present national econometric models are largely constructed on the macronotion that production in the economy is organized in such a way that the output is a single composite commodity—the real gross national product (GNP). From these models come estimates of GNP, the implicit price deflator, money supply, average interest rates, and similar macrovariables.

There are several research firms and organizations engaged in the business of providing long-range estimates of these variables for the economy. Among these firms, the forecasts performed by Chase Econometrics Associates are as good as any and were used as the basis for forecasting ton-miles in the transportation modes for 1985. As a point of comparison, Data Resources, Inc. (DRI), also prepares a set of macroeconomic forecasts. The Chase forecasts suggest a minor recession in 1978 and early 1979, whereas the DRI model does

Figure 7-1

TWO-STAGE COMMODITY FLOW ANALYSIS: FLOW CHART

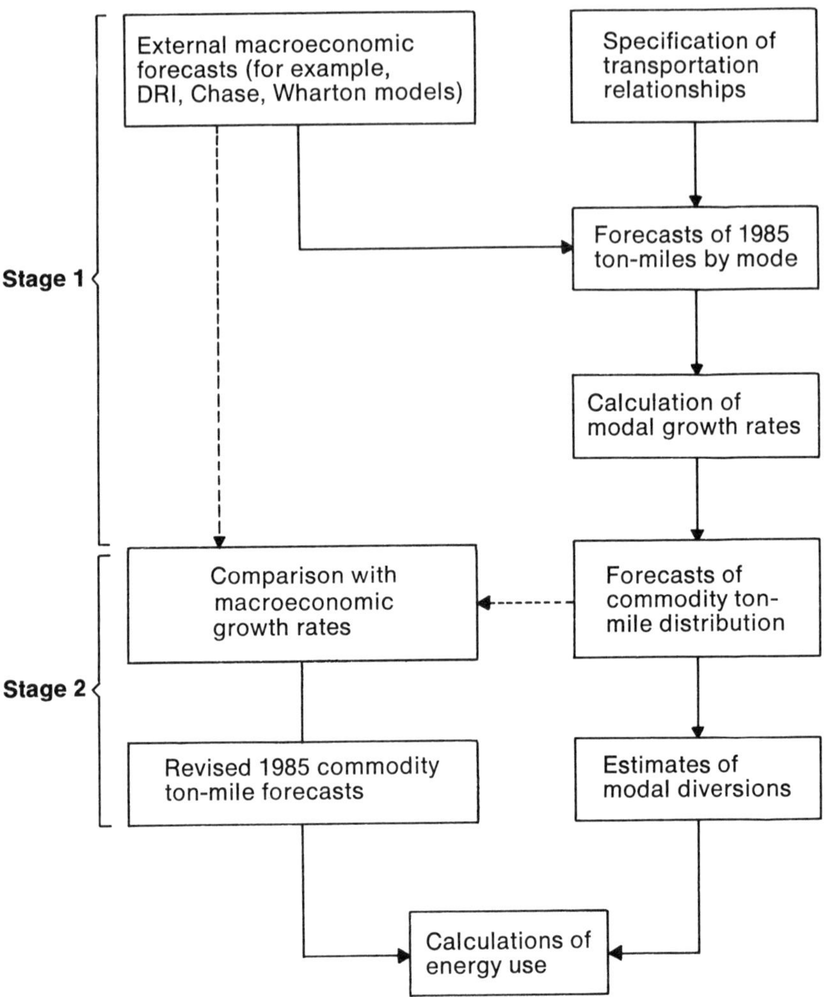

not. On the other hand, the Chase model is more optimistic than the DRI model on economic events in the 1980–1985 period.

With the Chase model results for selected macroeconomic forecasts being inserted into our transportation equations, forecasts of modal ton-miles are generated. Table 7-8 shows four regressions from the set of specifications that were attempted. These regressions (and others) were then used to forecast ton-miles by mode. These

Table 7-8

SELECTED ECONOMETRIC RESULTS FOR ESTIMATING INTERCITY TON-MILES

	Explanatory Variables[a]	R^2
Class I railroads	209.982 + 0.767 GNP (6.295) (15.459)	0.948
All motor carriers	11.387 + 0.568 GNP (10.569) (18.754)	0.972
Common and contract motor carriers	−15.062 + 1.367 GPDI + 5.632 i (−1.222) (6.512) (1.783)	0.946
Private motor operators	86.524 + 1.464 GPDI (5.791) (9.917)	0.891

[a] Terms in parentheses indicate t-ratios; all equations are based on time series data for the period 1960-1974, with the exception of the trucking industry equations for which the 1974 data are not yet available.

Note: GNP = gross national product (deflated), GPDI = gross private domestic investment (deflated), i = long-term government bond rate.

Source: Based upon forecasts performed by Chase Econometric Associates, Inc.

forecasts and their corresponding growth rates are presented in Tables 7-9 and 7-10.

In Table 7-9, forecasts for 1985 of ton-miles for the railroad and motor truck industries are presented. These forecasts are the outputs of the econometric models discussed above (and also shown in Table 7-8), and they are the principal focus of the *aggregate* level of analysis (Stage 1) used in the study.

In contrast, the *detailed* commodity shipment analysis (Stage 2) uses the aggregate analysis modal growth rates to provide base estimates for individual commodity flows in 1985—with the exception of the livestock and agricultural commodities. The U.S. Department of Agriculture has provided its own estimates of modal growth rates for all the major agricultural commodities for 1980. On the basis of the reputed USDA expertise, we have incorporated an extrapolation of the USDA growth rates to 1985 for the agricultural commodity flows. However, since the USDA growth rates are significantly lower than those of manufacturing, coal, and the other major commodities, the summation of the individual commodity flows in Stage 2 will be lower for rail, motor trucking, and the other movements (water and pipeline) than the totals generated by the models in Stage 1 (Table 7-9). In view of the recent long-term grain negotiations between the USSR

Table 7-9

TEN-YEAR FORECASTS OF RAILROAD AND MOTOR TRUCKING INDUSTRY TON-MILES

	1967	1970	1980	1985
Macroeconomic Variables				
Gross national product[a]	675.2	722.1	1,022.5	1,246.3
Gross private domestic investment[a]	101.2	104.0	160.4	205.7
Interest rate (percent)	5.07	7.37	9.24	7.86
Money supply[a]	154.5	159.6	156.7	165.8
Implicit price deflator (1958 = 100.0)	117.6	135.2	247.4	311.4
Ton-miles (in billions)				
Class I railroads	731.2	771.0	987.5	1,086.9
Motor trucking	388.5	412.0	617.7	738.2
Common and contract carriers	151.5	170.0	256.2	310.4
Private carriers	237.0	242.0	361.5	427.8
Total rail and truck	1,119.7	1,183.0	1,605.2	1,825.1
Grand total—four modes (rail, truck, inland waterway, and pipeline)	1,762.2	1,932.6	2,664.4	3,237.9

[a] In billions of 1958 dollars; based on estimates by Chase Econometrics Associates, Inc.

Note: Based on 1960-1974 time series data for all variables except the trucking industry's ton-miles series which does not include 1974.

Sources: U.S. Department of Commerce, *Survey of Current Business 1970-1974;* U.S. Department of Commerce, *Business Statistics, 1973,* biennial supplement to *Survey of Current Business;* American Trucking Associations, *Trucking Trends,* 1960-1974 editions; Interstate Commerce Commission, *Transport Statistics in the United States, Part I* (various issues); and Association of American Railroads, *Yearbook of Railroad Facts* (various issues).

and the United States (since the USDA reports were released), we believe that the USDA estimates might be pessimistic. As a consequence, we suggest that the reader who is interested in overall ton-mile growth rates refer to the analysis in Stage 1 while the reader who is interested in separate commodity movements use the data analyzed in Stage 2.

Commodity Shipment Analysis

On the basis of the aggregate analysis above and our detailed commodity shipment analysis,[7] the major commodity groups can be classi-

[7] In the original report the detailed commodity analysis was presented in appendixes 4 and 5, which are not included here.

Table 7-10

GROWTH RATES OF RAILROAD AND MOTOR TRUCKING INDUSTRY TON-MILES TO 1985

(percent)

	1967–1985	1967–1973	1973–1980	1980–1985
Class I railroads	48.6	16.5	19.9	10.1
Motor trucking	90.0	30.0	22.3	19.5
Common and contract carriers	104.9	39.9	20.8	21.2
Private carriers	80.5	23.6	23.4	18.3
Total rail and truck	63.0	21.2	18.3	13.7
Grand total—four modes (rail, truck, inland waterway, and pipeline)	83.7	25.4	20.6	21.5
Gross national product (deflated)	84.6	24.3	21.8	21.9

Source: See Table 7-9.

fied into six categories: (1) manufacturing, (2) agriculture, (3) coal, (4) mining and minerals except fuel, (5) crude petroleum, and (6) other commodities. A summary of each of these major commodity groups is presented in the following paragraphs.

Manufacturing. The primary data source for this group of commodities is the 1967 *Census of Transportation.* This reference distributes tons and ton-miles generated by the various modes for twenty-four different shipper groups. The information contained in the reference is perhaps the richest source of data on commodity flows, even though it is limited to manufactured items. Even so, the commodity flows represented by the twenty-four shipper groups constituted nearly two-fifths of all flows in 1967.

The forecasts were conducted in the following way: From the results of the macroeconomic models, aggregate growth rates were calculated for the railroad, the common and contract motor carrier, and the private operator industries. These growth rates were applied to the base 1967 data to produce ton-mile estimates for 1985 assuming that recent growth patterns continue. It was assumed that any internal or structural changes in the transportation industries are loosely accounted for in the Chase projections of future economic growth, which were used in the ton-mile projection process. The conclusion was that 1985 modal shares will shift in favor of the motor carriers.

Additional influences on modal growth rates or diversions were then estimated for each of the twenty-four shipper groups. These estimates were based both on an analysis of the mileage and weight data and on informed judgment about the major impacts that might stem from the proposed regulatory bills and from other trends not reflected in the macroeconomic forecasts. Each commodity was analyzed separately and a probable set of diversions was calculated. The final result is that the ton-miles generated by the manufacturing sector of the economy are expected to increase from 680 billion in 1967 to 1,265 billion in 1985, with an expected diversion in 1985 under the present structure of the bills of 35.2 billion ton-miles from rail to trucking (split about equally between common carriers and private operators).

Agriculture. The U.S. Department of Agriculture has developed over the years the richest reporting mechanism and data collection scheme of any federal agency. Time series data for the transportation of agricultural commodities, however, are difficult to discover, principally because such information may be nearly impossible to collect. There are some estimates provided by the USDA for selected years (1967, 1970) on the distribution of tonnage and ton-miles by mode for the major livestock and agricultural commodities. The USDA has also forecast these transportation variables for 1980.

Since there did not appear to be any more effective way to generate 1985 forecasts, the USDA growth rates from 1970 to 1980 were calculated for each commodity group and mode, and then they were extrapolated to 1985. Using this approach, the ton-mile forecast for all agricultural commodities in 1985 is 313.5 billion ton-miles. This figure represents a slow rate of growth for agricultural ton-miles in comparison to our model forecasts and relative to other commodity groups. Nevertheless, the forecast does rely on internal USDA judgment and presumably is reasonable, at least until 1980.

Agricultural movement ton-mile statistics are distributed into commercial truck and farm truck segments by the USDA. This distribution must be reconstituted as common carrier truck and private truck before final movement statistics can be determined. Farm truck is probably best classified as private truck. Commercial truck apparently consists of contract haulers, regular route common carriers, private trucks, and agricultural exempt owner-operators in some mix which is not readily available. It was necessary to assume percentages for each of these categories. The percentages assumed were based on informed estimates as follows: contract, 20 percent; common carrier, 10 percent; owner-operator, 50 percent; and private fleet, 20 percent.

This aggregated to 70 percent private truck and 30 percent common carrier truck overall. These percentages were then used to compute new figures for use in the summaries.

Coal. The effectiveness with which increased coal traffic is handled by the railroad and inland waterway networks is heavily dependent on both the aggregate level of coal shipped and the distribution of coal movements between regions. Railroads haul between 68 percent and 78 percent of all the coal mined in this country, with the average length of haul for rail in the range of 285 miles.[8] However, the average length of haul for barge carriers is much longer, giving these carriers a higher relative market share of total ton-miles transported.

Between 1975 and 1985, coal production and demand are likely to grow substantially. In the *Project Independence Report,* coal tonnage is expected by 1985 to be approximately double the 1973 figure of 550 million tons. Using this source, along with *Coal Traffic Annual* editions,[9] the total 1985 coal tonnage is expected to be about 1.04 billion tons. Assuming that the average lengths of haul will increase for rail to about 500 miles and will remain the same for water carriers, the 1985 ton-mile estimate is 520 billion.

Mining and Minerals except Fuels. This commodity group includes iron ore mining, nonferrous metal mining, miscellaneous mining excluding fuels, and various categories of minerals like stone, clay, glass, gravel, phosphate, sulfur, and limestone. The commodity data were collected from a combination of sources for various years and were then factored from 1965 to 1985 by use of the aggregate growth rate contained in the GNP forecasts produced by Chase. This figure then reflected a change in this composite commodity group's ton-miles from 205.4 billion in 1965 to 384.3 billion in 1985.

Crude Petroleum. In 1967, the total crude petroleum carried by all modes was 549.6 million tons. This commodity group is dominated by the pipeline companies and water carriers, which in 1967 carried 73.6 percent and 18.8 percent of the traffic, respectively. Using an assumed average length of haul of 600 miles, the total ton-miles generated in 1967 amounted to 329.8 billion. The estimate for 1985 is based on the expected average growth rate for the pipeline com-

---

[8] U.S. Department of the Interior, Bureau of Mines, and Federal Energy Administration, *Project Independence Report,* vol. 1, November 1975, p. 259.

[9] The *Coal Traffic Annual* is published each year by the National Coal Association, Washington, D.C.

panies and the water carriers for the 1967–1985 period (112.2 percent). The resulting forecast for this commodity then is 699.8 billion ton-miles.

Other Commodities. These commodities include basic chemicals, raw timber, fishery products, and other miscellaneous items not accounted for in the preceding categories. It was assumed that, since most of these commodities move by either rail or truck, the combined rail-truck growth rate between 1967 and 1985 could be applied to the base period data. The resulting ton-mile estimate for 1985 is 203.8 billion.

Estimation of Fuel Impacts Resulting from Diversions in 1985

The final step in the study is to estimate the fuel consumption impacts that would occur as a result of the expected diversions of traffic between the modes in 1985. After the diversions were calculated and totaled from the six major commodity groups in 1985, energy intensiveness factors were applied to these ton-mile diversions. These factors were derived from the industrial energy study prepared by Peat, Marwick and Mitchell, Inc., in 1974. They are presented in Table 7-11. Using these factors and sustaining the general assumptions regarding load factors and backhauls mentioned above, the differential energy cost is estimated to be approximately 14.9 million barrels of oil per year for 1985. This slight increase in the consumption of fuel (based on a current usage rate of 16 million barrels per day for the whole United States) can be attributed to the rather grim forecasts of the expected net diversions from railroads to the motor carriers.

Table 7-11

ESTIMATED ENERGY INTENSIVENESS

Mode	Approximate BTU per Net Ton-Mile	Net Ton-Miles per Gallon Diesel Fuel	Gallons Diesel Fuel per 1000 Net Ton-Miles	Estimated Ratio of Gross Ton-Miles per Net Ton-Mile
Railroad	700	198	5.05	2.5
Truck	2,800	50	20.00	2.2
Barge	500	277	3.61	1.8

Source: R. H. Leilich, J. C. Prokopy, and D. Ruina, *Industrial Energy Studies of Ground Freight Transportation*, vols. 1 and 2 (Washington, D.C.: Peat, Marwick, Mitchell, Inc., July 1974).

Concluding Points

One of the outstanding features of the proposed bills is that they promote unrestrained competition among the surface freight carriers. The outcome of the ensuing rivalry for market shares will be determined in part by the inherent technological advantages of the various modes. However, an equally important determining factor will stem from the talents and aggressiveness of carrier management. The studies by David Maister and D. Daryl Wyckoff and others support the view that private truck owner-operators should compete very strongly by offering prices at or near cost levels and by offering a high level of service. This, in turn, might force the large common carrier truck companies to adopt a more competitive attitude. In our opinion, these common carriers have the capability to lower rates and improve service while remaining profitable. These companies should remain as powerful forces in intercity freight transportation.

The reaction of railroad management to a fully competitive situation is more difficult to judge. Given that many railroad companies are fighting to stay solvent, it is doubtful that they would be able to match the rate and service changes introduced by the motor carriers. This leads to the conclusion that rail will lose a part of its markets to owner-operators and other truckers. However, this impact may be offset by the fact that many commodities presently moving by rail are not amenable to transport by motor carrier, a feature which may not be very consoling if the railroads are forced to haul only bulk, low-value commodities.

The diversion of commodities from rail to motor carrier will certainly lead to greater fuel use in transportation. The fuel efficiency advantage of rails over truck depends in large part on the terrain, type of cargo, and load factors. However, on a ton-for-ton basis, rail is by far a more efficient mode than truck.

It should be noted that the conclusions of this report on energy consumption are very sensitive to assumptions concerning average load factors. Furthermore, the question of load factors involves two main considerations, neither of which has been deeply studied. On the one hand, there is the percentage of total miles traveled during which a vehicle is empty. On the other hand, there is the percentage of available capacity used when a vehicle is loaded. We believe that trucks perform well on the first count and somewhat poorer on the second. In contrast, rail does poorly by the first criterion, but better by the second. In order that these criteria be quantified, the definitive analysis of rail and truck intensiveness in real world operations must await the collection of more data.

After considering the energy efficiency issue, this study concludes that diversions of freight from rail to truck in the more competitive commodity groups would lead to greater fuel consumption. Still, it should be emphasized that our quantitative estimates are subject to a range of error simply because of the uncertainty in the available load factor data.

In conclusion, we wish to point out that our projections include the impacts of the proposed legislation as well as other trends in the intercity freight industry. A composite analysis was conducted in this study simply because these industry trends and the provisions of the bills will certainly interact. However, it should not be concluded that the bills will solely cause or can solely abate these trends. The future survival of the railroads, for example, will depend on factors largely unrelated to provisions in the bills.

This study has not attempted to analyze two other impacts that the bills would have on freight transportation energy consumption. These are the changes in the overall level of freight transportation induced by changes in the level of service resulting from features of the bills, and changes in the location of production facilities. Although these impacts are expected to be less significant than the impacts considered in this study, their cumulative effects over a long period of time might be substantial.

This study estimated that the 1985 consumption of fuel in intercity freight transportation will be approximately 15 million barrels per year above the base level, assuming passage of the bills. Unfortunately, this projection is highly sensitive to several variables which cannot be projected with any degree of certainty. The first of these is the load factors on trucks mentioned above. The projection is also sensitive to the general state of the economy, which is, of course, also difficult to predict with any certainty. Finally, the projection is highly sensitive to changes in U.S. energy consumption patterns, which are expected to change radically over the next few years. This is because movements of fuels account for such a large proportion of total freight transportation.

The net result, then, of this study is to show that the combined energy effects of the diversion impacts of the proposed bills would cost approximately a day's worth of U.S. fuel consumption.

8

TRAFFIC DIVERSION AND ENERGY USE IMPLICATIONS: ANOTHER VIEW

Stephen Sobotka and Thomas Domencich

Introduction

There has been considerable discussion of the energy use implications of the proposed rail and motor carrier regulatory reform legislation. The only study directly applicable to this issue, however, was done by Paul Roberts and James Kneafsey.[1] This study was done as part of a larger, more broadly directed effort, and it was conducted under considerable time pressure.

The present paper is an independent attempt to assess the changes in fuel use that would result from modernization of truck and rail regulation. The paper does not pretend to be the definitive analysis of the energy implications of the proposed legislation. Any such effort would require massive detail on the operations of the two industries and their customers. The numerical estimates developed in this paper, therefore, should be regarded as highly uncertain and tentative. But they do suggest substantially different conclusions from those reached in the Roberts-Kneafsey study.

The changes in fuel use caused by regulatory reform arise from two sources: changes in the efficiency of operations and shifts in the

This paper is edited from a study entitled *The Energy Use Implications of the Rail and Truck Regulatory Reform Bills*, prepared for the U.S. Department of Transportation, October 1975.

[1] Paul O. Roberts and James T. Kneafsey, *Energy Use Implications of Proposed Changes in the Regulation of the Railroad and Motor Trucking Industries*, report prepared for the Federal Energy Administration, Office of Transportation Research, October 1975, and *Addendum* to the report, October 24, 1975 (hereinafter referred to as the Roberts-Kneafsey study). An edited version of this report appears in the present volume as Chapter 7.

market shares of the transport modes. As a result of regulatory reform, the motor carrier industry will operate more efficiently. Wasteful operating restrictions will be eliminated. The more efficient truck operators will be able to expand. Price competition will reduce the present reliance on costly service competition. As a result of these changes, intercity truck freight will be carried with fewer truck-miles. There will be less empty mileage and less circuity, and trucks will travel more fully loaded. The fuel savings from these efficiency improvements were not estimated in the Roberts-Kneafsey study. The estimates prepared in this paper indicate that they substantially outweigh the effects of traffic diversion as projected by Roberts and Kneafsey.

Diversion of traffic between the transport modes may increase or decrease fuel use, depending on whether traffic shifts to a more or less energy-intensive mode. The Roberts-Kneafsey study concludes that the regulatory reform legislation will divert a moderate amount of traffic from rail to truck. This would result in an increase in energy consumption in intercity freight transportation because rail is more energy-efficient on the average than motor carriage. As stated earlier, however, this increase in fuel use from traffic diversion is more than offset by the estimated fuel savings from increased operating efficiency.

Moreover, the Roberts-Kneafsey conclusion that regulatory reform would divert traffic from rail to truck is questionable. It is counter to most of the published literature on the subject. Most investigators agree that regulatory reform will enable railroads to compete more effectively with trucks because it will allow them to price their services competitively. Railroads are presently restricted by rate regulation from lowering rates to reflect their lower costs where it serves their interests to do so. Truck rates on truckload traffic by contrast are effectively deregulated. Hence, the rate flexibility provisions of the reform legislation should enable railroads to attract that traffic which is more economically served by rail but which is presently carried by trucks because of restrictive railroad rate regulation. If this is the case, traffic diversion will result in additional fuel savings in intercity freight transportation.

Before turning to the analysis of the effects on energy use of the proposed regulatory reform legislation, it is useful to put this issue in perspective. The objective of public policy is to improve economic efficiency, not energy efficiency. The efficient use of energy is just one element in the efficient use of resources. If regulatory reform actually results in diversion of traffic from rail to truck, it would do so because this is economically efficient. In a competitive market where prices reflect relative costs, diversion of traffic from one mode to another would only occur if it enabled shippers to reduce distribution costs. It would thus improve the efficient use of resources regardless of its effect on energy consumption.

Efficiency Savings in Fuel Use

To compute the efficiency savings in each of the sectors of the motor carrier industry, we first present estimates of future annual ton-miles of traffic for each truck sector. These are taken from the Roberts-Kneafsey study except where otherwise noted. The effect of the improvements in trucking efficiency caused by the legislation will be to reduce truck-miles for a given quantity of ton-miles. This can be represented in a number of ways but the most convenient in light of data limitations is as a change in average load factors. Thus, the next step is to develop pre- and post-legislation load factors for each trucking sector being considered. The following sectors of the motor carrier industry are examined: less-than-truckload (LTL) common carriage; truckload (TL) common carriage; contract carriage; unregulated for-hire (agricultural exempt) carriage; and private carriage.

The changes in load factors projected for each sector are then used to compute the changes in 1985 fuel use resulting from the improvements in operating efficiency caused by the proposed legislation. The Roberts-Kneafsey study recognizes some of the improvements in trucking efficiency that will take place as a result of the legislation. But the resulting savings in fuel use from these efficiency gains are not estimated in the Roberts-Kneafsey report.

Traffic Estimates by Sector of the Truck Industry. Table 8-1 shows estimates of 1985 ton-miles of traffic for each sector of the motor carrier industry being considered. The source is the Roberts-Kneafsey study's 1985 base-case forecast.[2] The only adjustment to the Roberts-Kneafsey data is the allocation of common carrier traffic to truckload and less-than-truckload traffic.[3] Data on the present shares of these

[2] Base-case traffic is the forecast amount before allowing for any assumed diversion between modes.

[3] Although the Roberts-Kneafsey study concentrates on the effects of the proposed legislation on TL traffic and presumably excludes the LTL market, no estimates are provided for the present traffic or the 1985 forecast. Instead, total common carrier traffic is broken down into regular and irregular route traffic. This is not the same thing as the required LTL and TL breakdown.

Table 8-1

1985 FORECASTED MOTOR CARRIER TRAFFIC BY SECTOR OF THE TRUCKING INDUSTRY

Industry Sector	Market Share (percent)	1985 Ton-Miles (billions)
Common and contract		
LTL	45	173
TL	45	173
Contract	10	38
Total	100	384
Private and exempt		
Private	70	189
Exempt	30	81
Total	100	270

Source: The market share estimates for contract, private, and exempt carriers and the total ton-mileage figures for "common and contract" and "private and exempt" were taken from Paul O. Roberts and James T. Kneafsey, *Energy Use Implications of Proposed Changes in the Regulation of the Railroad and Motor Trucking Industries,* prepared for the Federal Energy Administration, Office of Transportation Research, October 1975. It is assumed that TL and LTL ton-miles are about equal. The market shares were applied to the two total ton-mileage figures to get the individual sector ton-mile estimates. The ton-mile figures are taken from the 1985 base case, and they represent traffic before allowing for diversion between modes.

two sectors of common carrier trucking are not available. But it is thought that they each make up about half of the common carrier market, and this assumption is applied to the 1985 forecasts in Table 8-1 to get the required breakdowns. The remaining market shares were taken from the Roberts-Kneafsey study.

Pre-Legislation Load Factors. Table 8-2 presents estimates of pre- and post-legislation average load factors for each of the sectors of the trucking industry being considered. This section treats the pre-legislation load factors. They can be compared with the Roberts-Kneafsey load factors which are shown in Table 7-7 above. It can be seen that the Roberts-Kneafsey load factors differ substantially from those developed in this paper.

The load factor is computed as the percent of vehicle-miles on which some cargo is being carried multiplied by the average percent of vehicle capacity being utilized when the vehicle is carrying cargo.

Table 8-2

ESTIMATED LOAD FACTORS

Carrier Type	Pre-Legislation			Post-Legislation
	Percentage empty mileage	Percentage loaded[a]	Average load factor	Average load factor
Truck				
Common carrier				
LTL	25[b]	80	60	66
TL	25[b]	90	68	70
Contract carrier	45[b]	90	50	50
Unregulated for-hire (agriculture exempt)	32[c]	90	61	67
Private carrier	37[d]	80	50	62
Rail	44[a]	85	47	47
Barge	45[a]	95	52	52

[a] Figures taken from the Roberts-Kneafsey study; see Table 7-7 above.

[b] The basic source for the percentage of empty miles by truck category is the 1972 Federal Highway Administration (FHWA) truck weight studies. These data show that 28 percent of all ICC-regulated trucks in the 1972 survey were traveling empty. Thus, the empty mileage ratio should average 28 percent for ICC-regulated trucks, whether broken down by regular and irregular route carriers as in the Roberts-Kneafsey study or by LTL, TL, and contract as in this paper. Roberts's figures of 5 percent and 10 percent are clearly too low. The empty mileage figures in the table for the three categories of regulated carriers average 27 percent empty mileage using the market shares presented in Table 8-1 as appropriate weights. Contract carriers experience considerably more empty mileage than common carriers on average because of the use of dedicated, often specialized equipment. When trucks are empty, the TL/LTL distinction does not exist so the same "empty" percentages are used for both categories.

[c] The estimate of 32 percent empty miles for agricultural exempt carriers was taken from the FHWA figure for non-ICC-regulated semicombination trucks. The figure for all truck types in the non-ICC-regulated category is 34 percent, but this includes a number of noncommercial single-unit trucks (for example, pickup trucks). The slightly lower figure excludes these truck types.

[d] The estimate of 37 percent empty mileage for private carriers was taken from the FHWA figure for private carrier semicombination trucks. The total figure for private carriers includes a large number of noncommercial single-unit trucks and thus is inappropriate for the purposes of this analysis.

The chief difference between the Roberts-Kneafsey load factors and those estimated in this paper lies in the estimated empty mileage figures. The only comprehensive source of data on empty trucks is the Federal Highway Administration (FHWA) truck weight studies.

These data are used in Table 8-2, as explained in the footnotes to that table. The Roberts-Kneafsey empty mileage figures, based on estimates from industry sources, cannot be reconciled with the FHWA data. They are clearly too low, especially in the common carrier categories; hence, the estimated load factors are too high.

The Roberts-Kneafsey overestimate of average load factors gives the incorrect impression that there is little room for improvement in operating efficiency. The estimates based on the FHWA data show, however, that load factors are low on average, and there is substantial potential for efficiency gains.

Post-Legislation Load Factors. This section treats the post-legislation load factors for each of the sectors of the truck industry under consideration.

LTL common carrier trucking. This sector of the motor carrier industry deals with less-than-truckload shipments, usually under 10,000 pounds each, hauled by truck common carriers. LTL motor carriage will become substantially more efficient as a result of regulatory reform. Because this is a large sector of trucking, the resulting fuel savings will be sizeable. The efficiency savings in LTL trucking were not considered in the Roberts-Kneafsey report.

Improvements in LTL efficiency will arise from two sources. The more obvious source is the elimination of wasteful operating restrictions such as route and commodity restrictions, one-way authority, and the like. Up to 1964, of all certificates granted to motor carriers by the Interstate Commerce Commission, 19 percent provided only one-way authority after correcting for round trip authority on separate certificates.[4] In the case of commodity-restricted certificates the percentage is larger. These restrictions add to truck mileage but not to loads. Thus, they cause inefficient fuel use.

Less obviously, but more importantly, the bill will improve LTL efficiency by fostering price competition. Under the present regulatory system, price competition in LTL trucking is severely restricted. Carriers are forced to compete for LTL traffic by providing more frequent or more timely service rather than less costly service. The reliance on service competition rather than both price and service competition wastes resources, including fuel, by causing trucks to travel less fully loaded than they otherwise would.

[4] Interstate Commerce Commission, Bureau of Economics, *Profile of Property Industry Subject to ICC Regulation*, July 1965, p. 43.

The major goal of the proposed truck bill is to stimulate price competition and lessen reliance on wasteful service competition. This is done through the provisions which:

(1) establish a "no-suspend zone" within which carriers may freely adjust rates in response to competitive pressures;

(2) prevent the ICC from disallowing a proposed rate on the grounds that it is too low, so long as it covers the costs of the transportation services in question;

(3) allow for entry of a carrier which offers a rate-service combination not being provided by the existing authorized carriers; and

(4) place restrictions on the abilities of rate bureaus to control rates.

No direct estimates are available of the efficiency improvements from either the removal of wasteful operating restrictions or the stimulation of price competition. The effects on operations of the encouragement of price competition in LTL trucking are particularly difficult to quantify. Investigations into the effects of increased price competition in trucking have focused on the removal of regulatory restrictions from certain agricultural products and are not directly applicable to LTL movements.[5] Moreover, these analyses have concentrated on changes in prices rather than in service frequencies.

Several pieces of information are available which help to develop a rough order of estimates of the magnitude of efficiency gains in LTL trucking from regulatory reform. First, estimates can be constructed of the savings in private carriage from eliminating certain operating restrictions. In a subsequent section of the paper, a 3 percent improvement in the efficiency of private carriage arising from eliminating restrictions is estimated. The savings from eliminating LTL operating restrictions should be comparable.

Second, the savings from price competition should be substantially greater than those from eliminating operating restrictions. As mentioned earlier, this is the major thrust of the truck bill. We think that the savings from price competition will be approximately double

[5] James R. Snitzler and Robert J. Byrne, *Interstate Trucking of Fresh and Frozen Poultry under the Agricultural Exemption*, U.S. Department of Agriculture, Marketing Research Division, MRR-244, March 1958; idem, *Interstate Trucking of Frozen Fruits and Vegetables under the Agricultural Exemption*, U.S. Department of Agriculture, Marketing Research Division, MRR-316, March 1959; J. C. Winter and Ivan W. Ulrey, *Supplement to Interstate Trucking of Frozen Fruits and Vegetables under the Agricultural Exemption*, U.S. Department of Agriculture, Marketing Research Division, Supplement to MRR-316, July 1961.

the savings from the elimination of operating restrictions. We therefore assume that the bill will result in a 10 percent reduction in LTL fuel consumption, mostly from the reduction in service competition as a result of increased price competition. This seems to be the appropriate order of magnitude for the overall efficiency gains in LTL trucking, and it corresponds to a savings from price competition of 7 percent which is reasonable relative to the estimated savings of 3 percent for the elimination of operating restrictions.

An improvement of 10 percent in the operating efficiency of the LTL industry can largely be represented by a 10 percent increase in the average load factor. Increased price competition will result in lower average service frequencies and higher average loads. Removal of wasteful operating restrictions will reduce empty mileage and increase average loads. These changes all result in higher average load factors. The removal of certain route restrictions will reduce mileage without changing load factors. But these fuel efficiency improvements move in the same direction as those accounted for by increases in load factors and, given the roughness of the estimates, it seems safe to assume that they are incorporated in the 10 percent increase in load factors.

As can be seen in Table 8-2, a 10 percent increase raises the average LTL load factor from 60 to 66 percent. The estimated post-legislation load factor is considerably below the pre-legislation load factor used in the Roberts-Kneafsey report based on industry estimates. If, with regulatory reform, the LTL industry actually achieves the load factors that the Roberts-Kneafsey study assumes they are already achieving under the present system of regulation, the efficiency gains would be even greater than our figures indicate.

TL common carrier trucking. This sector of the truck industry deals with shipments of usually more than 10,000 pounds carried by either regular or irregular route common carriers. TL shipments frequently move directly from shipper to consignee so that there is less use of terminals with separate pickup and delivery movements than is the case with LTL.

The efficiency of TL operations will not be as greatly improved by the regulatory reform legislation as LTL trucking because TL trucking is already largely price-competitive. Much of the TL traffic moves under negotiated rates. Thus, the efficiency gains in TL trucking will largely be limited to the elimination of wasteful operating restrictions such as route and commodity limitations, one-way authority, and the like.

For LTL trucking, a rough estimate of 3 percent was used for the efficiency gains resulting from the removal of operating restrictions. The same figure is appropriate for TL trucking because the improvements stem from the same source.

Table 8-2 shows that the estimated pre-legislation load factor for TL motor carriage is 68 percent. This is higher than the corresponding LTL load factor because TL carriers generally travel with fuller loads. The estimated 3 percent increase in the TL load factor results in a post-legislative average load factor of 70 percent. Again, this is far lower than the comparable Roberts-Kneafsey load factors for common carrier trucking. This suggests that the estimated efficiency savings may be conservative.

Contract carriage. The proposed regulatory reform legislation will ease entry into contract carriage and will allow firms to expand. But it will not significantly improve operating efficiency or stimulate price competition in contract carriage. This is because there are no serious regulatory impediments to efficient operations in contract carriage, and this sector of for-hire trucking is already price competitive. Since we expect little change in efficiency, Table 8-2 shows no increase in post-legislative load factors for contract carriage.

Unregulated for-hire (agricultural exempt) carriage. This sector of the motor carrier industry consists of truckers who primarily carry agricultural goods where no ICC certificate is required. Carriers operating under this exemption are presently allowed to trip lease to certificated carriers. This allows them to reduce empty backhaul mileage. As can be seen in Table 8-2, however, the empty mileage ratio for exempt carriers is substantially greater than that for certificated common carriers.

The proposed legislation will significantly improve the load factors of exempt carriers. One provision of the regulatory reform bill enables smaller exempt carriers to haul regulated commodities on their backhauls without trip leasing to certificated carriers so long as they charge the regulated rate. In addition, the liberalized entry provisions will allow exempt carriers to obtain certificates to carry regulated commodities. And the liberalized pricing provisions will then allow them to publish their own tariffs and compete for cargo on the basis of price. These provisions will help agricultural carriers to balance their loads, increase their operating efficiency, and raise their load factors.

Those agricultural carriers who are eligible for the liberalized backhaul provision or who become certificated will be able to compete on an even basis with TL common carriers. Their load factors should equilibrate with those of the common carriers of TL shipments. They are likely to compete more directly with TL carriage than with LTL, even though LTL traffic generates higher revenues per ton-mile. This is because exempt carriers do not usually have access to terminal facilities, which are required in handling LTL cargo. Table 8-2 shows the post-legislative load factor for agricultural carriers increasing to almost the same level as that for TL common carriers. It is lower than the figure for TL common carriers, because we assume that not all agricultural carriers will become certificated or will be eligible for the liberalized backhaul provision, and because a slightly higher fraction of agricultural carriers than TL common carriers operate specialized equipment.

Private carriage. Firms are allowed to operate trucks to carry their own goods. Under the present regulatory system these private carriage operations are not allowed to carry for subsidiaries or affiliates or to trip lease to certificated carriers to utilize equipment on backhauls. The regulatory reform legislation will improve private fleet utilization by extending operations to corporate affiliates and subsidiaries and by allowing private carriers to trip lease.

A study by Drake-Sheahan provides data for making a rough estimate of the efficiency improvements from allowing private fleets to carry for affiliates and subsidiaries.[6] This study showed that for fourteen firms investigated, about 1.2 million of a total of 143 million private fleet-miles would be saved if intracorporate hauling were allowed. This is an efficiency gain of almost 1 percent.

The Drake-Sheahan study did not provide an estimate of the efficiency gains from allowing private carriers to trip lease. This is more difficult to estimate because it requires information on transportation movements outside the firms being investigated. The required data are not generally available. The trip lease provision should result in greater increases in the operating efficiency of private carriage than the intracorporate hauling provision because the former permits private carriers to avail themselves of more widespread opportunities to obtain backhaul cargo. For lack of a better estimate, we assume that this provision will cause efficiency savings about double those of the intracorporate hauling provision. Thus, the two private carriage provisions together should result in efficiency gains of 3 per-

[6] Drake Sheahan/Stewart Dougall, Inc., *Evaluation of Potential Changes to Federal Economic Regulation Governing Private Carriage*, report prepared for U.S. Department of Transportation, October 1974.

cent. This may be conservative because another way of looking at the potential savings from trip leasing is to assume that this provision causes the percentage of empty miles for private carriers to approximate that for exempt carriers who are now allowed to trip lease. This assumption yields an efficiency gain of about 9 percent (see Table 8-2).

A far more important impact on the average efficiency of private carriers will take place as a result of the regulatory reform provisions which allow common carriers to price competitively. Common carriers will be able to provide service tailored to the needs of individual shippers and to establish rates based on the costs of the specific transportation service being provided. The present system of regulation severely limits the range and diversity of rate-service combinations that regulated carriers can offer their customers. Consequently, firms that want a different service than is provided at the regulated rate turn to private carriage to meet their specific transportation preferences. There is ample evidence that the lack of rate-service flexibility in common carriage has induced firms to engage in private carriage.[7]

The rate flexibility provisions of the proposed legislation will enable common carriers to compete much more effectively with private carriage than they have in the past. This should cause substantial diversion from private to common carriage, particularly in LTL trucking where rate regulation has been most restrictive.

The expected diversion from private to common carriage will increase the efficiency of private carriage, on the average, because the less efficient private carriage operations will tend to be diverted to common carriage. The effects of diversion from private to common carriage are represented in Table 8-2 by an increase in the average load factor for private carriage to a level somewhat below the post-legislative LTL and TL figures. The reason it is somewhat lower is that a large fraction of private carriers operate specialized equipment.

It is important to emphasize that this substantial increase in the private carriage average load factor will be achieved by traffic being diverted from less efficient private carriage operations to more efficient common carriage operations. As discussed earlier, the efficiency increases in private carriage itself are expected to be small, on the order of 3 percent.

---

[7] Drake Sheahan/Stewart Dougall, Inc., *Private Carriage Motivation and Impact of Rural Location*, report prepared for the U.S. Department of Transportation, March 28, 1975.

Motor Carrier Fuel Consumption. In this section the pre- and post-legislation average load factors are used to estimate fuel consumption per ton-mile for each sector of the motor carrier industry. Both pre- and post-legislation fuel consumption factors are estimated. The difference between the two figures provides an estimate of the efficiency savings in fuel use per ton-mile in each sector of the motor carrier industry.

Table 8-3 shows the estimated fuel consumption factors. The estimates assume that trucks average 4.5 miles per gallon of fuel in all sectors. Truck fuel consumption usually averages from 4 to 5 miles per gallon, and 4.5 miles per gallon is a conventional estimate.[8] The average full load is assumed to be twenty-five tons for all carrier types. This is a conventional assumption for all except low-density commodities, and it corresponds to the new federal size and weight standards.

In Table 8-3, the average load factor is applied to the full load to estimate the average load. Then this is multiplied by miles per gallon to estimate ton-miles per gallon. The reciprocal is gallons per ton-mile. Column 11 shows the savings in gallons per ton-mile caused by the proposed legislation. This is the difference between columns 6 and 10.

Motor Carrier Fuel Efficiency Savings. In Table 8-4 the fuel savings in gallons per 1,000 ton-miles calculated in Table 8-3 are applied to the 1985 ton-mile forecasts presented in Table 8-2. The result is an estimate of the fuel efficiency savings in the motor carrier industry.

The only explanation required in presenting the results concerns the ton-mile estimate and the corresponding fuel consumption savings for private carriers. As will be recalled from the discussion of the expected change in the average load factor of private carriage, most of the increase is attributable to the diversion of traffic from private to common carriage. Thus, the average load factor in private carriage is increased. Because the post-legislation average load factors are the same in the two sectors, it is not necessary to estimate the expected traffic diversion in order to compute the fuel savings. Thus, Table 8-4 does not present estimates of the expected traffic diversion from private to common carriage.

---

[8] See, for example, David Maister and D. Daryl Wyckoff, *The Owner-Operator: Independent Trucker* (Lexington, Mass.: D. C. Heath and Co., 1975), p. 31. Consolidated Freightways reports that they average about four miles per gallon; see their *Annual Report*, 1974.

Table 8-3

MOTOR CARRIER FUEL CONSUMPTION PER TON-MILE

			Pre-Legislation				Post-Legislation				
Carrier Type	**Miles/ Gallon** (1)	**Full Load** (tons) (2)	Average load factor (3)	Average load (tons) (4)	Ton-miles/ gallon (5)	Gallons/ 1,000 ton-miles (6)	Average load factor (7)	Average load (tons) (8)	Ton-miles/ gallon (9)	Gallons/ 1,000 ton-miles (10)	**Savings in Gallons/ 1,000 Ton-Miles** (11)
Common carrier											
LTL	4.5	25	60	15.0	68	14.7	66	16.5	74	13.5	1.2
TL	4.5	25	68	17.0	77	13.0	70	17.5	79	12.7	0.3
Contract carrier	4.5	25	50	12.5	56	17.9	50	12.5	56	17.9	0.0
Unregulated for-hire (agriculture exempt)	4.5	25	61	15.0	68	14.7	67	16.8	75	13.3	1.4
Private carrier	4.5	25	50	12.5	56	17.9	62	15.5	70	14.3	3.6

Table 8-4

MOTOR CARRIER FUEL EFFICIENCY SAVINGS PER YEAR

Carrier Type	Ton-Miles (billions)	Savings in Gallons/ 1,000 Ton-Miles	Savings in Gallons (millions)
Common carrier			
LTL	173	1.2	208
TL	173	0.3	52
Contract carrier	38	0.0	0
Unregulated for-hire (agriculture exempt)	81	1.4	113
Private carrier	189	3.6	550
Total			923

Table 8-4 shows estimated fuel savings in the motor carrier industry as a result of efficiency improvements from regulatory reform to be 923 million gallons per year. This is an efficiency savings of 22 million barrels of fuel per year (based on 42 gallons per barrel). These efficiency savings, which were not estimated in the Roberts-Kneafsey study, far outweigh the losses in fuel use from traffic diversion estimated in that study. In the next section we consider the effects of traffic diversion on fuel consumption.

Traffic Diversion

Truck and rail transportation are affected differently by the present regulatory system and by the proposed regulatory changes. Thus, the regulatory reform legislation will alter the competitive balance between the two modes. This section describes the ways in which the legislation will affect the competitive relationship between truck and rail, and it assesses the traffic diversion that is likely to occur. The fuel use implications of the likely traffic diversion between the modes are then examined.

Motor Carrier Legislation. Much of the proposed truck legislation is directed at improving the efficiency of LTL transportation by eliminating various operating restrictions, liberalizing entry, increasing price flexibility, and fostering price competition. Although these aspects of the proposed legislation will greatly improve the efficiency of LTL operations, they will have little effect on the competitive relationship between truck and rail. The railroads have largely discontinued handling less-than-carload shipments, so they do not compete for LTL traffic.

The only provisions of the proposed truck legislation which will significantly affect truck-rail competition are those which deal with TL operations. As discussed earlier, common carrier TL costs will be reduced by the elimination of artificial restrictions such as one-way authority and commodity and route restrictions. Earlier we estimated that this would result in modest improvements in TL efficiency, on the order of 3 percent. This estimate is extremely rough and may be conservative. TL common carrier operations will not be greatly affected by the pricing flexibility provisions of the truck legislation because most TL rates are set competitively now.

Unregulated for-hire TL operations will be improved by the provisions of the legislation which liberalize backhaul authority, ease entry restrictions, and increase price flexibility. These provisions will enable agricultural exempt carriers to compete on a closer basis with common carrier operations for TL shipments of manufactured goods. This will increase the supply of truck capacity available for manufactured goods and will lower shipping costs and rates on TL shipments of both agricultural and manufactured goods. The efficiency improvements should be substantial, as estimated in the previous section of this paper.

Private carriage operations will be improved by the legislative provisions which liberalize intracorporate hauling and allow trip leasing to increase utilization on backhauls. We estimated earlier that these provisions would result in efficiency gains in private trucking of about 3 percent.

In summary, only modest cost reductions are anticipated in private and regulated common carrier TL operations as a result of the proposed truck legislation. Substantial improvements in the utilization of exempt carriers are expected. Their costs should drop to a level comparable with common carrier TL costs.

Rail Legislation. There are three main ways in which the rail legislation will affect the economics of the rail industry.

(1) Rate flexibility will be introduced, allowing railroads to set rates on the basis of the costs of the specific service being provided.

(2) Abandonment of branch lines will be made easier.

(3) Substantial federal grants, subsidies, and loan guarantees will be provided to upgrade railroad plant and equipment.

Of the three, the liberalization of rate regulation will have the most important and lasting impact on intermodal competition and efficient resource allocation.

The easing of abandonment will cause some rail traffic to be diverted to truck. Because the lines being abandoned carry little traffic, the amount of diversion will be small. Further, the effects of this diversion on fuel use will be negligible. Studies of branch line abandonments show that for short-haul movements the diversion to motor carrier reduces fuel use because of the reduction in interchanging. For long-haul movements, diversion to truck typically increases fuel use. But in either case, the change in fuel use is small.[9]

The provisions in the rail legislation for federal grants, subsidies, and loan guarantees will lower rail costs by providing capital to upgrade facilities. These funds can also be used to provide incentives to improve work rules, to develop and adopt improved rail technology, and to consolidate facilities through mergers and acquisitions. The impact of these actions would be improved productivity and a further reduction in rail costs.

The pricing provisions of the rail legislation will allow railroads increased flexibility in establishing lower rates to offset the superior service provided by motor carriers. Under the present regulatory system, railroads have been prevented by regulated rate minimums from taking advantage of their lower costs by reducing rates to attract traffic from trucks. Motor carriers, by contrast, have been able to set rates competitively on TL shipments, as most TL traffic is carried under negotiated rather than regulated rates. As a result of restrictive rail rate regulation, most independent observers feel that considerable intercity freight is now being carried by trucks when it could be more economically carried by rail, even taking into account the service disadvantages of railroads. Thus, allowing railroads to lower their rates where it serves their interests to do so should result in substantial diversion of TL traffic from truck to rail.

There are basically two situations in which it will be in the railroads' interest to lower rates and attract TL traffic. The first is where regulated rates exceed rail costs, including both operating costs and provision for capital replenishment. The second is where rates need not provide capital replenishment because continued invest-

[9] See John Fuller and William Hyman, *Energy and Environmental Effects of Railroad Branch-Line Abandonments*, report prepared for Wisconsin Department of Transportation, 1974.

ment in the facilities is not justified. It is generally agreed that, if the rail system were being constructed today, many of the existing lines would not be built. The issue is not merely one of uneconomic branch lines. There is considerable redundant capacity in the trunk line system. On those portions of the rail system which would not be built under today's economic environment, rail rates could drop substantially to attract TL traffic.

In summary, the rail bill should lead to increased operating efficiency as a result of the grant and subsidy provisions of the rail bill whereby capital and incentives to make needed changes will be provided. In addition, increased price flexibility should enable railroads to attract TL traffic by allowing them to price their product competitively.

To estimate accurately the effects of these provisions on truck-rail competition would require massive detail, by specific commodity movements, on such items as rates, costs, and redundant capacity. A number of studies, including the Roberts-Kneafsey study, have investigated truck-rail competition. Although none of these studies can be considered definitive, they do provide a range of estimates which can be used to establish reasonable bounds on the effects of regulatory reform on traffic diversion between truck and rail. The next section considers the results of these studies.

Findings of the Available Literature on Truck-Rail Competition. Most of the available published literature on the effects of regulation on truck-rail competition stems from the classic study by John R. Meyer and his colleagues.[10] They made detailed econometric studies of the relative costs of the two modes together with estimates of the costs to shippers resulting from the inferior service of railroads. The service attributes considered were time in transit and the railroads' larger minimum lot sizes. Based on these estimates, Meyer and his colleagues concluded that a significant amount of traffic is being carried by truck that could more economically be carried by rail if railroads were not restricted by rate regulation from pricing competitively. Specifically, the study concludes that even after adding the service differential to rail costs "37 percent more revenue ton-miles could be handled by rail than by truck for the same outlay."[11] Thus, the Meyer study clearly finds that rail rate flexibility would

[10] John R. Meyer, Merton J. Peck, John Stenason, and Charles Zwick, *The Economics of Competition in the Transportation Industries* (Cambridge, Mass.: Harvard University Press, 1960).

[11] Ibid., pp. 166-67.

result in a sizeable diversion of traffic from truck to rail, though the extent of the diversion is not specified.

A number of studies have attempted to update and expand the analysis of Meyer and his colleagues. These efforts have concentrated on updating the relative cost estimates and on making the measure of the service differential more comprehensive. It has been recognized that dependability of service and schedule frequency are more important for many shippers than speed in transit, and attempts have been made to include these factors in the measure of railroads' service handicap.

At the extreme end of this set of studies is the analysis by R.W. Harbeson, which concludes that competitive rate making would divert virtually all intercity TL traffic to rail.[12] Harbeson's findings are based on an updating of the cost and service differential estimates. He did not, however, attempt to extend the service attributes to include such factors as dependability of service, schedule frequency, or equipment availability. His conclusions, therefore, overestimate the amount of truck traffic that would be diverted to rail because truck provides more reliable arrival times than rail.

A recent study by Kenneth Boyer attempts to adjust the quality of service differential for the factors not included in the Meyer service differential.[13] His results indicate that these neglected factors are more important than the more easily measured factors included in the Meyer and Harbeson studies. Based on his estimates of the more comprehensive service differential, he concludes that competitive pricing would cause a 20 percent increase in rail ton-miles as a result of diversion from truck.

An independent effort to include reliability of arrival times, schedule frequency, equipment availability, and other minor factors in the service differential was made by D.W. Woods and T.A. Domencich.[14] This study concludes that competitive pricing would divert about 24 percent of the tonnage carried by common and private motor carriers to rail. This converts to an increase of 36 percent in rail ton-miles after adjusting by mileage blocks.

In contrast to these analyses, the Roberts-Kneafsey study con-

---

12 R. W. Harbeson, "Toward Better Resource Allocation in Transport," *Journal of Law and Economics*, October 1969.

13 Kenneth D. Boyer, "The Price Sensitivity of Shippers' Mode of Transport Selection and the Intermodal Allocation of Freight Traffic" (Ph.D. diss., University of Michigan, 1975).

14 D. W. Woods and T. A. Domencich, "Competition between Rail and Truck in Intercity Freight Transportation," *Transportation Research Forum*, 1971.

cludes that regulatory reform would result in a small diversion from rail to truck. They project a 4 percent decrease in rail ton-miles resulting from the truck and rail legislation. The Roberts-Kneafsey analysis of traffic diversion takes account of the efficiency improvements in TL trucking arising from the proposed truck legislation. The efficiency gains in TL trucking, as discussed earlier, are likely to be modest. The analysis does not take into account the effects of lower rail costs resulting from the federal grant and subsidy provisions or the increased competitiveness of railroads resulting from increased price flexibility. Thus, it is not surprising that the Roberts-Kneafsey study projects a diversion in traffic from rail to truck. Indeed, the small shift to truck is consistent with the modest improvements in TL operations indicated in this paper.

In summary, the literature on truck-rail competition indicates that rate regulation has severely hampered the railroads' ability to compete for TL traffic. It is easy to take issue with the specific cost estimates or measures of the service differential used in the various studies of truck–rail competition. But these studies do suggest that when account is taken of the competitive effects of increased railroad pricing flexibility, the truck and rail legislation should result in a net diversion of traffic from truck to rail. The magnitude of the expected diversion is uncertain. An increase in rail ton-miles on the order of 20 percent is possible. This is the Boyer estimate. It takes account of the improved price flexibility of the regulatory reform bills, but it does not incorporate the improvements in railroad operating efficiency that should result from the infusions of capital and the incentives to make needed changes in work rules and technology stemming from the grant and subsidy provisions of the rail bill. Thus, it may be a conservative estimate of the shift in traffic from truck to rail caused by the regulatory reform legislation.

Fuel Use Implications of Traffic Diversion. If regulatory reform results in a net diversion of traffic from truck to rail, then additional fuel savings should be added to the 30 million barrels per year estimated earlier for the truck efficiency savings. A rough estimate of these savings is made below. It should be stressed that this estimate is highly uncertain, for reasons which will be clear during the discussion.

Assume that traffic diversion increases rail ton-miles by 20 percent. A 20 percent increase in the Roberts-Kneafsey 1985 base-case

Table 8-5

FUEL USE EFFECTS OF ROBERTS-KNEAFSEY TRAFFIC DIVERSION ESTIMATES

Carrier Type	**Traffic Diversion** (billions of ton-miles)[a]	**Gallons Per 1,000 Ton-Miles**[b]	**Change in Fuel Use** (millions of gallons)
Truck			
Common carrier = TL	16.3	12.7	207
Contract carrier	3.6	17.9	64
Unregulated for-hire (agriculture exempt)	9.6	13.3	128
Private carrier	22.5	14.3	322
Rail	−33.3	5.05	−168
Barge	−18.7	3.6	−67
Total			486

[a] Data taken from Roberts-Kneafsey study, appendix 4.

[b] Data taken from Table 8-3, except for the figures for rail and barge which are taken from the Roberts-Kneafsey study.

projection of rail traffic is 183 billion ton-miles.[15] The 20 percent figure is taken from the Boyer study of traffic diversion and is itself uncertain. A more conservative estimate might be appropriate. If it were assumed, for example, that the actual diversion would be only half that estimated by Boyer, the fuel savings estimated below would be decreased accordingly. But the basic conclusions of this paper—that the regulatory reform legislation will result in savings in fuel use—would not be changed.

The next step is to calculate the fuel savings resulting from the estimated traffic diversion. Table 8-5 shows the average fuel use per 1,000 ton-miles for rail and for the various sectors of trucking. It can be seen that rail operations are less fuel intensive than truck operations, on the average, so the net effect of a diversion from truck to rail should be a savings in fuel consumption. A comparison of the post-legislation fuel consumption figure for rail and TL common carrier operations shows that TL operations use about 2.5 times as

[15] For perspective, this represents a 28 percent decrease in total 1985 base-case trucking ton-miles. It represents a decrease of about 38 percent in truck ton-miles after excluding LTL common carrier traffic, since this is assumed to be unaffected by rail competition. A portion of private truck traffic is also LTL. When an allowance is made for this, the estimated TL diversion is on the order of 40 percent or more.

much fuel per ton-mile as rail (that is, 12.7 versus 5.05 gallons per ton-mile).

However, the actual amount of the fuel savings may not be well reflected by the average fuel intensities of the two modes. The actual effect on fuel use of traffic diversion between the modes depends critically on the specific diversion that occurs. This can best be seen with a few examples.[16] Diversion can occur from the backhaul of one mode to the backhaul of another. If so, there would be very little change in fuel use regardless of the average fuel intensities. Alternatively, if traffic switches from a truck prime haul to a rail backhaul, the fuel savings will exceed the difference in the average fuel intensities because there will be little increase in rail fuel use and a substantial decrease in truck fuel consumption.[17] If the diversion occurs from prime haul to prime haul, the difference in average intensities may provide a reasonable approximation to the actual change in fuel consumption.

Under regulatory reform diversion of traffic from TL trucking to rail will tend to occur wherever regulated rail rates have been held above the long-run marginal costs of the specific movement in question. Thus, to provide a reliable estimate of the fuel use implications of the expected traffic diversion, it would be necessary to know where redundant capacity exists, where rail backhaul rates have been held up to parity with rail prime haul rates (an ICC rate regulatory practice to avoid "discriminatory" rates), where rail operations would become more efficient relative to truck as a result of the federal grant and subsidy incentives, and so forth. Because of the obvious impossibility of this, the only practical alternative is to use the average fuel intensities, recognizing that the actual fuel savings might be higher or lower than the resulting estimates.

Applying the difference in average fuel intensities to the projections of freight diversion, the following estimate of fuel savings is obtained:

183 billion ton-miles × (12.7-5.05) gallons/1,000 ton-miles
= 1,400 million gallons per year
= 33 million barrels per year at 42 gallons/barrel.

[16] A number of useful examples which show the complexity in estimating the energy implications of freight diversion are given in Alexander French, *Energy and Freight Movements*, Federal Highway Administration, paper presented at the Transportation Research Board, January 1976.

[17] If the diversion occurs from rail prime haul to truck backhaul, the savings will be less than the difference in the average intensities (that is, it will be about 5 gallons per 1,000 ton-miles, compared to about 12.7 gallons if the diversion is from truck prime haul to rail backhaul).

If it were conservatively assumed that the diversion would be half that estimated by Boyer, say, 92 million ton-miles, the estimated fuel savings would be 17 million barrels per year.

The Roberts-Kneafsey study concluded that the regulatory reform legislation would result in a net diversion of freight traffic from rail to truck. They project a 4 percent decrease in rail ton-miles. Although we believe that this conclusion is based on an improper understanding of the effects of increased rail price flexibility on truck-rail competition, it is still useful to examine the fuel use implications of their projected traffic diversion because they represent the most pessimistic case.

The Roberts-Kneafsey study estimates that as a result of the projected traffic diversion, fuel consumption would increase by 15 million barrels per year. This is half the savings in fuel use, estimated earlier, caused by improvements in motor carrier operating efficiency resulting from the proposed truck legislation. The efficiency gains were not estimated in the Roberts-Kneafsey study. Thus, based on these estimates, regulatory reform would result in a net savings in energy consumption of 15 million barrels per year.

The Roberts-Kneafsey estimate of the fuel use implications of their projected 4 percent decrease in rail traffic is too high, however, for two reasons. First, the increase of 15 million barrels per year is based on an average truck fuel efficiency of 20 gallons per 1,000 ton-miles for common and contract carriage. This assumes that, at a 100 percent load factor, common and contract carriers use 15.53 gallons per 1,000 ton-miles.[18] Since heavy diesel trucks get between four and five miles per gallon, this translates into sixty to seventy-five vehicle-miles per 1,000 ton-miles, or an average maximum load of thirteen to sixteen tons. Since vehicle capacity is about twenty-five tons, actual fuel efficiency is higher (fuel consumption is less).

The Roberts-Kneafsey estimates of the fuel use implications of their projected traffic diversion are adjusted for this overestimate in truck fuel consumption in Table 8-5. The fuel consumption estimates used in Table 8-5 were developed earlier in the analysis of fuel efficiency savings. They are based on average maximum loads of twenty-five tons, and they also take into account the effects of the proposed legislation on load factors in each sector of the truck industry. Table 8-5 shows that, after correcting for the underestimate in truck fuel efficiency, the Roberts-Kneafsey projections of traffic

[18] Roberts-Kneafsey study, appendix 3.

diversion yield an increase in energy use of 486 million gallons per year, or 11 million barrels per year (at 42 gallons per barrel).

Earlier in this section the uncertainties arising from the use of average fuel efficiencies were discussed. When traffic is diverted from truck to rail, the difference in the average fuel intensities may understate or overstate the actual fuel changes. If traffic is assumed to be diverted from rail to truck, however, the difference in the average fuel intensities is likely to overstate the change in fuel use. This is because it overstates the change in fuel use for either a backhaul to backhaul traffic shift or a rail prime haul to truck backhaul shift.[19] Thus, the estimate of 11 million barrels per year probably represents some sort of upper bound to the estimated increase in fuel use resulting from the Roberts-Kneafsey projected diversion from rail to truck. This is half the estimated fuel savings from the improvements in truck efficiency caused by the motor carrier regulatory reform legislation. Thus, under the most pessimistic assumptions, the regulatory reform legislation is projected to result in savings in fuel consumption.

Summary

The conclusions of the paper are summarized as follows:

(1) The expected improvements in the efficiency of truck operations resulting from regulatory reform are estimated to save 22 million barrels of fuel per year by 1985.

(2) Regulatory reform is expected to result in diversion of freight traffic from truck to rail, which is estimated to save an additional 33 million barrels of fuel per year. Thus, total savings are estimated to be on the order of 55 million barrels per year by 1985.

(3) The Roberts-Kneafsey study, representing the most pessimistic estimate of the fuel use implications of regulatory reform, concludes that traffic will be diverted from rail to truck. Based on their traffic diversion projections, they estimate an increase in fuel use of 15 million barrels per year.

(4) Since the estimated fuel savings from efficiency improvements exceed the Roberts-Kneafsey projections of the effects of traffic diversion, the regulatory reform legislation

[19] These two cases work in opposite directions for diversion from truck to rail.

is expected to result in fuel savings even if the most pessimistic estimates of traffic diversion are accepted. The net savings would be 7 million barrels per year using the Roberts-Kneafsey estimates of the fuel implications of their traffic diversion projections.

(5) The Roberts-Kneafsey study overestimates the fuel use implications of their traffic diversion estimates.

  (a) The average fuel consumption per ton-mile of trucks is overstated. Correcting for this overestimate reduces their estimate of increased fuel use from 15 million to 11 million barrels per year.

  (b) The effects of traffic diversion on fuel consumption are overstated because of the use of average fuel consumption figures in converting intermodal shifts in traffic to changes in fuel use. The magnitude of the overestimate is not known. The firmest conclusion that can be reached is that the Roberts-Kneafsey projections of traffic diversion imply an increase in fuel consumption of between zero and 11 million barrels per year.

(6) If the Roberts-Kneafsey analysis of traffic diversion is used, regulatory reform is estimated to result in fuel savings of between 11 million and 22 million barrels per year. This is the net effect of fuel efficiency gains of 22 million barrels per year minus the effects of diversion of zero to 11 million barrels per year. The appropriate amount within that range depends on the extent to which the method used in converting traffic diversion to changes in fuel use overstates the increase in fuel consumption.

PART FIVE

REFORMS OF OPERATING RESTRICTIONS AND COMMERCIAL ZONES

The Ford administration's trucking reform proposal contained provisions to lower the legal barriers to entry into the trucking industry and to provide carriers with greater operating flexibility by removing a number of restrictions imposed by the Interstate Commerce Commission. The paper by Norman Jones, a private economic consultant, analyzes the effects of eliminating some of these restrictions—namely, the backhaul restriction and the so-called gateway restriction. As background to his analysis, Jones reviews the structure of the industry and describes two models which afford a means for attaining quantitative assessments of changes in regulation. The administration's proposal also provided for expanding the so-called commercial zones, the area surrounding metropolitan centers within which trucking is exempt from economic regulation. The paper by W. Bruce Allen, a professor of economics at the University of Pennsylvania, examines the economics of expanding the commercial zones with particular reference to Philadelphia. Both of these studies were undertaken for the U.S. Department of Transportation as part of its research program into motor carrier regulatory reform.

9

ON REMOVING OPERATING AND BACKHAUL RESTRICTIONS

Norman H. Jones, Jr.

Introduction

The consequences of regulation of the motor carrier industry have been well and extensively detailed. Operating costs and rates in the regulated sector of the industry are higher than otherwise would be the case. Both the regulated and the nonregulated segments have substantial excess capacity. The annual "costs" of these aspects of regulation of the motor carrier industry were estimated to have amounted to between $1.5 billion and $2.9 billion per year in 1968. Their elimination in that year would have reduced the nation's motor carrier freight bill by some 6 to 15 percent.

For almost fifteen years each national administration has pressed for regulatory reform and has urged the Congress to enact legislation which would reduce the economic regulation of surface transportation and place greater reliance on competitive forces to control and direct the industry. No such legislation has been adopted, and change in regulatory policies and procedures of the Interstate Commerce Commission has been minimal. The inability to enact modernization legislation reflects in part the strong political power of the surface transportation industry. It also, however, reflects the inability of the proponents of change to marshal strong political support for that change. Put another way, the "public" does not perceive the benefits of regulatory change as being worth the costs and the risks that will be associated with that change.

This paper is edited from a study entitled *Examining the Impact of Change in Motor Carrier Regulation*, prepared for the U.S. Department of Transportation, October 1974. A slightly revised version of this study appeared in Allen R. Ferguson and Leonard Lee Lane, eds., *Transportation Policy Options: The Political Economy of Regulatory Reform* (Washington, D.C.: Public Interest Economics Foundation), pp. 107-28.

Regulatory change, if it is effective, will lead to changes in transportation rate structures and consequently in the profitability of shippers and consignees. The American Trucking Associations predicts that in the case of the motor carrier industry a consequence of change will be "chaos" comparable to the early 1930s. In the view of the ICC, regulatory change would lead to: a "law of the jungle atmosphere"; "the harmful and wasteful effects of unrestrained random operation"; and the "creation of destructive competition, carrier instability, and regulatory chaos." Further, the commission believes that any lower rates that might result from such action would be purely temporary in nature since "once the 'king of the hill' emerges and controls the market without the restraints of balanced competition, prices would rise higher than before."

These fears of the ATA and the ICC are the focus of this chapter. Specifically, two kinds of regulatory change are examined in an effort to identify the consequences for the motor carrier industry and its shippers and consignees. These changes are:

(1) the consequences of removing all gateway restrictions on motor carriage, and

(2) the consequences of eliminating empty backhauls through relaxing commodity restrictions on motor carriage.

The immediate effects of the first of these changes (elimination of gateway restrictions) would be to reduce the cost to the motor carrier of particular traffic flows—that is, those where direct routes involving less mileage, less time, and hence lower cost are feasible in terms of the service requirement. This could be expected, in a free market, to set in motion: (1) a reallocation of resources among markets (services) by the carriers so affected; (2) price changes; (3) changes in the service levels in the various markets and in aggregate.

Elimination of backhaul restrictions would set in motion two sets of forces. First, individual firms would have a tendency to increase the expected revenue of inbound traffic and, thus, the revenue of round trips. Second, by allowing all carriers with authority between two points to participate in all traffic between those points, the move would serve to break down market distinctions based on commodity definitions. Again, these changes would be expected in a free market to set in motion a reallocation of resources among services, changes in prices, and changes in the overall availability of service.

The primary interest here then is to identify the way these possible regulatory changes will lead to changes in:

(1) rate levels;

(2) service levels;

(3) firm numbers, firm size, and, if possible, firm stability (that is, length of life in a given market).

The starting point of the investigation is a description (model) of the industry.

The Industry

Firm Characteristics. Firm size in the motor carrier industry can be very small. A single tractor-trailer and driver can be defined as the smallest producing unit (if terminal needs are ignored for the moment). Thus, investment needs per production unit are small. Further, an active secondhand market facilitates easy entry and exit, so that the formation of a firm, or its withdrawal, can take place easily and with substantial assurances of liquidity. Finally, it would appear that terminal size in general may be scaled to the number of production units included in the firm. Thus, capital (entry) costs can be closely scaled to the expected level of output. In such an industry one would not expect to have significant economies of scale emerge, and on the face of it one would expect an industry comprised of many small firms.

In general, the numbers would seem to bear out those expectations. In 1971 the number of motor carrier firms reported to the ICC was 15,117. These included 1,597 Class I motor carriers, whose revenues exceeded $1 million; 2,169 Class II motor carriers, whose total revenues fell between $300,000 and $1 million; and 11,351 Class III motor carriers, whose revenues were less than $300,000 per year. These federally regulated motor carriers accounted for 41 to 42 percent of the total motor carrier traffic. In addition to the regulated carriers are (agricultural product) exempt carriers—estimated to have been about 20,000 firms in 1960—and a substantial number of private carriers. The motor transport industry as a whole would seem to be composed of more than 50,000 individual firms and firm-type producing units. Clearly, such a large number of firms relative to the overall market would suggest that without regulation no one firm could influence price. Further, the easy mobility of assets would suggest that, in general, individual submarkets also would be competitive in the sense that no one supplier alone could affect price. (This probably exaggerates the case for some of the more sparsely settled areas.)

Moreover, several statistical studies have suggested that significant economies of scale are not present in the motor carrier industry, thus bearing out the intuitive evidence above. Nonetheless, there are very large differences in firm size and important evidence of concentration in the regulated portion of the industry. For example, the 1,597 Class I carriers accounted for almost 80 percent of the total regulated carrier revenues in 1971. The mean revenue of Class I carriers was almost thirty-nine times the mean revenue of Class II and Class III carriers in 1970. The extent of concentration in the industry is shown even more dramatically in Figure 9-1. There the percentage of total revenue is compared with the percentage of the total population of the regulated firms, using a traditional Lorenz curve.

To review the earlier statistical studies, a Cobb-Douglas production function was fitted to ton-mile data for a sample of Class I and Class II carriers.[1] The choice of a Cobb-Douglas, or log-linear, production function was purely on the grounds of the convenience of interpreting the coefficients of the independent variables. That is, in the case of the Cobb-Douglas, the coefficients are elasticities and their sum indicates increasing, constant, or decreasing returns to scale if it is greater than, equal to, or less than one, respectively. The results are shown below, with standard errors in parentheses. The relationship is:

$$\text{log ton-mile} = a + b_1 \text{ log labor input} + b_2 \text{ log assets.}$$

	Constant (a)	*Labor Coefficient* (b_1)	*Capital Coefficient* (b_2)	R^2
All carriers	2.923	0.242	0.793	0.65
	(1.113)	(0.070)	(0.071)	
Class I carriers	3.592	0.322	0.657	0.56
	(1.084)	(0.094)	(0.092)	
Class II carriers	7.720	−0.361	0.281	0.05
	(0.961)	(0.113)	(0.117)	

[1] Source for the data was *TRINC's Blue Book of the Trucking Industry* (Washington, D.C.: TRINC Transportation Consultants, 1971). A sample of 525 firms was drawn from the firms reported in TRINC's to have less than 50 percent local freight transportation. The sample was drawn randomly and no attempt was made to stratify. The distinction between Class I and Class II carriers in the analysis here is made on the basis of 1970 revenues.

Figure 9-1

LORENZ CURVE PLOTTING PERCENT OF REVENUE AND PERCENT OF FIRMS IN THE MOTOR CARRIER INDUSTRY, 1962

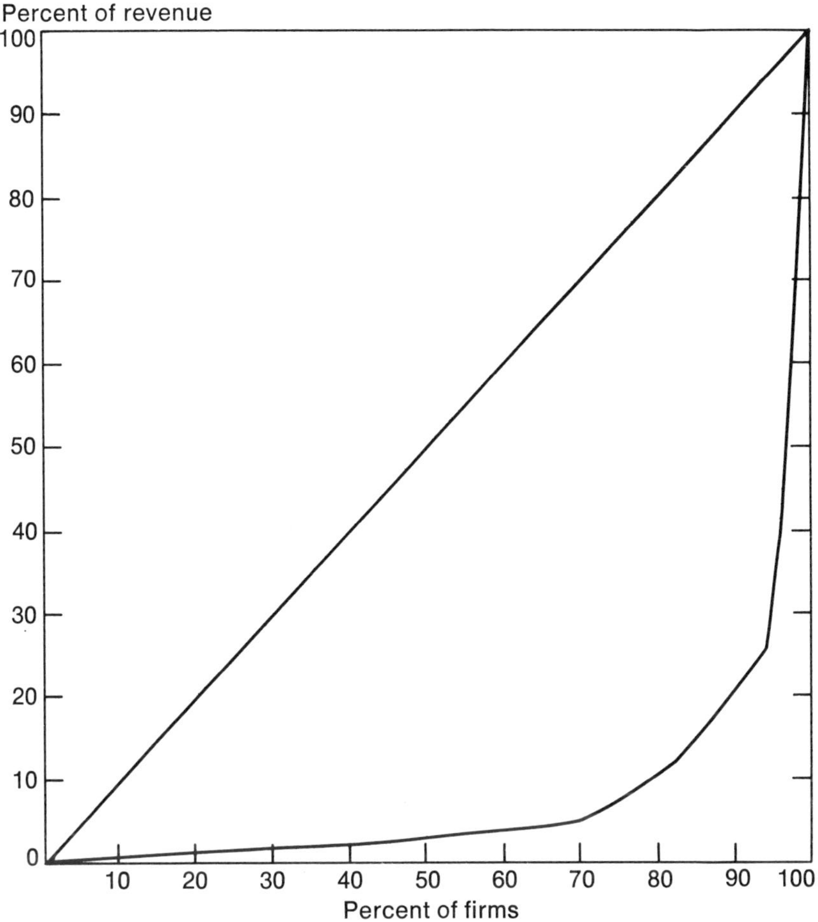

Source: Interstate Commerce Commission, *78th Annual Report, 1964,* p. 149.

Labor is measured in terms of the number of employees, and assets are measured in terms of dollar value.[2] These figures are taken from the annual reports of the carriers to the ICC.

[2] An alternative asset series was constructed to account for the large amount of truck leasing that has emerged in the industry. Using this series, the R^2 was improved slightly—about eight points—but the regression coefficients did not change in a statistically significant fashion.

The results for the entire sample indicate that the industry operates under constant costs—that is, the sum of the labor and capital coefficients is not statistically different from one. Put another way, the results indicate that a doubling of the labor force and the capital stock of the firm would lead to a doubling of output. The results for the Class I carriers are essentially the same as that for the entire sample. Although the coefficients of the Class I component are different from those of the entire sample, their difference is not statistically significant at high orders of confidence. The results for the Class II carriers in the sample, however, are disturbing. They would indicate that these carriers had essentially no returns to scale —that is, doubling the firm size would have no impact on output. This, of course, is nonsense. What the results do reflect, though, is the great heterogeneity of the firms falling into the Class II category. This is emphasized by the very small R^2 of the regression.

In contrast with the evidence that the industry as a whole (as reflected in the sample) and Class I carriers in particular operated under constant returns to scale, the relationship of unit costs (costs/ton-mile, costs/shipments) to output measures (ton-miles, shipments) provides directly contrary evidence. Very briefly, the evidence is that costs/ton-mile (and costs/shipments) decline as the volume of output and ton-miles (and shipments) increases. This is shown in the regression results presented below. Again, logarithmic form was used since the coefficient for the independent variable (that is, the measure of output) shows the percentage change in cost/unit given a 1 percent change in the level of output. Standard errors of the coefficients are in parentheses.

	Constant (log *a*)	*Ton-Mile Output Coefficient* (*b*)	R^2
All carriers	1.499	−0.349	0.44
	(0.736)	(0.017)	
Class I carriers	2.477	−0.424	0.50
	(0.694)	(0.024)	
Class II carriers	3.371	−0.624	0.66
	(0.566)	(0.032)	

In all instances the sign of the coefficient is negative, indicating that an increase in output is accompanied by a decrease in unit costs. Even more surprising is the fact that the regression equation for the sample of Class II carriers shows both a sharper decline in unit costs as output increases and evidence of a better fit (as shown by the R^2).

As a final test of the cost-output relationship of the sample, a quadratic polynomial was fitted to the logarithms of costs/ton-mile and ton-miles, that is:

$$\log \text{cost/ton-mile} = \log a + b_1(\log \text{ton-miles}) + c(\log \text{ton-miles})^2.$$

The results are summarized below:

	a	b	c	R^2
All carriers	5,311	−1.845	0.076	0.58
Class I carriers	20,836	−1.940	0.075	0.66
Class II carriers	104	−0.651	−0.016	0.86

In all three categories, the R^2 value is substantially greater than the preceding set of equations, indicating significantly "better fits" to the sample data. In the case of the Class I carriers and the sample as a whole, the results indicate that costs/ton-mile are virtually constant over a very wide range of output, rising only at the extreme ranges of output (as measured by ton-miles). In the case of Class II carriers, however, costs continue to decline over the relevant range of output.[3]

A large part of the decrease in unit costs as output expands appears to be "explained" by the spreading of terminal costs over the increasing output. "Terminal costs" in this instance refers to the non-transportation costs of the carriers. In the case of the Class II carriers, the spreading effect shows up most noticeably below where a 1 percent increase in ton-mile output is accompanied by an almost 1 percent decrease in unit nontransportation (terminal) costs. In the case of the Class I carriers in the sample, the decline in unit non-transportation costs as output increases is much less rapid (and the regression fit much less good). These results are summarized below, where

$$\log \text{nontransportation cost/ton-mile} = \log a + b\ (\log \text{ton-miles.})$$

	a	b	R^2
All carriers	0.90880	−0.359	0.38
Class I carriers	1.84707	−0.427	0.45
Class II carriers	5.52592	−0.981	0.82

[3] Among other things, these results suggest that the present criteria for distinguishing between Class I, II, and III carriers are not well related to cost differences among the carriers.

Fitting a quadratic polynomial to the logs of the sample data again yields a substantially improved fit in terms of the R^2. And the results tend to confirm the speculation that the increasing costs/ton-mile encountered by Class I carriers at high levels of output stem from rising per-unit terminal costs at those levels of output. Class II carriers, on the other hand, appear to enjoy decreasing unit terminal costs over their full range of output. The statistical results are shown below:

$$\log(\text{terminal cost/ton-miles}) = \log a + b(\log \text{ton-miles}) + c(\log \text{ton-miles})^2$$

	a	b	c	R^2
All carriers	8,215	−1.924	0.081	0.52
Class I carriers	15,466	−2.011	0.078	0.62
Class II carriers	4	0.054	−0.063	0.82

From all of this it would seem that:

(1) Size of firm, when measured in conventional fashion, appears to play no role in the scale of return. The cost evidence clearly indicates that unit costs decrease or are constant as output increases over virtually the entire scale of production of the firms in the industry. The decrease is most sharp over the range of output of the smaller firms in the industry, as they spread their nontransportation costs over increasing output.

(2) The distribution of revenues in the industry is sharply skewed with the few larger firms receiving most of the industry revenues. (In 1962, out of a total of 6,123 general commodity carriers, 103 firms received 47.5 percent of the general commodity carrier revenues.)

Market Characteristics. Legislation (and the ICC) has effectively divided the total motor carriage market into three primary components:

(1) the for-hire carriers, composed of the common carriers and the contract carriers;
(2) the exempt commodity carriers; and
(3) the private carriers.

ICC regulation (and service as cartel manager) extends over the for-hire market. It also, however, participates in the definition of the boundaries between that market and the other two. In this respect, the ICC tends to behave as one might expect and seeks to expand its dominion over activities in the other markets through the definition of both the exempt commodities and the role of private carriage.

The ICC further partitions the motor carrier market through the issuance of certificates of public necessity. In this way it controls entry in terms of geographic points to be served, the commodity or commodity categories to be served, and the nature of the service. This procedure virtually insures that the submarkets of the motor carrier industry are both discriminatory and oligopolistic in nature. That is, shippers do not have full freedom of choice with respect to the carriers that can serve them and thus discrimination among shippers is institutionalized. Further, the submarkets are characterized by a scarcity of firms and by no significant product differentiation. Consequently, there is a high interdependence of price and output decisions among firms.

In response to these factors, the rate bureaus and the ICC have taken on much of the appearance of cartel managers pursuing the accommodations of member firms to the goals of the group. Perhaps nothing speaks more eloquently to this than the role of the rate bureaus in opposing single carrier attempts at rate reduction or service innovation, and the success the bureaus enjoy before the ICC in such cases.

For the purposes of this paper it is proposed that motor carrier markets be categorized in the following manner:

(1) markets which are primarily served by several large carriers and in which there may be many small carriers;

(2) markets in which there is one large carrier and several small carriers;

(3) markets which are served principally by small carriers.

The first set of markets comes close to the traditional oligopolistic markets. In general, actions by the smaller firms will not generate strong response unless they threaten to cut into the joint traffic of the large firms. In such markets the rate bureaus play a key role as cartel managers, policing the tacit or explicit agreements that may have been reached with respect to market shares, et cetera. Such markets are not likely to be marked by price competition, although competitive activity on other levels (such as scheduling, equipment condition, and the like) may be substantial. Demand shifts (increases) are easily accommodated in the market, although demand decreases may well come at the expense of the smaller firm. The cartel will tend to guard against differential shifts in costs that may result from regulatory change since they would change the balance among major firms.

In the second set of markets the dominance of the large firm will tend to stabilize the extent of competition. The modest cost advantage that the larger firm generally enjoys will tend to restrict price competition in this type of market. So long as small carrier action does not threaten an important share of the larger firm's part of the market, the larger firm is not likely to respond with significant price or service changes. The role the rate bureau may play in this environment is not really obvious, that is, its contribution as cartel manager is clearly less significant in this situation. For a variety of quasi-political reasons, however, the dominant firm in the market may prefer to rely on the bureau to maintain stability. Although shifts in costs growing out of regulatory changes would be destabilizing, they would not pose the threat to market stability that they would in the first set of markets.

It would appear that the potential for traditional competition would be greatest in the third market category. The attraction of costs decreasing with output might lead the firms into price and/or service competition. The consequences would depend on the nature of the demand for service in the market and the willingness of the firms to stabilize shares of the market. This set of markets would seem to come closest to experiencing the unrestricted competition that the ATA and the ICC fear. On the face of it, changes in costs could be destabilizing in this category of market.

Obviously, individual firms may well find themselves in more than just one category of market, and many firms will find themselves in all three. Moreover, decisions in these various market categories will be interdependent through rate bureaus and the presence of competitive firms and through competing shippers. Clearly then, the firm's decision problem in its effort to maximize a profit function will be greatly complicated.

To summarize, the motor carrier industry when viewed in the aggregate takes on many of the technical characteristics that are commonly associated with a competitive industry, including: a large number of firms, constant costs over a wide range of output and increasing unit costs at high levels of output (that is, no scale effect), and the relative ease with which production units can be added to or subtracted from the industry. Only the constraints imposed on new firm entry and pricing by regulation mar the picture of the motor carrier industry in aggregate as a competitive industry. Viewed market by market, however, the motor carrier presents the very different characteristics of an oligopolistic industry—that is, an industry in which the behavior of any one firm has a direct impact on the well-being of others in the market. This, of course, is true because the restraints on entry imposed by regulation have their explicit impact on individual markets.

Analytic Models. Assessing the impact of regulatory change calls for an examination of: (1) the overall impact of the change in terms of the aggregate supply of services and price levels of the industry, and (2) the impact of the change on individual transportation markets and carriers in terms of the distribution of resources among markets and changes in the income and wealth positions of individual carriers. The dual character of the motor carrier industry described above presents a significant problem to any attempt to carry out such examinations. In effect, the nature of the industry is such that, although an industry model such as that described below will meet the needs of the first task, it will not permit an accurate assessment of the impacts in individual transportation markets. A market model (or model of firms) such as that described below, on the other hand, calls for substantial data detailing for specific firms cost environments, market conditions, competitive situations, and objectives. These data demands and processing limitations necessarily limit the application of the model in terms of the number of markets and firms that may be evaluated at any one time. In summary, at the present time it is necessary to pursue two approaches to the assessment of regulatory change. The approaches are conceptually consistent, but they may not readily merge in empirical application.

An industry model. The industry model described below uniquely permits estimates of the aggregate impact of regulatory changes on the quantities and prices of motor carrier services offered, on the incomes generated in the motor carrier industry, and on the distribution of those income changes between the capital and labor resource owners. The model is derived from the conventional model of a competitive industry. The model was initially developed to assess the impact of different federal government subsidy programs on the employment of labor and capital in various industries.[4] In slightly

[4] Systan, Inc., *Analysis of Alternative Subsidy Programs: Impact on Regional Development,* prepared for U.S. Department of Commerce, Economic Development Administration, August 1973.

different form this model has been employed to analyze the industry-by-industry impact of proposed rail abandonments in the northeastern United States. The model has yielded estimates of the employment and income consequences of those abandonments by industry and by community.

The model of the motor carrier industry consists of six equations (with the same number of unknowns). The model serves to delineate the elements of production, demand, factor use, and factor availability. A normalization procedure has been adopted which aggregates the behavior of the representative firm in order to provide effects for the total industry. Each firm within the industry is assumed to be identical, to follow profit-maximizing behavior, and to regard output price and factor costs as given. For the entire industry, variation in firm behavior produces variation in output price and repercussions in the factor markets. That is, each firm is assumed to have no effect on output or factor prices, whereas the impact of all firms in concert will affect output prices and costs.

For purposes of analytical convenience, a "firm" is defined as a standard unit of capital denoted as $\overline{K}$. Thus, a "firm" is, in reality, an arbitrary unit of capital so that an "industry" consisting of N "firms" comprises, in total, $N\overline{K}$ units of capital. For this reason there is no way to distinguish between a firm of 10 units of capital versus one with 100 units of capital. For the purposes here, the two firms together entail 110 units of capital or 110 "firm" units. Although it is an obvious oversimplification of the real world, given the nature of the basic motor carrier production process (that is, one driver, one vehicle), this normalization procedure does not do great violence as an analytic and computational convenience.

The firm's production function, F, relating capital and labor services employed to the flow of physical value added, is assumed homogeneous of degree one so that $X/\overline{K}$ can be expressed as a function of labor per unit of capital (firm) $L/\overline{K} = Q$. Without any loss of generality, $\overline{K}$ can be set equal to one, and X can be reinterpreted to represent physical value added per "firm," L to represent labor per "firm," and Q can be dropped as variable. Equation 1′ represents the proportionate differentiation of equation 1, where the asterisk (*) refers to proportionate rate of change:

$$X = F(\overline{K},L) = \overline{K}\cdot f(L/\overline{K}) = \overline{K}\cdot f(Q) \qquad (1)$$

$$X^* = \alpha Q^* = \alpha L^*. \qquad (1')$$

The demand curve faced by the industry in the market relates price per unit of value added, P, to industry output $N\cdot X$. Proportionate differentiation of equation 2 gives the percentage change in price as a function of the elasticity of demand, η, and change in industry output $(N^* + X^*)$:

$$P = g(N\ X) \tag{2}$$

$$P^* = 1/\eta \cdot (N^* + X^*) = 1/\eta \cdot (N^* + \alpha L^*). \tag{2'}$$

The representative firm following profit-maximizing behavior employs labor to the extent that the wage rate (marginal equals average cost per unit of labor) coincides with the marginal value product of labor. F_L represents the marginal physical product of labor and is a function of the ratio of labor per unit of capital (firm). Proportionate differentiation of equation 3 determines the percentage change in the wage rate in terms of L^* and P^* where ν is the elasticity of the marginal product of labor:

$$w = F_L\, P \tag{3}$$

$$w^* = F_L{}^* + P^* = \nu L^* + P^*. \tag{3'}$$

Equation 4 embodies the assumption of profit-maximizing behavior where the discounted net marginal value product of the annual flow of capital services coincides with the present value of the cost of capital services. Implicit in this formulation is the notion that capital is a continuous variable so that capital is replaced as it is used up. Further, it is assumed here that capital is acquired via the issuance of debt instruments so that the annual cost of a unit of capital services, $P_K r$, represents the price per unit times the loan rate r or the annual service or interest costs incurred. Expression 4 is a condensation of a more complicated formula for the present value of cash inflow and outflow:

$$\int_{\delta}^{n} rP_K e^{-r_a t} + P_K e^{-r_a \nu} = \int_{\delta}^{n} F_K P e^{(r_a - \delta)t}$$

where r is the loan rate, r_d the decision maker's discount rate, ν the maturity of the loan, and δ the rate of depreciation of physical capital. Such a condensation rests on the premise that doses of capital can continuously be added to existing capital and that refinancing is always possible. Equation 4′ is the proportionate differentiation of equation 4, assuming that the price of physical capital remains unchanged $(P_K{}^* = 0)$ but allowing for variation in the loan rate r:

$$P_K r = F_K P \tag{4}$$

$$r^* = F_K + P^* = \nu L^* + P^*. \tag{4'}$$

The final set of equations portrays the supply conditions that prevail for labor and capital services, respectively. Equations 5 and 6 entail the assumption that additional factor services are available to the industry at an increasing price. Expressing each equation in proportionate terms captures the notion that the supply functions need to be specified by their respective supply elasticities, ϵ_L and ϵ_K. It should be noted that factor market curves pertain only to the industry. Firms perceive the same marginal (equal average) factor rental rates, and monopsonistic behavior is ruled out.

$$w = h(N \cdot L) \tag{5}$$

$$w^* = \frac{1}{\epsilon_L} (N^* + L^*) \tag{5'}$$

$$r = j(N) \tag{6}$$

$$r^* = \frac{1}{\epsilon_K} N^*. \tag{6'}$$

Summarizing the industry specification in terms of the parameters defined above, it should be noted that factor and output markets are respectively identified via the supply elasticities ϵ_L and ϵ_K and the demand elasticity η. Production relationships are interdependent and specified by α and σ. However, for a linear homogeneous production function the following relationships between α, σ, and the elasticities of marginal factor products can be established:

$$U = \alpha/\sigma > 0$$

$$\sigma \equiv -Q^*/(F_L/F_K)^* = \frac{1}{u - v}$$

$$v = \frac{\alpha - 1}{\sigma} < 0.$$

A market model. In a limited set of circumstances the industry model described above may be used to assess in the aggregate what may happen in a given market set in response to a change in regulatory policy. Assume, for example, a traditional oligopolistic market equilibrium where each firm confronts a limited demand schedule (that is, price decreases will be met quickly by price decreases of competitors, price increases will not be met by competitors) and a regulatory change which permits new firms to enter the market. Accommodation of new firms can only take place by reducing the market shares of firms presently in the market. Output of present firms can be maintained only by expanding industry output and lower prices. If the market demand is very elastic the change in price required to accommodate new firms will be small, and the impact on the income of firms already in the market will be relatively small. If, on the other hand, the demand for service is inelastic, accommodating new entrants will require sizeable declines in price and a consequent considerable impact on the earnings of firms already in the market.

The industry model described above can be adapted to estimate the extent of the declines in income that would be associated with such a policy change. If we assume that factor supply elasticities and factor shares are as given, the impact of declining prices to accommodate new entrants on the nonlabor income of firms already in the industry (for various service demand elasticities) will be as shown in Figure 9-2. These purely hypothetical results serve to explain in part the strong opposition that regulated motor carrier firms generally mount to efforts that would expand the number of firms in a given market.

Figure 9-2

IMPACT ON INCOME OF DECLINING PRICES TO ACCOMMODATE NEW FIRMS

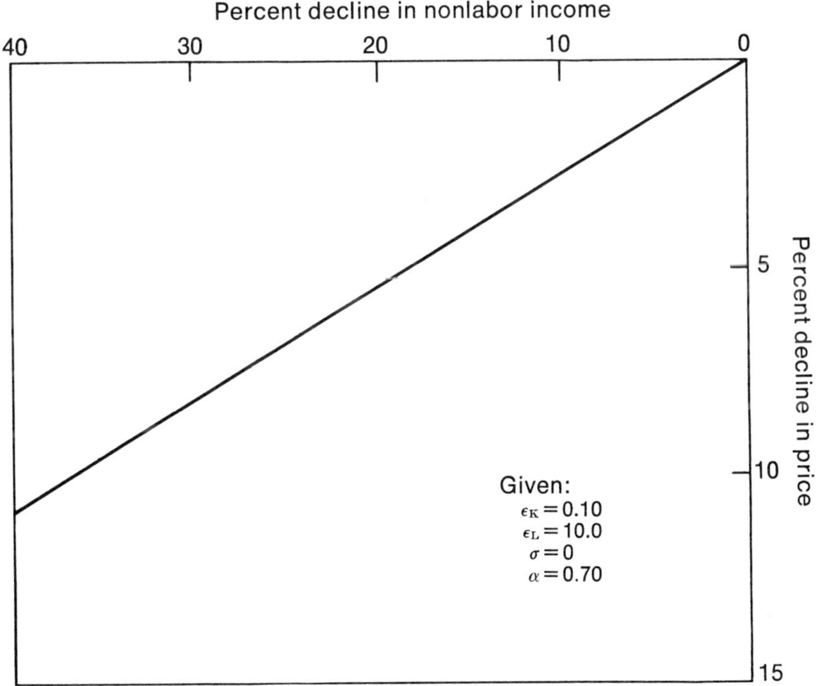

The industry model may be used to obtain empirical measures of aggregate impacts within a market set. However, the model will not provide quantitative estimates regarding either the change in the distribution of resources among markets or the change in the distribution of products in the various markets. As noted above, this calls for focusing on the decision environments of the individual firms—the technology, the structure of the markets involved, and the relationship of firms to each other in the various markets in which they participate.

The market model described here represents an extension and an adaptation of a conventional linear programming model to take into account the fact that there are several firms in a market and that each firm will generally participate in more than one market. Solution of the model may be found through the application of conventional quadratic programming computer procedures. The basic model firm is as follows:

$$\text{Max } z = \sum \Pi_{ij} X_{ij}.$$

Subject to:

$$A_{ij} X_{ij} \leqslant B_j$$

$$X_{ij} \geqslant 0$$

$$\sum_j X_{ij} = T_i, \text{ where } T_i = f(P_i)$$

$$\text{and when } \Pi_{ij} = P_i - \sum c_b b_{ij}, \text{ given } C_b = q(B_j).$$

The equations for T_i and C_b describe the demand schedule for service in the individual markets and the supply schedules of inputs confronting the motor carrier firms. The A_{ij} describes the (proportional) input requirements of each firm in each market. This market model has been employed in the analysis of investment choices. The model is presently being adapted to assist in the evaluation of the impact of changes in regulatory policy and procedure on the incentive to innovate in the regulated industries and among their suppliers.

Implementation of the models. The need for change in federal economic regulation in general, and in the case of the motor carrier industry in particular, has become a popular topic. There is little concrete evidence, however, to describe the consequences of such change in terms of the benefits to society, or to the users of the regulated services, and in terms of changes in the regulated industries themselves. A program for change, including priorities for action, cannot be implemented in the absence of such evidence.

The two models described in this paper afford a quick, efficient, and accurate means of attaining quantitative assessments of changes in the regulatory environment of the motor carrier industry. They represent two related views of the industry: an aggregated view of the industry as a whole, and a microview of selected markets and firms. Conceptually, they may be integrated into a single model. Full implementation of such a model would be extremely time-consuming and expensive. A much more reasonable and useful effort is to focus on an aspect of regulatory change that is important for a particular policy issue. Thus, the aggregative resource and distributional consequences of the elimination of "gateways" or of "backhaul restrictions" (or of some other proposed change) may be examined first. Then, if the results are judged promising, the microconsequences of the change in terms of resource allocations among markets, the degree of competition, the gains and losses of individual firms (or categories of firms) may be identified and assessed.

The data requirements needed to implement the models are substantial, but much of the data collected can be used for a variety of simulations. The broad requirements are:

(1) Aggregative model

- Specification of the market area—markets of regulated carriers may be expressed in two ways in the model: in terms of geography and/or in terms of certificate category.
- Estimates of the demand for service as expressed by the price elasticity of demand.
- Estimates of the supply of inputs as expressed by the price elasticity of their supply.
- A description of the production process as reflected by labor's share and the elasticity of substitution.
- Identification of the impact of the regulatory change—this may be expressed as a change in the demand schedule, a change in the productivity of inputs, a change in the supply of inputs (leasing changes), a change in the process of producing the service.

(2) Market model

- Identification of the market(s) to be evaluated.
- Identification of the production characteristics of firms in the market(s) to be examined—these ultimately must be expressed in terms of physical input/output relationships.

- The level of service in the market(s) and the distribution of market(s) shares among the firms.
- Specification of constraints on the performance of service by individual firms (or firm groups) in terms of the markets to be served, commodities carried, et cetera.
- Identification of the demand for service in the market(s) examined, in terms of price elasticities.
- Description of the supply of inputs in terms of price elasticities.
- Specification of the regulatory change—in terms of changes in production requirements, changes in service constraints, changes in the demand for service, changes in the supply price of inputs, et cetera.

Elimination of "Gateways"

Introduction. Gateways arise where two or more motor carrier authorities are "joined" at a common point—a gateway—by a regulated motor carrier. Provision of service from Point A on one authority to Point B on the other authority through the gateway is then possible for the carrier. No data appear to be directly available regarding the number of potential gateways and their geographic or commodity distribution. One measure of the number, however, is the response to the ICC's recent "80 percent ruling" on gateways. By virtue of this rule making, gateways that were in use may be eliminated in those instances where the direct mileage is not less than 80 percent of the authorized routing. Some 15,000 letter requests seeking to change present gateway service to direct service have been filed with the commission on the basis that the service falls within the 80 percent limit. Another 500 requests were filed for authority to perform direct routing service in situations where the service through gateways exceeded the 80 percent rule. Another measure of the number is the distribution of grants of authority by firm. The latest data available are those for 1964, when it was estimated that grants of authority were distributed in the following manner:

Carrier Class	*Number of Firms*	*Grants*
I	1,208	40,858
II	2,502	19,195
III	10,191	31,282

Thus, in 1964, there were approximately 6.6 operating rights for all classes of carrier firms. Class I carriers, naturally, had the largest number of operating rights per firm, 33.8, and the Class III carriers had the smallest number per firm, 3.1. In 1964, tacking or joinder of rights was not permitted on some 2,600 of the rights.

Gateway elimination, as the term is used here, would allow irregular route carriers to serve any points identified in their authorities in whatever fashion met their market needs.[5] Primarily, of course, carriers would be able to serve any pair of points identified in their authorities with direct routing. Gateway elimination, as defined here, would make more profitable that traffic where carriers can substitute direct routing for gateway routing. Regression analysis of the cost data for the sample of carriers described above indicates that total cost of the firm declines almost proportionally with respect to vehicle-miles, a 0.8 percent reduction in costs for every 1 percent reduction in vehicle-miles in the case of Class I carriers, and a 0.33 percent reduction in costs for each 1 percent decline in vehicle-miles in the case of Class II carriers. This would suggest that the greatest part of the cost saving associated with gateway elimination would accrue to the larger firms—those which have by far the largest number of gateways per firm and whose costs prove to be more sensitive to vehicle-mileage.

At the same time, gateway elimination would expand significantly the market opportunities of firms. That is, gateway elimination would, in effect, place all carriers in a given market on essentially an equal cost footing by allowing all firms to use direct routing if justified by the market and by their other operational demands. This means that firms would be able to compete effectively in markets where they had previously been precluded. Thus, we would expect to see firms expanding into such markets, using resources freed elsewhere as a consequence of the gateway elimination, and drawing new resources into motor carrier activity. This response will be conditioned by the costs of entry into the new markets and by the competitive environment they find in their present markets as a consequence of gateway elimination. Finally, gateway elimination will change the relative attractiveness of various markets to the individual carriers, leveling resource reallocations among markets.

The two models described above (that is, the industry model and the market model) may now be used to obtain quantitative measures

[5] Regular route carriers would presumably continue to serve their routes as before.

of the impact of gateway elimination on the industry as a whole and on individual markets and/or firms.

Aggregative (Industry) Impact. Two aspects of gateway elimination are of primary concern here: (1) the resource saving which results from the reduced haul distance, and (2) the consequences of the changed competitive environment, in which all firms in a given market may use direct routing.

Resource saving. Elimination of enforced circuity means that the motor carrier industry would be able to provide the present level of service with fewer resources or expanded levels of service with the same resources. In the industry model described above, this may be simulated by shifting the industry supply schedule to the right (increased output for the same level of inputs) by the amount of the resource saving,[6] and calculating the consequences in terms of output prices, et cetera (see Figure 9-3). This, of course, requires data, or assumptions, regarding the elasticity of supplies, demand, et cetera.

To demonstrate the use of the model in this role, the following assumptions with respect to the key parameters were made:

- price elasticity of demand equals −2.0;
- price elasticity of capital supply equals 10.0;
- elasticity of substitution equals 0;
- labor's share equals 0.70.

Finally, it was assumed that the efficiency gain was 5 percent. Put another way, it was assumed that the excess mileage traveled by the regulated carriers in the industry because of gateways was perhaps 6 to 8 percent. Unfortunately, no information is available to evaluate this crude assumption other than the claims presented in the ICC proceedings on gateway eliminations.

Rather than attempt a single point estimate of the impact, the range of output changes that would be associated with different price elasticities of the supply of labor were calculated along with the associated increase in payrolls and the decrease in price that would clear the market.

[6] This may be simulated most easily in the terms of the model by assuming that the resource saving is a proportional shift in both inputs, so that the increase in efficiency may be reflected as an increase in the price per unit of physical value added. This is a computational convenience for this paper rather than a characteristic of the model.

Figure 9-3

IMPACT OF GATEWAY ELIMINATION,
USING THE INDUSTRY MODEL

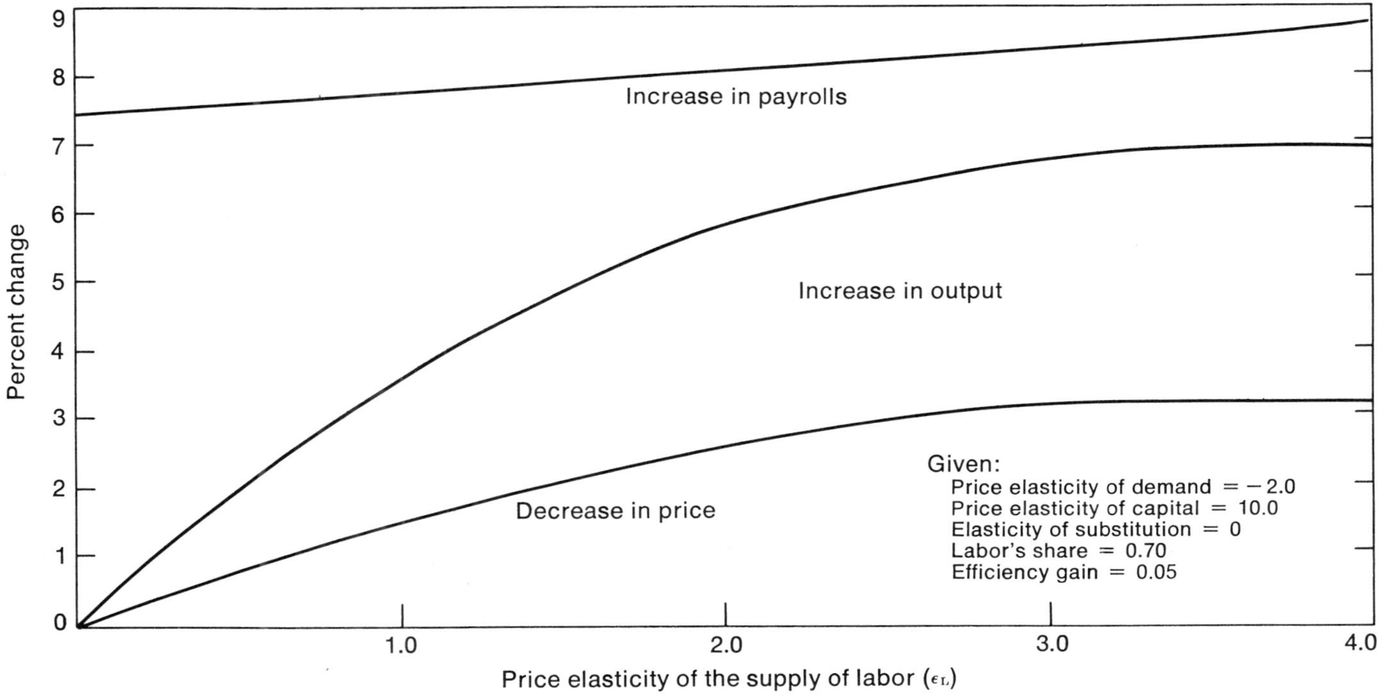

The results of the model simulation are summarized in Figure 9-3. There the vertical axis represents the percentage change in payrolls, output, or price. The horizontal axis represents the price elasticity of the supply of labor. Given the assumptions with regard to the other parameters, the response of the industry to gateway eliminations will be shaped in an important way by the elasticity of the supply of labor. If that elasticity is high—that is, labor is relatively abundant and is available to the firms in the industry at little price increase—then the output response will be substantial. On the other hand, if labor is not abundant to the industry—that is, increases in supply will be available to firms in the industry only as a consequence of cost increases—output increases in response to gateway eliminations will be small and most of the "savings" will be captured by labor in higher wage rates and/or other benefits. In effect, then, the more effective the monopoly control over the supply of labor to the motor carrier industry, the less will be the distribution of the benefits to motor carrier users in the form of lower rates and/or expanded service.

To show the sensitivity of the results to different price elasticities of the demand for service, the simulation was rerun to obtain estimates of output changes with the other elasticity parameters held constant. The results are summarized in Figure 9-4. There the vertical axis measures the percentage change in output. The hori-

Figure 9-4

SENSITIVITY OF OUTPUT CHANGES TO DEMAND FOR SERVICE, USING THE INDUSTRY MODEL WITH OTHER ELASTICITY PARAMETERS HELD CONSTANT

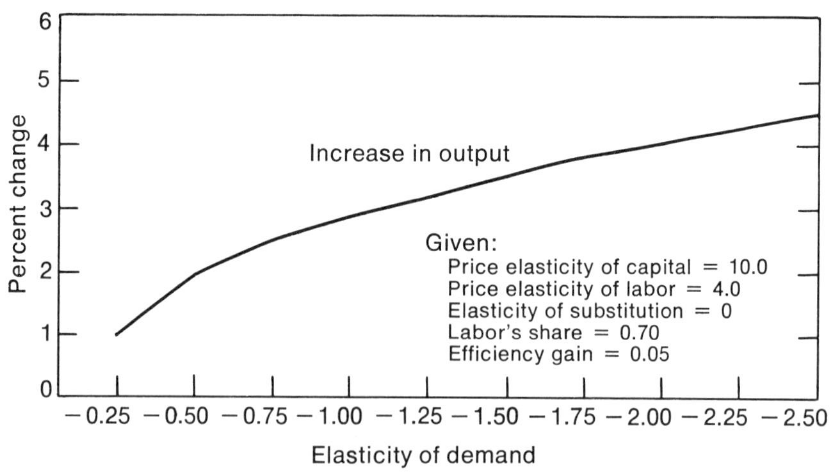

zontal axis represents the increasing elasticity of demand. The increase in output arising in response to gateway elimination increases at a decreasing rate, as demand elasticity grows. The results indicate, as one might expect, that the more inelastic the demand for service, the smaller will be the share of the gain passed forward in the form of output increases.

These brief results from using the model to simulate the consequences of "resource saving" in the industry (whether from gateway elimination, or from elimination of commodity restrictions, or from some other change) emphasize two points with respect to the distribution of the "saving":

(1) For motor carrier users to realize any benefit in the form of reduced rates and increased service, motor carrier rates must be allowed to decline appropriately.

(2) Even if motor carrier rates are flexible, benefits in the form of lower rates and increased service will not generally be realized by the users if the demand for service is very inelastic, or if the supply of inputs to the industry is highly price-inelastic upward (that is, monopolized).

Increased competition. The aggregate industry model is able to give an accurate picture of the overall industry response to gateway elimination in terms of the availability of resources in total, and in terms of aggregate levels of service. However, the model provides no basis for evaluating changes in specific market structures. In effect, the model cannot differentiate as to the nature of the response to gateway elimination—that is, whether it is increased output from existing firms in present markets, a shifting of firms among markets, or the introduction of new firms into the industry. These issues are the target of the extended linear programming model.

Market (and Firm) Impacts. The primary concern in this section is to identify the response among individual firms and within selected markets regarding the resource saving and the increased competition that may be expected to grow out of gateway elimination. Of particular concern is the impact of these changes on: (1) the allocation of resources among markets by individual firms; and (2) the implications of changed competitive conditions on the structure of various markets. The approach adopted here is to simulate the change in regulatory environment and the firm response, given information about firm objectives, the elasticity of the demand for service in the various markets, and the elasticity of supply and resources to the firm. In the examples presented below, all firms are assumed to be profit maximizers. As a matter of convenience, the resources available to the firm are assumed to be fixed, and the elasticity of demand is assumed to be infinite. Implementation of the full extended linear programming model would permit relaxing each of these assumptions.

Technical parameters of the examples are summarized in Table 9-1. Firm I is assumed to have authorities to serve markets 1, 2, and 4. Firm II is assumed to have authorities for markets 2 and 3. Further, it is assumed that Firm I serves market 2 via a gateway, which increases its input requirements in that market per unit of

Table 9-1

TECHNICAL PARAMETERS OF EXAMPLES

Production requirements per unit of output

	Firm 1	
	Truck-hours	Man-hours
Market 1	0.5	10.0
Market 2	1.2	2.0
Market 4	3.1	4.0

	Firm 2	
	Truck-hours	Man-hours
Market 2	0.96	1.6
Market 3	1.9	2.45

Resources available

	Truck-hours	Man-hours
Firm 1	32	50
Firm 2	32	50

Market rates per unit of output

Market 1	$5.00
Market 2	3.50
Market 3	5.00
Market 4	7.20

Note: These parameters have been assumed rather than estimated.

output. Firm II, on the other hand, serves market 2 via a direct route.

The initial profit-maximizing, market-clearing equilibrium position of the firms is show below:

	Market Output				
Firm	1	2	3	4	*Total Revenue*
Firm I	0	19.29	0	2.86	88.11
Firm II	0	31.25	0	0	109.38
Total	0	50.54	0	2.86	197.49

Both firms serve market 2, with Firm I getting slightly less than 40 percent and Firm II getting slightly more than 60 percent of the market. Firm I also serves market 4, while Firm II concentrates all of its resources in the more profitable market 2. At this equilibrium position, Firm I utilizes all of its resources fully, while Firm II fully utilizes its man-hours, but has some excess truck capacity.

If the gateway restriction on Firm I is eliminated, its resource requirements to serve market 2 will be identical with those of Firm II. If the demand for service in market 2 were perfectly elastic, the new equilibrium position for the two firms would be that shown below, that is, Firm I would shift all of its resources into market 2 and would cease entirely serving market 4. Interestingly enough, Firm I, which had previously been using all of its labor and truck resources fully, would now have some excess truck resources.

	Market Output				
Firm	1	2	3	4	*Total Revenue*
Firm I	0	31.25	0	0	109.38
Firm II	0	31.25	0	0	109.38
Total	0	62.50	0	0	218.76

Obviously, the demand for service in market 2 is not likely to be perfectly elastic. In this particular example, however, the firms would end up at this allocation of resources, so long as the elasticity of demand in the market was greater than −2. If the demand for service in market 2 were less elastic than that, Firm II would tend to shift resources from market 2 to market 3 (assuming that such a shift would have no impact on the price in market 3). As a result, at a demand for service in market 2 that is more inelastic than −2, output will tend to fall closer to the original equilibrium level, and price will tend to stay closer to the original equilibrium point. The effect, however, will be to shift the resources out of market 4, primarily into market 2, but there will also be some small production by Firm II for market 3. Finally, even with price flexibility, some resources may go unemployed.

Price flexibility, however, is by no means assured in the present regulatory environment. If price changes are not to be allowed, then three sets of consequences may emerge:

(1) Competition for market shares will spill over into other markets.

(2) Some resources will go unemployed at the original market share equilibrium.

(3) Resources may be devoted to competition not involving price or they may become committed to "featherbedding" (that is, they will be underemployed).

Two examples of the first consequence are shown below. The first example is an instance in which firms are assumed to attempt to maximize the sum of the joint profits. In this instance, the market share of Firm II in market 2 is reduced and some resources are shifted to market 3 (the calculations assume that the resource shift will not significantly affect the price or market shares of market 3).

	Market Output				
Firm	1	2	3	4	*Total Revenue*
Firm I	0	34.11	0	2.86	104.98
Firm II	0	26.43	3.14	0	106.01
Total	0	50.54	3.14	2.86	210.99

In this example, Firm I continues to use fully all of its resources. Interestingly enough, Firm II will utilize more of its truck resources than in preceding examples, and it will continue to utilize fully its labor resources as before. Both firms will suffer revenue losses from the optimal position that might have been achieved in a free market environment. More important, however, is the fact that this adjustment calls for Firm II to suffer a loss in revenues from its original position. That is, while Firm I enjoys a substantial revenue gain as a consequence of the gateway elimination, Firm II will suffer a revenue loss.

The second example of market accommodation assumes that the extant shares in market 2 are maintained, and that Firm I seeks to employ the resources freed as a consequence of the gateway elimination in other markets. The results of the effort by Firm I are summarized below. This effort is less than completely successful, however, and some of each resource is left unemployed.

	Market Output				
Firm	1	2	3	4	*Total Revenue*
Firm I	0.176	19.29	0	4.24	98.92
Firm II	0	31.25	0	0	109.38
Total	0.176	50.54	0	4.24	208.30

Clearly, from the point of view of Firm I, this last alternative is not particularly attractive. If an accommodation could be made with Firm II, it would pay Firm I to cover the loss experienced by Firm II in the joint profit-maximizing case. The likelihood of such an accommodation is not easy to assess. One point stands out, however. In the example chosen, the payoff to Firm I from expanding its share of market 2 is substantial. As a result, Firm I would be willing to expend considerable resources and to take considerable risks to expand its share of that market. As a result, Firm II would experience a great deal of competitive pressure from Firm I and would be forced to expend resources and to take risks itself, merely to preserve its share of the market. Obviously, the temptation for accommodation, whether explicit or tacit, in such instances will be strong.

Finally, the competitive pressures generated in market 2 as a consequence of gateway elimination will spill over into other markets, as shown by the fact that both firms will turn to other markets to employ resources released. The extent and importance of this spillover can be assessed by incorporating more markets and firms into the model.

Conclusions. The following conclusions emerge from the foregoing analysis of gateway elimination:

- Price inflexibility will limit sharply the benefits to be enjoyed by gateway elimination. In the absence of rate reductions (throughout the system) unemployment and underemployment of resources will take place.

- In all but the most rigid of market situations, some redistribution of income among firms and some reallocation of resources among markets will take place.
- The competitive pressures in various markets, as firms seek to develop or expand market shares, can be expected to become intense.
- The more complete the monopoly control over the supply of some inputs, the greater the share of the "savings" resulting from gateway elimination that input will capture in the form of price and/or benefit increases or "makework."
- In the absence of rate flexibility, collusive or semicollusive agreements as to market shares can be expected to prove attractive in some market settings.

Elimination of "Backhaul Restrictions"

Introduction. Virtually any transportation system is going to face an "empty backhaul" problem. Seldom, if ever, will the loads in one direction precisely match the loads in the reverse direction and some "respotting" of vehicles will be necessary for even the largest and most efficient of carriers. The ICC in its effort to restrict the supply of service through route and commodity restriction, however, has exacerbated this backhaul problem. The consequence is that regulated vehicles return empty about 38 percent of the time and private vehicles return empty more than 62 percent of the time.[7] These figures imply more than 15 percent excess capacity in the regulated sector of the motor carrier industry and an excess capacity in the private and exempt sectors of perhaps 30 percent. In short, the excess capacity in the industry as a whole resulting solely from restrictions on market and service performance may total 20 percent.

In assessing here the implications of regulatory changes that would eliminate the empty backhaul, a distinction is maintained between the regulated and the nonregulated segments of the motor carrier industry. In the case of the regulated segment, the empty backhaul may be dealt with through an extension or an expansion of present operating rights, the elimination of commodity restrictions, a wider range of routes, the elimination of the "to________

[7] Edward Miller, "Effects of Regulation on Truck Utilization," *Transportation Journal*, Fall 1973.

from__________" clause, and the substitution of "between__________ and__________" in the present operating rights. The result will be a breakdown of the market segmentation on which the present oligopolistic nature of individual markets within the regulated segment is based. Elimination of the empty backhaul of private and exempt carriers implies the granting of operating rights on backhaul traffic for such carriers and ultimately an almost complete relaxation (other than financial and safety) of entry controls.

Industry Impact. The initial focus here is the regulated segment of the industry and its accommodation to make explicit the concealed excess capacity in that portion of the industry. If rates remain fixed, that accommodation ultimately can only come in the form of resources reallocated within the industry and resources released from the industry. Accompanying these changes will be a redistribution of income (and wealth) among the firms and resources. So long as rates remain fixed, many of the resources released from empty backhaul may be redirected into nonprice competition, that is, extra services, more frequent or timely service, et cetera. As a result, competitive pressures in the industry will tend to build as firms seek to expand their shares of the traffic. Excess capacity will be made explicit with the reduction of empty backhaul, and there will be higher returns per production unit. Thus, the penalties for losing traffic shares will become more important for the individual firm.

Pressures for rate adjustments (reductions) can be expected from several directions, including: (1) shippers—at least some of whom will seek to gain a share of the cost sharing through lower rates; (2) resource supplies—labor and capital owners faced with unemployment as an alternative; (3) motor carrier firms themselves—as they seek to gain expanded shares of the market and to meet successful service competition through lower rates.

In the absence of a change in regulatory procedures, rate levels (and thus traffic, employment, and profit levels) will be shaped in hearings before the ICC. Obviously, it is not possible to predict where rates might stabilize as a consequence of the regulatory bargaining process before the commission. It is possible, however, to simulate the way the industry would respond—if firms in the industry were free to act independently on price and output decisions—to the increase in productivity represented by the elimination of empty backhauls. (For this simulation certain assumptions would have to be made regarding the nature of the market for service, the production processes, and the supplier of inputs.)

The dominant factor in shaping the response, and the point where the industry would stabilize, is the elasticity of the demand for service. If demand is relatively elastic—that is, if reduced rates increase more than proportionally the amount of traffic offered—the adjustment process would be relatively "easy." That is, modest rate reductions would increase the demand for service, and thus the resources released from empty backhaul could be employed in "new" traffic.

If, on the other hand, the overall demand for service is relatively inelastic, stabilization of the market will require deeper rate reductions and a greater release of resources from the industry. The extreme, of course, would be the case where the demand for service was perfectly inelastic (insensitive to price). Although individual firms might seek to increase their share of the market through rate reductions, these rate reductions, as they are spread through the market, would not lead to an overall increase in the demand for service. Both rate reductions and release of resources would be greatest in this circumstance. This, of course, is the "cutthroat competition" environment that the ATA conjures up when faced with proposals for market freedom.

Simulation results, based on the character of the industry as described above and on "reasonable" assumptions regarding the availability of capital and labor to the industry, are shown below. In developing the simulations it was assumed that the gain in productivity represented by eliminating backhaul restrictions was about 10 percent for the regulated segment of the industry. Two sets of results have been prepared: the first shows the overall rate level, output, and resource employment changes in the environment of an inelastic (−0.5) demand for service; the second shows the changes in the environment of an elastic (−2.5) demand for service.

Simulation Results
(percentage changes)

Environment	*Rates*	*Traffic*	*Labor Employment*	*Capital*
Inelastic demand	−13.3	6.7	−3.6	−3.3
Elastic demand	− 5.0	11.7	0.6	3.2

The results indicate that in the most likely case (that is, the inelastic demand case) competition would level substantial rate reductions, declining incomes, and some release of resources from the industry (including some small reductions in the number of firms).

If the overall demand for service were quite rate-sensitive (not reflected in the available data), the industry would stabilize with slightly lower rates than before, a substantial increase in output, and some increase in the employment of labor and capital (and some small increase in the number of firms).

Market Impacts. The initial focus here is on the reduction of empty backhaul in the regulated segment of the market—that is, relaxation of the market entry constraints imposed in operating rights. Simulation is again used as a tool of analysis, drawing on the two-firm, four-market example described earlier to examine the consequences of eliminating backhaul restrictions on rates, on the allocation of resources among markets, and on the competitive condition in the industry.

As in the earlier gateway example, the starting position may be described by the following equilibrium position of the firms and markets.

	Market Output				
Firm	1	2	3	4	*Total Revenue*
Firm I	0	19.29	0	2.86	88.11
Firm II	0	31.25	0	0	109.38
Total	0	50.54	0	2.86	197.49

Let us assume in this example that market 3 represents the backhaul of market 4 for Firm I and that market 4 is the backhaul of market 3 for Firm II. If the backhaul restrictions incorporated in the initial example are eliminated for both firms (and if price in all markets is assumed to be perfectly elastic), the following profit-maximizing pattern of output would emerge for the two firms. Both firms would shift essentially all their production resources into the now very attractive markets 3 and 4. If this shift could be realized at prevailing prices, both firms would realize substantial gains in revenues and profits.

	Market Output				
Firm	1	2	3	4	*Total Revenue*
Firm I	0.93	0	10.17	10.17	128.78
Firm II	0	0	16.84	16.84	205.45
Total	0.93	0	27.01	27.01	334.23

In the short run, under ICC regulation the relative rates among markets will remain constant, but in that event the ability of markets 3 and 4 to absorb the increase in supply represented by Firms I and II would be sharply limited. If markets 3 and 4 were in equilibrium at the beginning (that is, if supply of service were equal to the demand at the rates), the ability of Firms I and II to shift resources into those markets would be limited by the willingness of the firms already in the markets to reduce their market share, either through shifting resources to other markets (perhaps in response to the elimination of backhaul constraint) or as a result of unemploying resources.

Obviously, as a consequence of eliminating the backhaul restrictions on Firms I and II, the competitive pressure on firms in markets 3 and 4 will grow substantially and their feeling of insecurity and instability will increase accordingly. At the same time, if market 2 is opened up to backhaul competition, the competitive pressures on Firms I and II will also grow and their sense of insecurity and instability will increase accordingly. Obviously, in such a climate the task of maintaining cartel discipline and stable rates (especially if we consider the product to encompass ancillary services as well as intercity service) will be difficult. This difficulty will grow as the formerly concealed resource underemployment of the empty backhaul is made more and more explicit.

Elimination of backhaul restrictions without rate flexibility will lead, as in the earlier gateway example, to an intensification of institutional competition and possibly to collusion to stabilize market environments. It will also lead to income shifts within the regulated segment of the industry and between its suppliers. Without rate flexibility these changes will bring limited benefits to the user of regulated motor carrier services and to consumers in general, except as resources released from this segment of the industry are reemployed elsewhere.

If the elimination of backhaul restrictions in the regulated sector is accompanied by rate flexibility, a substantial shifting of resources and firms among markets can be expected to result. By and large, the extent of this shifting will be conditioned by the elasticities of demand in the various markets.

This may be illustrated in the following example. It is assumed that prices are flexible in all markets. The distribution of resources of Firm I and Firm II among the four markets, given different relative prices among the markets, is shown in Table 9-2. In effect, the price relationships between markets 2, 3, and 4 are assumed in each instance to be those that will clear the supply offered by Firms I and II

Table 9-2

IMPACT OF ELIMINATION OF BACKHAUL RESTRICTIONS ON DISTRIBUTION OF RESOURCES AND FIRMS AMONG MARKETS

	Market				Total Revenue
	1	2	3	4	
Case A					
Price	5.00	3.50	5.00	7.20	
Firm I	0.93	0	10.17	10.17	128.78
Firm II	0	0	16.84	16.84	205.45
Totals	0.93	0	27.01	27.01	334.23
Case C					
Price	5.00	4.18	2.72	6.05	
Firm I	0	19.29	2.86	2.86	105.69
Firm II	0	0	16.84	16.84	147.69
Totals	0	19.29	19.70	19.70	253.38
Case E					
Price	5.00	4.94	2.23	5.65	
Firm I	0	25.00	0	0	123.50
Firm II	0	31.25	0	0	154.38
Totals	0	56.25	0	0	277.88

(assuming that other producers do not alter their supply to these markets).

If prices were to stay fixed, Firm I and Firm II would seek a distribution of resources like that depicted in Case A of Table 9-2. That distribution of resources, however, would yield market prices like those shown in Case B (and the corresponding distribution of resources by Firms I and II). Given the assumptions, equilibrium would be achieved at the prices and distribution of resources depicted in Case C. At these prices, however, the revenue of firms already in markets 3 and 4 would decline significantly (35 percent in the case of the firms in market 3, and 15 percent in the case of firms already in market 4) if all the resources that were formerly employed were maintained in use.

Clearly, to the extent possible these firms initially in markets 3 and 4 will seek to transfer resources to markets where they would be more adequately rewarded. In this way, the impact of elimination of backhaul restrictions would spread through all markets. In the event of a large-scale elimination of backhaul restrictions, however, the opportunities for "adequate reward" will not be many. That is, the returns to inputs and firms will decline unless it is:

(1) possible to shift resources out of the industry to other pursuits at little or no loss of income;

(2) possible through explicit or tacit collusion to maintain prices through market-sharing arrangements.

The possibility of the first is clearly limited, while the second runs the risk of legal penalties.

The competitive pressures (and price movements within the regulated sector) will be exacerbated or eased depending on the ability of the regulated portion of the industry to absorb the resources released by the elimination of backhaul restrictions. That is, the more inelastic the demand for regulated motor carrier service, the greater will have to be the price adjustment and the greater the share of released resources that will have to find employment outside the industry.

In general, then, the impact of eliminating backhaul restrictions in an environment of rate flexibility will be much more drastic and widespread than the impact of the same elimination in an environment of fixed rates. There will be substantially more instability and uncertainty in the motor carrier industry and a significant shifting of resources among markets. This will also confront shippers with uncertainties and changing market positions. Absorbing the excess capacity represented by the empty backhaul will be a trying exercise for the regulated motor carrier industry, and some of the burden will fall disproportionately heavily on some firms and resource suppliers to the industry. A key point which must be emphasized is that the benefits of backhaul elimination—in terms of a more efficient utilization of resources and consequent lower transportation charges—can be realized only in an environment of rate flexibility.

Conclusions

The basic characteristics of the motor industry are those generally associated with a competitive industry: ease of entry and exit, and resource mobility between firms and regions. The skew in firm size and revenue distribution as well as the declining number of firms and the oligopolistic nature of markets in the regulated sector are essentially products of economic regulation.

Eliminating economic regulation of entry, rates, and service procedures would lead to:

(1) A substantial redistribution of activities between markets within the industry;

(2) Lower rates in general and most likely lower incomes to firms and the release of resources from the industry in the process of transition;

(3) Changed relationships among individual rates and markets which, in turn, will have substantial impact on the competitive positions of shippers and consignees (although shippers may welcome lower rates in general, more important to the individual shipper is his rate relative to his competitors).

Concern has been voiced that particular segments of the economy would suffer disproportionately in the event of the relaxation of economic regulation, notably small shippers and small communities. The implication, of course, is that the present regulatory environment has led to the efficient cross-subsidization of those groups. So far, evidence is lacking to substantiate that claim. Indeed, only in the case of the regulated motor carrier does the institutional structure exist by which to facilitate such a cross-subsidy. This is not to say that individual shippers or shipper groups may not be subsidized by a carrier, but rather to say that such subsidization is essentially an individual carrier's decision and not a product of the regulatory process.

Further, the extent to which small shippers and small communities have been unprofitable markets for carriers may stem in part from the restraints on entry and the consequent higher costs of servicing traffic over all. The efficiency gains from eliminating entry and rate controls may serve to make formerly unprofitable markets more attractive, just as the shifting of resources and rate adjustments will make some of the formerly very profitable markets less so. Finally, whether some shipper groups should be subsidized is a social policy decision that properly belongs to Congress and not to the ICC or the motor carrier rate bureaus.

A further concern has been voiced that the benefits of relaxing economic controls will be only temporary and that once a "king of the hill" is established those benefits will disappear into monopoly profits and higher prices. The thrust of the industry description presented in this paper is that there is no economic advantage to size in the motor carrier industry other than that conferred by economic regulation. In the absence of regulation of rates and service, carriers of widely disparate size can compete on equal terms in individual markets. What may not be true is that carriers are able to do so on equal terms in the supplier markets. That is, larger carriers may enjoy price and service advantages in their supplier markets that smaller carriers cannot realize. This, of course, is outside the scope of the present regulation. (It is interesting to note that the large carriers have not been able to convert these advantages—if they exist—into significant cost advantages.) The emergence of a "king of the hill" is not a very likely consequence of motor carrier deregulation.

As we have seen, the costs of transition associated with the relaxation of economic regulation of the motor carrier industry can be quite high. Most recent proposals for regulatory change pay lip service to these costs and their policies. Thus, they reflect "initial steps to deregulation," implying that more steps will come. Two problems result. First, by being limited in scope, they fail to yield significant gains in resource use and efficiency, while at the same time they destabilize the industry, its customers, and its suppliers. Second, because they are limited in scope, they are seen as "experiments" that can be drawn back from if things do not go well. This, of course, creates still more uncertainty for the industry, its customers, and its suppliers, increasing their incentive to avoid the change.

10

ON EXPANDING THE COMMERCIAL ZONE EXEMPTION

W. Bruce Allen

This paper presents evidence reflecting the movement over time of residences, businesses, and industry in relation to cities and metropolitan areas. Although most of the evidence presented herein pertains specifically to the Philadelphia Commercial Zone, the evidence on suburbanization of both residences and places of employment nationwide is becoming well documented.[1] Thus, although the data presented here are idiosyncratic, I believe that, for the most part, the conclusions may be generalized.

Preliminary Considerations

The Interstate Commerce Commission has asserted that it does not create commercial zones but merely recognizes economic facts. Al-

---

This paper is edited from a verified statement prepared for use in support of a U.S. Department of Transportation position in a proceeding before the Interstate Commerce Commission, Commercial Zones and Terminal Areas, Ex Parte No. MC-37 (Sub-No. 26), October 1975. The original statement contained a number of maps which have not been reproduced here. Also in the original statement, following the section on the spatial economic structure of Philadelphia, the author undertook a discussion of a number of specific questions posed by the ICC in the proceeding. Although this detailed discussion has not been included here, the main points are noted in the paper's concluding summary.

[1] Edgar Hoover and Raymond Vernon, *Anatomy of a Metropolis* (New York: Anchor Books, 1962); Edwin Mills, *Studies in the Structure of the Urban Economy* (Washington, D.C.: Resources for the Future, 1972); Richard Muth, *Cities and Housing* (Chicago: University of Chicago Press, 1969); John Niedercorn and Edward Hearle, *Recent Land Use Trends in Forty-Eight Large American Cities* (Santa Monica, Calif.: Rand Corp., 1963); and Leon Moses and Harold Williamson, "Location of Economic Activity in Cities," *American Economic Review*, vol. 57 (1967), pp. 211-22.

though this may have been true when the zones were first formed, the assertion today ignores the impact that the formation of the zone has on the location of economic activity. Transportation considerations have been diminishing in importance as a determinant of industrial location, partly because of the general ubiquity of transport systems in the United States.[2] They are, however, still a factor of secondary importance in the location process, and they can play an important part in deciding upon the actual location (the microlocation) once the general area (the macrolocation) has been determined. There are certain advantages to being located within the commercial zone: more carriers allowed to serve the location, general use of the main city as the rate base, et cetera. Thus, one could expect that, other things being equal, the commercial zone location would be chosen over the noncommercial zone location. In fact, some evidence does exist to suggest that the commercial zone does influence the location process.[3] But, of course, everything else is not equal and location does take place outside of the commercial zone. Nevertheless, the commission must recognize that it is not a neutral observer to the process of the "economic fact" which determines commercial zones. To some extent, the suburbanization process which the United States is observing today is occurring in spite of the commission; that is, employment is moving beyond the zone when the benefits of the outlying areas exceed the benefits of the artificially created zone. The point is that the commission has a role in determining current "economic fact."

A second consideration is the current predilection of the commission to reward economic continuity and contiguous plots of economic activity. At a time when the United States has become vitally aware of its environment and, especially on the local level, has embarked on a policy of some land use planning and land use control (all of which may preclude contiguous economic development), it would seem that the commission's general feelings in this area should be reviewed. If good planning requires open space but

[2] Melvin Greenhut and Marshall Colberg, *Factors in the Location of Florida Industry* (Tallahassee, Fla.: Florida State University Press, 1962); Edward Smykay, Donald Bowersox, and Frank Mossman, *Physical Distribution Management* (New York: Macmillan Co., 1961); Eva Mueller and James Morgan, "Location Decisions of Manufacturers," *American Economic Review: Papers and Proceedings* (Nashville, Tenn., 1962), pp. 204-17; Herbert Gishlick, "Plant Location in Manufacturing: A Testing of Some Hypotheses" (Ph.D. diss., University of Pennsylvania, 1973); and Benjamin Stevens and Carolyn Brackett, *Industrial Location* (Philadelphia: Regional Science Research Institute, 1967).

[3] David Yaseen, "The Interstate Commercial Zone: An Industrial Location Factor," *Land Economics*, February 1966, pp. 107-12.

good commercial zones require continuous development, something has to give; both cannot prevail.

The following discussion addresses five different geographic areas in the Philadelphia context. These are (in general order of area size):

(1) The existing commercial zone (as explicitly defined by the commission);
(2) The urbanized area of Philadelphia (as defined by the U.S. Bureau of the Census);
(3) A population-mileage formula distance of twenty miles from the corporate limits of Philadelphia;
(4) A population-mileage formula distance of twenty-five miles from the corporate limits of Philadelphia; and
(5) The Philadelphia standard metropolitan statistical area (SMSA; Bucks, Chester, Delaware, Montgomery, and Philadelphia counties in Pennsylvania and Burlington, Camden, and Gloucester counties in New Jersey).

Two other areas were initially considered:

(1) The standard consolidated statistical area (SCSA), which comprises the Philadelphia SMSA; the Trenton, New Jersey, SMSA (Mercer County); and the Wilmington, Delaware, SMSA (New Castle County, Delaware; Salem County, New Jersey; and Cecil County, Maryland).
(2) The Philadelphia BEA-OBE (Bureau of Economic Analysis —Office of Business Economics) area, which comprises Philadelphia, Bucks, Montgomery, Chester, Delaware, Berks, Lehigh, Northampton, Schuylkill, Carbon, and Monroe counties in Pennsylvania; Warren, Mercer, Burlington, Ocean, Camden, Gloucester, Atlantic, Salem, Cumberland, and Cape May counties in New Jersey; New Castle County in Delaware; and Cecil County in Maryland.

For reasons of time and data availability, only the above-mentioned five areas were examined.[4]

Most of the points within the Philadelphia Commercial Zone are within five miles of the corporate limits of Philadelphia. Many places—especially in New Jersey, but also in Pennsylvania—are

---

[4] The major source of data on detailed economic activity was the Delaware Valley Regional Planning Commission (DVRPC), whose jurisdiction includes just the eight-county Philadelphia SMSA and the one-county Trenton SMSA.

within five miles of the corporate limits of Philadelphia but are not in the current zone.

A vast amount of data has been assembled in order to demonstrate that the economy of the Philadelphia region is more spatially diverse today than it was in the 1930s when the commercial zone was established. Only two changes have been made to the Philadelphia zone during the last forty-five years. The first change occurred almost immediately after the zone was established, when some New Jersey communities were added. The second occurred in 1964, when the remainder of Fort Washington Industrial Park (approximately 458 acres) was added; a part of the industrial park was already in the zone.

Most of the data is from the Delaware Valley Regional Planning Commission (DVRPC). Data gathered prior to 1960 is not regarded as accurate by the DVRPC, and most of the information presented herein will refer to the period 1960–1970 (the latter year being the latest available data).

The data include detailed spatial breakdowns of employment by type, population, and land use. The summary tables which are presented in this paper detail the changes which have occurred over time in the five geographic areas considered herein. The results of a study of the location of manufacturing activity on the two-digit Standard Industrial Classification (SIC) level are also presented.

The Philadelphia Spatial Economy

Detailed employment by municipality is available for the year 1970 (with the exception of some data which cannot be revealed because of disclosure problems). With the exception of a few communities in Delaware County, Pennsylvania (Nether Providence, Swarthmore, and Springfield), and the 1964 addition of the Fort Washington Industrial Park (in upper Dublin Township, Montgomery County, Pennsylvania), the Philadelphia Commercial Zone follows municipal boundaries. Thus, the correspondence of data to the commercial zone is quite good. The four communities mentioned above are included in the commercial zone since more disaggregate data than community was not available; their inclusion biases the commercial zone figures upward.

Employment data for 1960 were also collected by the DVRPC. However, such data was not collected by municipality. It was collected by data collection districts (DCD). Such districts are generally aggregates of municipalities (except in large population areas like

Philadelphia and Camden where they are disaggregates). In the outlying regions, many municipalities are aggregated to form one DCD. The correspondence of data and the commercial zone was therefore less precise in 1960 than it was in 1970. Judgment was used in determining whether a DCD should be included in the zone or out of it. Elements entering into that judgment were: area in the zone compared to area out of the zone; personal knowledge of the spatial, economic nature of the area; et cetera. In general, the selection process was done with a bias toward increasing the data attributable to the commercial zone.

Unfortunately, the detailed levels of employment data for 1960 and 1970 are not totally comparable, and agricultural employment must be subtracted from the 1970 total employment to make it comparable with the 1960 total employment. However, by aggregating two categories of 1960 and 1970 employment, manufacturing and trade, a category can be established that is virtually identical in composition in each period. This category does not include employment in the armed services, finance, insurance, real estate, government, construction, transportation, communication, or utilities. The combined category makes up 52.7 percent of the total employment in the Philadelphia SMSA. A third category, mining, should be added to make the years compatible. However, in 1970 only 1,386 jobs existed in mining in the Philadelphia SMSA out of an employment base of 2,019,874. The aggregation of manufacturing and trade is quite convenient because it probably puts together two major (potential) consumers of trucking service (much more so, for example, than finance, insurance, and real estate).

The data shows that approximately 64.7 percent of all SMSA manufacturing and trade employment and approximately 70.8 percent of all SMSA manufacturing and trade firms were located within the commercial zone in 1970. By comparison, 67.6 percent of all employment in the SMSA was in the zone while 72.8 percent of all firms in the SMSA were in the zone. Some categories like finance, insurance, and real estate have much higher ties to the urban core (81.4 percent of employment and 80.7 percent of the firms) because of the need in these categories for face-to-face contact and other specialized services that are offered in the core.

The data above should be put into perspective. One item of this perspective is the impact that the commercial zone has on the location process, as has already been discussed. A second item of the perspective is the basic inertia inherent in the industrial location process. A new location, in general, would not be sought until the

Table 10-1

COMPARISON OF COMMERCIAL ZONE EMPLOYMENT WITH SMSA EMPLOYMENT, 1960 AND 1970

	Manufacturing, Trade, and Mining Employment			**Total Employment**		
	Commercial zone	SMSA	Percentage in commercial zone	Commercial zone	SMSA	Percentage in commercial zone
1960	765,847	973,221	78.7	1,362,525	1,606,398	84.8
1970	689,012	1,066,523	64.6	1,283,304	2,010,955	63.8
Percentage change	−10.0	+9.6		−5.8	+25.2	

Source: Calculated by author from Delaware Valley Regional Planning Commission (DVRPC), Philadelphia, Pa., computer run of 6/4/75 and DVRPC Plan Report No. 1, *1958 Regional Projections for the Delaware Valley Supplement.* The first yielded 1970 figures and the latter 1960 figures.

net benefits of the new location (which include capital outlays) exceed the net benefits of the old location. Since the capital outlays are a variable expense item in the consideration of the new location, but a fixed expense item in the old location, significant advantages must be available at the new location before a move will occur. Some of the likely advantages of the newer areas are lower crime and vandalism, lower taxes, land availability for one-story technology and for expansion, nearness to the interstate highway system, proximity to management personnel residences, et cetera.

Another perspective is the comparable data for 1960. In that year 78.9 percent of the SMSA employment was in the commercial zone (the number of firms is not available for 1960) and 79.9 percent of total employment was in the commercial zone.

Although there are several ways for relative shares to change, Table 10-1 shows that the shift here occurred in a manner which strongly supports the argument that economic activity which benefits by the commercial zone concept is moving out of the commercial zone. For example, SMSA manufacturing and trade employment increased from 1960 to 1970 by 9.6 percent, but commercial zone manufacturing and trade employment decreased from 1960 to 1970 by 10 percent.

Thus, evidence exists to substantiate the claim that the current population-mileage formula is inadequate since it does not reflect the current economic facts. Were earlier data available, they undoubtedly

Table 10-2
DENSITY FUNCTIONS FOR PHILADELPHIA

		1920	1930	1940	1948	1954	1958	1963
Population	γ	0.25	0.37	0.36	0.31	0.27	0.25	0.23
	D	67,595	62,034	59,789	53,264	45,714	41,868	38,268
Manufacturing	γ	0.32	0.35	0.32	0.33	0.30	0.29	0.26
	D	7,586	7,332	5,243	9,229	7,863	6,896	5,765
Retailing	γ		0.47	0.39	0.37	0.44	0.30	0.26
	D		4,493	3,118	4,182	5,797	2,855	2,229
Services	γ			0.49	0.43	0.42	0.39	0.36
	D			1,243	1,604	1,685	1,720	1,710
Wholesaling	γ		0.70	0.63	0.59	0.49	0.44	0.37
	D		4,384	2,934	4,139	3,058	2,529	1,891

Source: Edwin Mills, *Studies in the Structure of the Urban Economy* (Washington, D.C.: Resources for the Future, 1972), pp. 45-46.

would show that the commercial zone's share of employment was much higher in 1950 and 1940.

Some secondary evidence exists to support this hypothesis. In a study published in 1972, Edwin Mills estimated the employment density function over time for many municipalities, including Philadelphia.[5] The density function is written as

$$D(u) = D\, e^{-\gamma}\, u,$$

where

$D(u)$ = the density, that is, employment per unit of land area, u miles from the center;

e = the base of the natural logarithm;

D, γ = parameters to be estimated from the data.

D is the measure of density at the city center and γ, which is positive, is the measure for the rate at which density declines with distance from the center. If γ is large, density falls off rapidly, that is, there is a high concentration of employment near the center. If γ is small, density falls off slowly, that is, there is a dispersion of employment. If a time series of γ estimates shows γ falling over time, then the conclusion is that employment is relocating from the center city.

Table 10-2 shows Mills's estimates of γ for population, manufacturing, retailing, services, and wholesaling over time for Philadelphia. In general, most Ds decline with time as do most γs. This is

[5] Mills, *Structure of the Urban Economy.*

consistent with the decentralizing hypothesis stated above. Since Mills's estimates only cover up to 1963, they provide a complement to the data derived within this paper. Mills's data shows that decentralization has been going on since World War II and, in fact, since the inception of commercial zones.

A further bit of evidence comes from the work of John Blair,[6] who follows on some earlier work of Britton Harris.[7] Blair has determined the manufacturing center of gravity for two-digit SIC manufacturing firms by output within the five Pennsylvania counties of the Philadelphia SMSA for 1957. The center of gravity is, of course, a resolution of various vectors of forces, and it does not necessarily depict the actual location of the industry. Like any average, it can be strongly influenced by data outliers, that is, data far away from the mean.

Blair has also determined the center of gravity for all new locations between 1957 and 1968 for each two-digit SIC group. The centers of gravity for both the 1957 firms and the new locations between 1957 and 1968 are shown in Table 10-3. The center of gravity of the new locations of five of the eighteen SICs (that is, 20, 28, 34, 37, and 38) is outside of the commercial zone. Only SICs 22 and 39 seemed to be centralizing. Since these are averages, nothing is revealed about the actual locations. However, the general outward movement and the fact that some locations had to be beyond the commercial zone to pull the center of gravity out in that direction are not to be disregarded.

The work of Harris traced the new location process prior to 1957. It too shows the general outward migration of manufacturing firms away from the Philadelphia core.

The next area of interest is the urbanized area as defined by the Bureau of Census. The urbanized area includes a central city of at least 50,000 population and the surrounding closely settled territory. The latter is defined as incorporated places with a population greater than 2,500 or with a population less than 2,500 but with some part having at least 100 housing units closely settled. Also included are small parcels of land normally less than one square mile having a population density greater than 100 per square mile. Finally, small areas in unincorporated territory with lower popula-

[6] John Blair, unpublished Ph.D. diss. research on industrial location in Philadelphia, University of Pennsylvania, 1975.

[7] Britton Harris, et al., *Industrial Land and Facilities for Philadelphia*, report to the Philadelphia City Planning Commission by the Institute for Urban Studies, University of Pennsylvania, 1956.

Table 10-3

GEOGRAPHICAL CENTERS OF GRAVITY FOR MANUFACTURING FIRMS IN PHILADELPHIA

(coordinate points)

SIC[a]	New Locations 1957–1968	1957 Location
20	10.0W, 3.3N	2.1W, 3.3N
22	0.6W, 4.7N	2.7W, 4.7N
23	2.9W, 2.5N	2.7W, 3.1N
24	4.5W, 10.2N	6.6W, 4.0N
25	2.1W, 6.9N	2.6W, 5.1N
26	4.5W, 2.8N	5.0W, 4.2N
27	3.6W, 1.9N	3.3W, 1.2N
28	12.2W, 4.2N	3.1W, 5.3N
29	3.1W, 0.6S	2.2W, 2.7S
30	6.6W, 1.9S	8.1W, 9.1N
32	6.2W, 7.2N	5.7W, 8.9N
33	8.4W, 6.7N	5.8W, 8.2N
34	3.0W, 10.9N	2.8W, 6.6N
35	1.4W, 6.7N	3.0W, 3.7N
36	6.3W, 5.3N	2.6W, 4.1N
37	10.0W, 11.7N	2.7W, 4.3N
38	10.5W, 3.2N	2.0W, 9.3N
39	0.9W, 3.7N	3.9W, 6.6N

[a] Standard Industrial Classification.

Note: Point (0,0) is City Hall, Philadelphia; distance is in miles; W = West, N = North, S = South, E = East.

Source: John Blair, unpublished Ph.D. research on industrial location in Philadelphia, University of Pennsylvania, 1975.

tion densities are allowed in order to eliminate enclaves, to close indentations of less than one mile, and to link outlying areas which otherwise qualify and are less than 1.5 miles away from an existing urbanized area.

The urbanized area is much more responsive to the shifts in population and industrial and commercial activity that have occurred in the last forty years. With the noted exception of the New Jersey side of the Delaware River, the urbanized area is almost always within five miles of the existing commercial zone except for three fingers which go out to meet Malvern in Chester County, Norristown in Montgomery County, and Bristol in Bucks County. In a small number of places—like Whitemarsh and Upper Dublin in Montgomery County—the urbanized area is within the commercial zone.

This increase in territory, which is not enormous, increases the 1970 share of SMSA manufacturing and trade employment to approximately 79.2 percent and the 1970 share of SMSA manufacturing and trade firms to approximately 84.4 percent. The 1970 share of total SMSA employment becomes 81.1 percent.

The tremendous impact that suburbanization has had on employment can be noted by comparing the share of SMSA employment which the urbanized area had in 1960 with that in 1970. In 1960 the percentage shares for manufacturing and trade employment and for total employment were approximately 94.7 percent and 95.6 percent, respectively. Between 1960 and 1970 the urbanized area fell in manufacturing and trade employment by 8.4 percent, while the SMSA total in such employment grew by 9.6 percent. In total employment, the relative share of the urbanized area fell. Total employment in the urbanized area grew, but its rate of growth was only 6.3 percent, which is well below the SMSA growth rate in total employment of 25.2 percent.

A word of caution is in order regarding these figures. Since the urbanized area does involve parts of unincorporated municipalities, much judgment must be used in determining the areas whose data should be included in the 1970 urbanized area figures. In addition, because several of the fingers stretch out to the outer reaches of the region, the 1960 DCDs involved are quite large. Again, judgment was involved. Because of the lack of specification possible, these figures should be regarded in a much more tentative fashion than the commercial zone figures. These figures are displayed in Table 10-4.

The appeal of using the urbanized area as the Philadelphia Commercial Zone is that the level of economic activity and the level of population are closely related phenomena. Virtually the whole employment of trade is population-serving, and so locations of trade facilities generally tend to be where the people are. Because of the virtual ubiquity of the highway system, much industrial activity is more footloose than it was previously. Much activity seems to *follow* population (note the generally higher γs in Table 10-2 for the non-population items).

Since the decennial and special censuses provide the opportunity to redefine the urbanized area periodically, the definition has a type of built-in responsiveness—unlike the current system. In addition, as mentioned above, the distribution of population and economic activity are closely correlated.

Table 10-4

COMPARISON OF URBANIZED AREA EMPLOYMENT WITH SMSA EMPLOYMENT, 1960 AND 1970

	Manufacturing, Trade, and Mining Employment			Total Employment		
	Urbanized area	SMSA	Percentage in urbanized area	Urbanized area	SMSA	Percentage in urbanized area
1960	921,621	973,221	94.7	1,535,740	1,606,398	95.6
1970	844,481	1,066,523	79.2	1,631,507	2,010,955	81.1
Percentage change	−8.4	+9.6		+6.3	+25.2	

Source: See Table 10-1.

Several drawbacks exist. The first drawback is that the finger development mentioned above makes for an octopus-type zone. Some type of arcing process is a possible solution. This process would fill in the gaps. The second drawback is that the definition basically requires continuous development. As mentioned before, environmental goals or community differences may dictate that diversity in land use occur or that planned industrial development be buffered from existing population. However, accommodation of local land use planning and the use of the urbanized area could be a forceful tool for using the commercial zone definition to plan for the future rather than reacting to the past.

Thus, although the growth in current manufacturing and trade employment appears to be occurring beyond the urbanized area (subject to the data caveats mentioned above), the urbanized area represents a significant increase in the percentage of SMSA employment covered and an area increase which will generate fewer protesters than the larger increases to be mentioned below.

It might also be added that of the 249 industrial parks in the SMSA only 67 are in the commercial zone. If the area were enlarged to include the 1970 urbanized area, 78 or more industrial parks (or 31.3 percent) would be added. Moreover, the 1970 urbanized area covers many of the new suburbs and the areas involved in the fastest growth on the New Jersey side and the closer-in growth areas on the Pennsylvania side.

The remaining two areas are population-mileage formula expansions to twenty and twenty-five miles from the corporate limits

Table 10-5

COMPARISON OF 20-MILE AREA EMPLOYMENT WITH SMSA EMPLOYMENT, 1960 AND 1970

	Manufacturing, Trade, and Mining Employment			Total Employment		
	20-mile area	SMSA	Percentage in 20-mile area	20-mile area	SMSA	Percentage in 20-mile area
1960	927,707	973,221	95.3	1,541,428	1,606,398	96.0
1970	1,010,558	1,066,523	94.8	1,919,190	2,010,955	95.4
Percentage change	+8.9	+9.6		+24.5	+25.2	

Source: See Table 10-1.

of Philadelphia, including all areas of incorporated municipalities which meet those limits. It should be noted that both the twenty- and the twenty-five-mile areas include Trenton and Wilmington. The twenty-five-mile area includes virtually all of the Trenton SMSA. With the exception of a significant area of western Chester County, a very small amount of northern Montgomery County, a relatively small amount of northern Bucks County, a trivial part of Gloucester County, and a relatively small part of Burlington County (of which all is in the Pine Barrens), the twenty-five-mile limit covers the Philadelphia SMSA, plus significant areas to the northeast and southwest of the SMSA. As can be seen below, this area includes virtually all of the SMSA employment.

In 1970 the manufacturing and trade sectors located within the twenty-mile area made up approximately 94.8 percent of the SMSA manufacturing and trade employment and approximately 95.8 percent of the SMSA manufacturing and trade firms. The comparable 1960 employment figure was 95.3 percent. The 1970 total employment share was 95.4 percent, while the 1960 share was 96.0 percent. See Table 10-5.

These numbers also involved judgment in determining which municipalities to include in the twenty-mile area and which to exclude. The same judgmental factors ruled as in the above cases. The 1970 figures have an overstatement bias since they were calculated by subtracting communities not in the twenty-mile area from the SMSA total (the bias results from the underreporting of some data in the areas outside the twenty-mile area because of disclosure problems).

Table 10-6

COMPARISON OF 25-MILE AREA EMPLOYMENT WITH SMSA EMPLOYMENT, 1960 AND 1970

	Manufacturing, Trade, and Mining Employment			Total Employment		
	25-mile area	SMSA	Percentage in 25-mile area	25-mile area	SMSA	Percentage in 25-mile area
1960	956,387	973,221	98.3	1,580,120	1,606,398	98.4
1970	1,046,065	1,066,523	98.1	1,974,436	2,010,955	98.2
Percentage change	+9.4	+9.6		+25.0	+25.2	

Source: See Table 10-1.

The manufacturing and trade sectors located within the twenty-five-mile area made up approximately 98.1 percent of the SMSA manufacturing and trade employment in 1970 and approximately 98.4 percent of the SMSA firms. The comparable 1960 employment figure was 98.3 percent. The 1970 total employment share was 98.2 percent, while the 1960 share was 98.4 percent. The same caveats that apply to the twenty-mile area apply to the twenty-five-mile area. The figures appear in Table 10-6.

Although these areas cover virtually all of the SMSA employment (and add a significant amount of activity from Wilmington and Trenton), they also add vast amounts of virtually unoccupied land to the commercial zone.

A potentially appealing aspect of the expansion of the population-mileage formula to a twenty- or twenty-five-mile maximum would be the inclusion of Wilmington and Trenton in the Philadelphia Commercial Zone. However, although interaction does occur with both of these cities, the ties between Philadelphia and Wilmington and Trenton are less than the ties to other areas.

The last area is the SMSA. Its data has already been presented as the basis for comparison for the other four areas. Although expansion of the Philadelphia Commercial Zone to be coextensive with the SMSA is thought to be too large for reasons analogous to those given for the twenty- and twenty-five-mile areas, expansion to the SMSA has significant advantages in many cities.

Tables 10-7 and 10-8 show that expansion of the Philadelphia Commercial Zone to the urbanized area vastly increases the amount of available land (over sixfold). Of the various expansion possi-

Table 10-7

LAND USE AND LAND AVAILABILITY BY AREA TYPE, 1970
(in acres)

				Industrial Zoned Land		
	Available Land	Manu-facturing Land	Com-mercial Land	Total	Vacant	Per-centage vacant
Commercial zone	45,024	8,826	7,436	36,539	9,368	25.6
Urbanized area	284,083	16,857	15,834	108,219	59,702	55.2
20-mile area	842,103	21,702	22,168	191,639	131,701	68.7
25-mile area	1,166,578	23,452	24,430	212,825	149,709	70.3
SMSA	1,637,019	24,630	26,569	226,037	161,188	72.3

Source: Computed by author from Delaware Valley Regional Planning Commission, computer run of June 4, 1975.

Table 10-8

LAND USE AND LAND AVAILABILITY BY AREA TYPE AS PERCENTAGE OF SMSA TOTALS, 1970

	Available Land	Manu-facturing Land	Com-mercial Land	Industrial Zoned Land	Vacant Industrial Zoned Land
Commercial zone	2.8	35.8	28.0	16.2	5.8
Urbanized area	17.4	68.4	59.6	67.1	37.0
20-mile area	51.4	88.1	83.4	84.8	81.7
25-mile area	71.3	95.2	91.9	94.2	92.9
SMSA	100.0	100.0	100.0	100.0	100.0

Source: See Table 10-7.

bilities, expansion to the urbanized area provides for the largest marginal jump in manufacturing land, commercial land, and industrial-zoned land (that is, the highest change in percentage points as one reads down Table 10-8). Again, expansion to the urbanized area adds a proportionately large amount of land which is currently used or is available for use in economic activity which benefits by being within the commercial zone. The expansion of the commercial zone to the urbanized area will almost double the manufacturing acreage

Table 10-9
POPULATION BY AREA TYPE, 1960 AND 1970

	1960	Percentage of SMSA Population	1970	Percentage of SMSA Population	Percentage Change, 1960 to 1970
Commercial zone	2,842,836	65.5	2,857,438	59.3	0.5
Urbanized area	3,748,890	86.4	4,079,477	84.6	8.8
20-mile area	4,138,883	95.4	4,537,699	94.1	9.6
25-mile area	4,221,409	97.3	4,688,688	97.2	11.0
SMSA	4,377,416	100.0	4,820,040	100.0	11.1
Population outside 25-mile area	116,007	2.7	134,352	2.8	15.8

Source: See Table 10-7.

covered by the zone. (It will not, however, double the employment because of the land intensive nature of the suburbanized firm—that is, the one-story production process.)

The same pattern holds for population, as is shown in Table 10-9. The biggest marginal jump in population is from the commercial zone to the urbanized area. The share of SMSA population in the commercial zone has dropped because of its small population growth relative to the SMSA's growth. In fact, all areas grow slower that the SMSA, except the areas outside the twenty-five-mile area. However, the urbanized area growth rate is much more in line with the SMSA growth rate than is the current commercial-zone growth rate, and the figure for the urbanized area is biased downward since it contains the figure for the commercial zone. Since much economic activity is population-serving, the new growth relative to the existing zone seems ripe for servicing by an expanded commercial zone.

The above analysis presents significant evidence that the current Philadelphia Commercial Zone definition is outmoded from an economic point of view. The surrounding areas are growing in population and in industrial and commercial activity. The commercial zone is stagnant or is experiencing negative growth. Industry is migrating to the outlying areas because of relocation forced by the construction of the Delaware Expressway or because of any number of location-influencing factors.

These are economic facts. An alternative definition of the zone should be adopted which recognizes these economic facts. Such a definition should account for a significant increase in the coverage of population, of manufacturing and commercial land use, of industrial land availability, and of employment in manufacturing and trade. The urbanized area accounts for 84.6 percent of the 1970 SMSA population (versus 59.3 percent for the commercial zone); 68.4 percent of the SMSA land used in manufacturing (versus 35.8 percent); 59.6 percent of the SMSA land used in commercial activities (versus 28.0 percent); 67.1 percent of the industrial-zoned land (versus 16.2 percent); 79.2 percent of SMSA employment in manufacturing and trade (versus 64.6 percent); and 81.1 percent of total SMSA employment (versus 63.8 percent). All of this increase in coverage is accomplished with a relatively small increase in area—especially in relation to the five-mile population-mileage limit which would exist if the Philadelphia Commercial Zone were not specifically defined.

The urbanized area is a flexible concept that can change as conditions change. Ample land availability (284,083 acres) can allow for a diverse, balanced growth. Subject to the feedback relationship of the existence of the commercial zone and the location of economic activity, the high population-employment correlation will allow the economic system to define the commercial zone. This will eliminate the need for an arbitrary definition imposed by the commission. However, amendments to the urbanized area that are proposed by land use planners could be entertained by the commission.

Summary

In summary, the case for the outmodedness of the current Philadelphia Commercial Zone can be strongly made. Industry and trade have moved out; employment in the area of the commercial zone is falling. The new growth is outside the existing commercial zone. This growth has been going on since the formation of the zone in the 1930s. Ample evidence is available to document this decentralization phenomenon. Thus, on the "demand" side, the case for an expanded zone is quite good. The urbanized area as defined by the Bureau of Census is suggested as the best candidate for expanding the Philadelphia Commercial Zone at this time.

On the "supply" side (that is, carriers) and on the environmental side, the results are less specific and the conclusions to be drawn are less clear. In the case of truckload movements, it seems most likely that fewer vehicle-miles will be performed, less fuel used, and less equipment required if the commercial zone is significantly expanded. The results of a case study in the Fort Washington area shows that more competition occurs, with resultant improvements in rates and service quality. However, the magnitude of these improvements is such that they are not perceived as significant by all shippers. It is difficult to determine (because the *rate* of turning to private carriage may have been slowed), but we did observe that some firms in the zone continued to turn increasingly to private carriage. On net, however, the conclusions for truckload movements were positive.

With respect to less-than-truckload movements, few clear-cut conclusions could be drawn. Competition certainly increased and service improvements resulted when Fort Washington was incorporated into the Philadelphia Commercial Zone. Rate improvements were not perceived to be significant by the shippers. The effects on operating efficiency, conservation of scarce resources, and impact on the environment are not clear. Since LTL requires pickup and delivery and terminal operations, it is possible that an increased zone could involve more vehicle-miles, more fuel consumption, more air and noise pollution, and more scarce resource consumption. Of course, the exact reverse could occur. The result depends on the shipping patterns. No conclusion can be drawn here; the information at hand does not permit it.

A slight amount of information does exist on what happens to truckers whose exclusive authority is effectively eliminated. A before-and-after study of the truckers who served the Fort Washington addition to the Philadelphia Commercial Zone showed initial injury to their operations but subsequent growth to beyond their pre-expansion levels. The lesson indicated is that the time for zonal expansion should be a time when general growth is occurring.

From the supply side too, the evidence seems to point to expansion. A modest expansion would be to the urbanized area which would, nevertheless, be large enough to show demonstrable effects in the area of operating efficiency, conservation, and impact on environment.

PART SIX

MARKET STABILITY IN A LESS REGULATED ENVIRONMENT

Motor carriage of unprocessed agricultural commodities is generally exempt from economic regulation by the Interstate Commerce Commission. Proponents of reduced motor carrier regulation cited the exempt agricultural trucking experience as evidence of the benefits of deregulation (lower prices, better service, reduction in private carriage). Critics argued that the exempt agricultural experience either was not applicable or showed contrary results (market instability, high carrier mortality and turnover, and shipper dissatisfaction). The paper by Walter Miklius and Kenneth L. Casavant presents the results of their study prepared for the U.S. Department of Agriculture analyzing the stability of exempt agricultural trucking. Their study provides strong indications of effective and sustained market performance by companies outside of regulation.

11

STABILITY OF MOTOR CARRIERS OPERATING UNDER THE AGRICULTURAL EXEMPTION

Walter Miklius and Kenneth L. Casavant

Introduction

Some industry representatives and even some economists maintain that in the trucking industry absence of public regulation would lead to excessive competition. The "excessive" ("destructive" or "cut-throat") competition is typically described as a situation where an easy entry into the industry results in overcapacity, which in turn leads to pricing below short-run variable costs. Yet, in spite of losses, the excess capacity is not withdrawn by disinvestment and does not discourage a constant influx of new owners and capital into the industry.

Hence, the industry is plagued with a chronic redundancy of capacity relative to demand. It may never reach an equilibrium or be moving in that direction.

The main evidence supporting the claim of excessive competition comes from the instability of the motor carrier industry during the depression of the 1930s. By now, however, it is generally admitted that this evidence is largely irrelevant. The instability of the industry during the depression has been highly exaggerated and, in any case, could be attributed to the economy-wide fall in the level of economic activity.

Furthermore, the experience of the countries that have deregulated their trucking industries is inconsistent with excessive com-

---

This paper is edited from a report prepared for the U.S. Department of Agriculture, August 1975. The report was prepared at the Department of Agricultural Economics, Washington State University.

petition. The industries in these countries appear to be stable and efficient.[1] Nevertheless, the excessive competition argument continues to play a major role in deliberations about changes in transport policies.

The for-hire transportation of unmanufactured agricultural commodities by truck in interstate commerce is exempt from economic regulation by section 203(b), subsection 6 of the Motor Carrier Act of 1935 as amended. This section is known as the "agricultural exemption," and the for-hire carriers hauling agricultural commodities exclusively are known as "exempt carriers."

The agricultural exemption, however, does not create an isolated, nonregulated segment of the motor carrier industry. According to the court interpretation and a subsequent amendment to the agricultural exemption, any motor vehicle hauling an exempt commodity is free from economic regulation as long as nonexempt commodities are not moved in the same vehicle at the same time. Thus, in addition to exempt carriers, other motor carriers participate in transportation of agricultural commodities. The exempt carriers, in turn, are indirectly affected by regulation.

In spite of these linkages, in the United States the carriers hauling agricultural commodities probably approach closest to a sector of the motor carrier industry free from economic regulation. Therefore, the nature of competition prevailing among exempt carriers may be indicative of the nature of competition which would prevail in the absence of regulation in the rest of the motor carrier industry.

Time and resource constraints did not permit us to undertake a comprehensive study of the nature of competition among exempt carriers. Instead, this study has a more limited objective. Its purpose is to examine one possible implication of excessive competition—the instability of motor carriers operating under the agricultural exemption. The instability is defined as a significantly higher entry and exit rate and a lower survival rate than in other similar industries.

Although no historical data on turnover rates among exempt carriers are available, the high turnover rates have been asserted on several occasions. For example, W. M. McCurdy, president of Perishable Commodity Carriers Association, stated at congressional hearings in 1961 that the turnover among exempt carriers "has reached a frightening proportion" and that "about one-third of the small exempt

[1] See J. C. Nelson, "Implications of Evolving Entry and Licensing Policies in Road Freight Transport," paper presented at the International Conference on Transportation Research, Bruges, Belgium, June 18-21, 1973. In recent years Australia, Canada, Great Britain, the Netherlands, Sweden, and Switzerland have either completely or materially deregulated their surface transport.

truckers go out of business each year."[2] Furthermore, the so-called Doyle Report concludes that "the Nation has to pay for economic waste such as that caused by the rapid turnover of exempt carriers."[3]

This study concentrates on the three aspects of stability: the entry of new firms, the survival of firms from previous time periods, and the exit of firms from the industry. The following section discusses various types of entry and exit and their effects on efficiency and wealth distribution. The subsequent section presents estimates of entry and exit rates into and out of exempt trucking and compares these rates to those in other lines of business. The final section summarizes the major findings of the study.

The available statistical data on transportation are largely a by-product of government regulation. Since the exempt carriers are not regulated, the information needed for this study was not available from the agencies normally engaged in collecting such data. A disproportionate amount of time and effort, therefore, had to be devoted to collecting primary data. The sources, nature, and scope of data used in the study are described in the appendixes which were attached to the original report.

Entry and Exit and Their Implications on Efficiency and Wealth Distribution

Entry and exit occupy a prominent role in economic theory. The entry of firms into an industry is counted upon to eliminate excess profits, and the exit of firms is expected to reduce excess capacity and to weed out inefficient producers. Similarly, legal restrictions to entry into business and occupations have been used extensively as a public instrument to transfer wealth among selected groups of individuals in the society, and occasionally in situations where restricted entry would improve efficiency (for example, public utilities, common property resources, et cetera). In spite of this, there appears to be considerable confusion about the consequences of turnover among business firms. Perhaps the best example is the statement from the Doyle Report quoted above. The purpose of this section is to discuss various types of entry and exit and their effects on economic efficiency and distribution of wealth.

[2] U.S. Congress, Senate, Subcommittee on Surface Transportation of the Committee on Interstate and Foreign Commerce, *Hearings on Problems of the Railroads*, Part 2, 87th Congress, 1st session, 1961, p. 1005.

[3] *National Transportation Policy* (Doyle Report), preliminary draft of a report to the Senate Committee on Interstate and Foreign Commerce, 87th Congress, 1st session, 1961, p. 524.

Entry may be defined as the extent to which new owners become established in an industry either through the establishment of a new business or through the purchase of existing firms. The two types of entry have different effects and should be treated separately. When an entrepreneur establishes a new business, resources are drawn into the industry and away from alternative uses; that is, real economic costs are being incurred, and the industry capacity expands. A mere transfer of ownership, on the other hand, does not impose any real costs nor does it cause any changes in the industry's capacity. Depending on the expected profitability of the business, the previous owner may have made a capital gain or suffered a capital loss. In both cases, however, these wealth transfers do not impose any costs on society in general, since the loss of one person or firm is offset by the gain by another member of society.

Ownership transfers, however, may have an effect on efficiency. A buyer may offer to buy a firm if he thinks he knows how to run a business better than the present owner. The new owner pays less than he thinks he can earn with the firm, while the old owner gets more than he thinks he could earn. If the buyer is correct, resources are used more efficiently. If he is wrong, he will have to bear the loss.

Several alternative ways are available for exit of the firms from an industry. The most notorious is through bankruptcy. The term bankruptcy is used generally to describe legal proceedings undertaken in a court when a debtor is unable to pay or to reach an agreement with his creditors. Exits via bankruptcy account for a relatively small percentage of all exits. Like the business transfers, the bankruptcy process itself does not incur economic costs since no real resources are consumed when debts are discharged. The process merely acts as a mechanism of wealth redistribution. Although the initial impact of a business bankruptcy is on its creditors, who usually receive a very small amount of their claims, these losses are passed on to the creditors' purchasers and are ultimately borne by the consumers. The main beneficiaries, in addition to the bankrupt, are those who operate the system (referees, trustees, attorneys, and others).[4]

In the majority of cases, the firms simply discontinue business, discharge employees, sell off assets, and shut down. When this happens the resources formerly used there revert to their next best source of income. Aside from the general state of economy, one of the main

---

[4] For a more complete discussion of the bankruptcy process, see D. T. Stanley and M. Girth, *Bankruptcy: Problems, Process, Reform* (Washington, D.C.: The Brookings Institution, 1971).

determinants of the impact is the mobility of these resources, which in turn depends on their specialization. Other things being equal, the employees of an industry that requires skills specific to that industry will suffer greater decreases in income than the employees of an industry that utilizes easily transferable skills. Similarly, owners of specialized assets locked into specific locations will suffer greater capital losses.

On both counts, relative to other industries, the impact of exits from exempt trucking should be minimal. Drivers' skills are easily transferable among all sectors of the motor carrier industry as well as to the private firms. The truck, truck-tractor, and most trailers are neither specialized nor irrevocably committed to specific markets or regions. The existence of a secondhand equipment market allows a greater fraction of the initial investment to be recovered on liquidation.

The firms may also exit by sale or merger. The exits via merger, which are rather important in the case of regulated carriers, should rarely be observed among the exempt motor carriers. One of the merger motives among regulated motor carriers is to remedy regulation-induced inefficiencies. The regulated motor carriers are restricted in their operating authorities to specific points or territories to and from which a carrier may render the specified service and to routes and gateways over which operations may be conducted. A carrier may be further restricted to specific commodities or prohibited from soliciting or obtaining traffic on return haul, serving intermediate points along designated routes, et cetera.[5] The fragmentation of operating authority may leave a carrier with an inefficient operation, and the only practical remedy may be to acquire operating rights of other carriers through mergers or outright acquisitions.

A partial indicator for the value of improvement in efficiency is provided by the sale of "naked" operating rights.[6] A study by W. Adams and J. B. Hendry found that the "giant" carriers (that is, carriers with total operating revenues of more than $2.5 million in the period between January 1, 1950, and June 27, 1956) paid an average price of $45,852 for "naked" operating rights. The maximum paid for these rights was $200,000. "Other" carriers bought operating rights at an average price of $12,157, with the maximum price

[5] See J. C. Nelson, "The Effects of Entry Control in Surface Transport," in *Transportation Economics* (New York: Columbia University Press, 1965), pp. 381-422.

[6] That is, no other assets are included in the sale.

of $49,000.[7] More recently it has been estimated that the operating authorities possessed by individual regulated motor carriers are typically valued as a rule of thumb at 10–15 percent of their annual operating revenues. Since the operating revenues of regulated motor carriers were $16.7 billion in 1971, the total value of these operating authorities is on the order of $1.67 billion to $2.5 billion.[8] Unfortunately, the value of "naked" operating rights also includes the capitalized value of monopoly rents resulting from legal restrictions of entry into the trucking industry. In any case, since the exempt motor carriers do not hold operating rights, their exit is more likely to be through bankruptcy, sale of assets, or transfer of operations to other areas rather than through merger or sale of the firm.[9]

Finally, it must be emphasized that not all firms exit from the industry for economic reasons. An Office of Business Economics study estimated that less than one-half of business discontinuances and only one-fourth of all business transfers were liquidated by the original owners in order to prevent or minimize a loss.[10]

In short, "high" turnover rates of business firms in general, or of exempt motor carriers in particular, do not impose significant costs on society. The main result is a transfer of wealth among members of society with the gains offsetting the losses. Whether these wealth transfers are "good" or "bad" depends on one's value judgment. This judgment is similar to that which must be made, for example, about whether an individual should have a right to make decisions that pertain to his own welfare, whether he should be permitted to benefit from making "correct" decisions and be required to suffer the consequences for making the "wrong" ones. More broadly, these wealth transfers may be considered desirable or undesirable when judged against some ethical standard, or they may merely be less preferred by politically powerful groups to the wealth attainable through a political process.

---

[7] W. Adams and J. B. Hendry, *Trucking Mergers, Concentration, and Small Business: An Analysis of Interstate Commerce Commission Policy, 1950-1956,* U.S. Senate, Hearings before the Select Committee on Small Business, 85th Congress, 1st session, 1957, pp. 234-35.

[8] *Improving Railroad Productivity,* final report of the Task Force on Railroad Productivity to the National Commission on Productivity and the Council of Economic Advisers, November 1973.

[9] W. A. Jordan found this difference in the means of exit between regulated airlines and the relatively unregulated California intrastate carriers. See Jordan, *Airline Regulation in America: Effects and Imperfections* (Baltimore: The Johns Hopkins Press, 1970).

[10] B. C. Churchill, "Recent Business Population Movements," *Survey of Current Business,* vol. 34 (January 1954), pp. 11-16 and 24.

Entry, Exit, and Survival

This section contains the empirical core of the study. Its purpose is to report estimated entry, exit, and survival rates among exempt motor carriers and to compare these rates with similar rates for other industries.

The empirical work encountered several difficulties. The first major difficulty pertains to the definition of an "exempt motor carrier." As we have defined it, an exempt motor carrier is a carrier that operates solely under section 203(b), subsection 6 of the Motor Carrier Act of 1935 as amended. According to our estimate, some 11,000 motor carriers operating in 1974 fit this definition. However, according to this section of the law, any motor vehicle hauling unmanufactured agricultural commodities in interstate commerce is exempt from economic regulation by the ICC. In other words, it is the nature of the commodity transported that determines the regulatory status of the vehicle, regardless of legal or other classifications of the carrier firm operating the vehicle. Thus, motor carriers holding ICC operating rights and regulated intrastate motor carriers may and do operate vehicles free from economic regulation. But for most purposes the basic unit of analysis is the firm rather than the vehicle. This creates a problem since, strictly speaking, there is no such thing as an exempt motor carrier.

To compound the problem, according to our estimate, in 1974 some 11,000 motor carriers holding ICC operating rights and/or operating as regulated intrastate carriers participated in interstate transportation of exempt agricultural commodities. These carriers have registered as "exempt carriers" in states requiring registration of all motor carriers operating in the state. Thus, an "exempt motor carrier" could be defined as any carrier that hauls agricultural commodities exempt from the ICC regulation. This definition would include motor carriers holding ICC operating rights and/or regulated intrastate carriers as long as they are registered as an "exempt carrier" in at least one state.

To differentiate between the two definitions we will identify them as a "narrow" and a "broad" definition, respectively. Although the broader definition may be quite useful for a number of purposes, it has a distinct drawback. It may be argued that the conclusions regarding stability of exempt carriers are likely to be affected by the revenue some carriers are able to earn by transporting regulated commodities.

Unfortunately, in some situations it was not possible to exclude motor carriers holding ICC operating rights and/or regulated intrastate carriers. In these circumstances we have used estimates based on both definitions. The estimates based on the narrow definition are hereafter identified as MCEAC* and those based on the broad definition as MCEAC. Motor carriers of exempt agricultural commodities that hold ICC operating rights and/or operating as regulated intrastate carriers are identified as MCEAC**.

The second difficulty pertains to selection of comparison industries. In order to determine whether the entry and exit rates into exempt trucking of agricultural commodities are "high" or "low," it is necessary to compare our estimates with similar estimates for other industries. Ideally, one would like to compare exempt motor carriers with industries that have similar characteristics. In selecting these industries, it would be necessary to decide what characteristics ought to be considered; this, in turn, requires knowledge of the determinants of entry and exit rates.

A priori, one would expect entry into an industry to be a function of the initial capital requirement, expected profits, and the probability of a failure. Unfortunately, information on expected or even realized profits and probability of failure are not available either for exempt trucking or for other industries or for both. It is known, however, that little capital is required to enter into trucking of exempt agricultural commodities. The size of most exempt carriers, as measured by size of their truck-tractor fleet, is relatively small. About 38 percent of firms operating in 1974 had only one truck-tractor, and 78 percent had five truck-tractors or less.

In 1970 the cost of truck-tractors was estimated at about $21,000. There is more variation in the cost of trailers since they are more likely to be designed for transportation of specific commodities. For example, a tandem-axle aluminum grain trailer, capable of hauling a payload of twenty-four tons, would have cost about $7,000,[11] while the aluminum "pot" trailer, with a dropped center section and two to four loading decks used for carrying live animals, would have cost about $15,000.[12] Nevertheless, in comparison with other industries, a relatively small amount of capital is needed to enter trucking of exempt agricultural commodities.

---

[11] L. D. Schnake and J. R. Franzman, *Analysis of the Effects of Cost of Service Transportation Rates on the U.S. Grain Marketing System*, U.S. Department of Agriculture, Technical Bulletin No. 1484, 1973, p. 11.

[12] P. P. Boles, *Cost of Operating Trucks for Livestock Transportation*, U.S. Department of Agriculture, Marketing Research Division MRR-982, 1973, p. 6.

The entry is further encouraged by a flourishing secondhand equipment market which allows a sizeable reduction in the initial capital requirement, and readily available financing. The most common loan is for 80 to 85 percent of the value of the equipment, thus requiring only a 15 to 20 percent down payment. The length of the loan is most commonly forty-eight months on new tractors and trucks, and sixty months on trailers.[13]

In general, therefore, if profit opportunities and risks were the same, one would expect the entry of new firms into exempt trucking to be greater than into industries requiring more capital. This suggests the initial capital requirement as a partial criterion for selecting comparison industries. However, our search for data on initial capital required to enter various industries or for an appropriate proxy variable was not successful. We are forced, therefore, either to disregard the differences in inter-industry characteristics entirely or to use our judgment in selecting comparison industries.

Estimation of Entry Rates. The survey of exempt motor carriers conducted in 1974 provided the basis for estimating the distribution of carriers by year of entry for newly established firms as well as those entering through the transfer of ownership.

The estimated distributions of MCEAC* and MCEAC** populations by year of entry are shown in Table 11-1. The MCEAC* firms on the average are younger than the MCEAC** firms, although the differences are considerably smaller than might be anticipated. As expected, because of the regulatory restriction of entry by new firms, the entry via transfer of ownership is more prevalent in the case of MCEAC** than in the case of MCEAC* (Table 11-2).

Table 11-3 shows the percentage distribution of firms by year started in three selected comparison industries: eating places (Standard Industrial Classification 5812); dry cleaning establishments (SIC 7216); and auto repair (SIC 7538). All of these industries share a common characteristic of a relatively easy entry and the predominance of small, single-unit firms. The estimated distributions are based on random samples of establishments drawn for each industry from the Dun and Bradstreet files.[14] The MCEAC* firms are generally younger than dry cleaning and auto repair establishments but older than eating places.

---

[13] R. G. Hutchinson, A. R. Hutchinson, and M. Newcomer, "Study in Business Mortality," *American Economic Review*, vol. 28 (September 1938), pp. 497-511.

[14] The sample sizes were 1,641, 1,645, and 1,433 establishments, respectively.

Table 11-1

ESTIMATED DISTRIBUTION OF MCEAC BY YEAR STARTED AND TYPE OF CARRIER, 1974

	MCEAC*		MCEAC**	
Year	Number	Percent	Number	Percent
1974[a]	73	0.7	90	0.8
1973	1,275	11.7	922	8.6
1972	945	8.6	703	6.7
1971	781	7.1	599	5.6
1970	774	7.1	548	5.1
1969	560	5.1	511	4.8
1968	551	5.0	377	3.5
1967	287	2.6	314	2.9
1966	277	2.5	314	2.9
1965	301	2.8	279	2.6
1964	377	2.5	267	2.5
1963	185	1.7	185	1.7
1962	254	2.3	195	1.8
1961	199	1.8	216	2.0
1956–1960	1,012	9.2	1,093	10.2
1951–1955	687	6.3	818	7.6
1946–1950	898	8.2	1,181	11.0
1941–1945	247	2.3	386	3.6
1936–1940	337	3.1	398	3.7
1931–1935	199	1.8	314	2.9
1930 and earlier	703	6.4	862	8.0

[a] Part of the year.

The basic weakness of the preceding data is the exclusion of any firm that discontinued business before 1974. That is, the sample includes only those firms that survived to 1974. However, the number of surviving firms depends on two factors: the entry of firms in prior years and the survival or business mortality functions specific to each industry. Thus, the interindustry differences in age distribution, shown in Tables 11-1 and 11-3, may merely reflect the differences in time-growth patterns of these industries.

Furthermore, the entry rate estimates based on surviving firms would be biased downward. The bias, however, is likely to be less significant for 1973 than for the earlier years. According to our estimate, 1,275 MCEAC* firms were established in 1973. This gives

Table 11-2

ENTRY VIA TRANSFER OF OWNERSHIP AS A PERCENTAGE OF TOTAL ENTRY, MCEAC* AND MCEAC**, 1974

Year	MCEAC*	MCEAC**
1973	6.2	19.1
1972	7.9	24.7
1971	8.4	23.0
1970	12.0	18.7
1969	14.7	21.8
1968	6.6	20.8
1967	8.8	15.9
1966	14.3	19.0
1965	11.3	25.3
1964	12.7	20.3
1963	13.7	11.1
1958–1962	8.4	24.1
1953–1957	7.6	16.4
1943–1952	4.6	15.5
1933–1942	1.7	6.4
1932 and earlier	5.5	7.4

Table 11-3

PERCENTAGE DISTRIBUTION OF BUSINESS ESTABLISHMENTS BY YEAR STARTED, SELECTED INDUSTRIES, 1974

Year	Eating Places (SIC 5812)	Dry Cleaning (SIC 7216)	Auto Repair (SIC 7538)	MCEAC*
1973	8.4	2.8	3.1	13.2
1972	9.4	3.8	4.0	8.2
1971	7.7	3.9	4.3	7.3
1970	8.2	3.7	6.0	7.0
1969	7.0	4.9	3.9	4.8
1968	6.9	3.4	3.7	5.3
1967	5.4	2.7	3.8	3.0
1966	3.7	4.6	3.6	2.2
1965	2.9	3.9	3.4	2.6
1964	4.0	3.5	3.1	1.8
1963	4.0	2.9	3.2	2.4
1958–1962	11.0	14.2	15.4	10.4
1953–1957	7.4	13.0	12.7	6.6
1945–1952	8.5	22.0	19.0	11.4
1944 and earlier	4.0	10.5	10.3	12.0

Source: Dun and Bradstreet, Inc.

Table 11-4

ENTRY RATES, SELECTED INDUSTRIES, 1954, 1958, 1963, AND 1967

SIC Code	Industry	1954	1958	1963	1967
5812	Eating places	12.3	14.6	18.1	7.4
7216	Dry cleaning establishments	4.3	6.5	5.5	2.3
7538	Auto repair	5.6	8.0	12.4	4.3

Note: Ratio of the number of establishments not in business at the beginning of the year to the number of establishments operated all year.

Source: U.S. Bureau of Census, Census of Business.

us an approximate entry rate of 11.7.[15] It is comparable to historical entry rates into the restaurant industry and is higher than historical entry rates into two other comparison industries (Table 11-4). However, even this entry rate may be atypical; that is, the entry into trucking of exempt agricultural commodities in 1973 may have been significantly affected by the surge in demand for truck transportation which followed the U.S. sale of wheat to the U.S.S.R.

An attempt was also made to estimate the exit rate for 1973 from the information supplied by the survey. The respondents were asked if they knew any truckers of exempt agricultural commodities who went out of business in 1973 and, if so, to list their names and addresses. Unfortunately, the respondents did not identify exempt carriers who went out of business in sufficient detail for verification and elimination of duplicates. It was not possible, therefore, to estimate the exit rate even for a single year.

Exits via Bankruptcy. A different source of data was available to estimate the exempt motor carrier exit rate via bankruptcy. The business failure statistics are compiled by the Business Economics Department of Dun and Bradstreet. According to their records, 79 establishments belonging to SIC 4213 (trucking, except local) declared bankruptcy in 1972, and 68 establishments declared bankruptcy in 1973. On January 1, 1974, the Dun and Bradstreet file contained records on 24,724 establishments belonging to SIC 4213. Thus, the annual failure rate per 10,000 operating concerns was a relatively low 27.5.

[15] Ratio of the number of MCEAC* firms established during 1973 to estimated population at the beginning of 1974.

It may be argued that the failure rate was relatively low because of the expected low rate among regulated motor carriers. Unfortunately, our attempt to identify the bankrupt carriers by type was only partially successful. The following breakdown was established:

	1972	*1973*
Exempt motor carriers	20	16
Regulated motor carriers	11	15
Intrastate motor carriers	3	5
Unable to identify	45	32

Now, suppose that we allocate unidentified carriers in proportion to those we were able to identify. According to this allocation, thirty exempt motor carriers declared bankruptcy in 1973. However, it has been estimated that the Dun and Bradstreet bankruptcy file covers approximately 90 percent of court cases.[16] Adjusting for the missing 10 percent of cases, we obtain an estimated total of thirty-three bankruptcies among exempt motor carriers in that particular year.

This estimate includes other exempt carriers in addition to exempt carriers of agricultural commodities. To be conservative, we assume that the proportion of exempt carriers of agricultural commodities is the same as the proportion on our list (that is, 57.75 percent). This gives us an estimated total of nineteen bankruptcies among exempt carriers of agricultural commodities and a failure rate of 8.75 or 17.37 per 10,000 operating concerns, depending on whether the population estimate based on the "broad" or the "narrow" definition of exempt carrier is used. This failure rate is very low as compared with that in other lines of business. It is lower than in any of the manufacturing industries (Table 11-5) and is among the lowest in retail lines (Table 11-6).

Our results are consistent with the results of a similar study of bankruptcy rates in Great Britain.[17] W. M. MacLeod and A. A. Walters estimated bankruptcy rates in road haulage prior to introduction of the licensing system. They then compared these rates to the bankruptcy rates in other lines of business where: "As in road haulage, the small man with a limited amount of capital does hope to enter . . . with the aid of a mortgage, and with some degree of

[16] Letter from Rowena Wyant, manager of the Business Economics Department, Dun and Bradstreet, Inc., dated February 5, 1975.

[17] W. M. MacLeod and A. A. Walters, "A Note on Bankruptcy in Road Haulage," *Journal of Industrial Economics*, vol. 5 (November 1956), pp. 63-67.

Table 11-5
MANUFACTURING INDUSTRIES RANKED BY FAILURE RATE, 1973

Line of Industry	Failure Rate per 10,000 Operating Concerns
Leather and shoes	94
Transportation equipment	76
Apparel	76
Electrical machinery	70
Furniture	63
Textiles	57
Chemicals and drugs	56
Paper	50
Printing and publishing	48
Lumber	41
Metals, primary and fabricated	39
Food	36
Machinery except electrical	34
Stone, clay, and glass	30

Source: Dun and Bradstreet, Inc., Business Economics Department.

success, and the very small and very large business exist side by side."[18] Their results provide no justification for the claim that the bankruptcy rate in the road haulage industry, before licensing, was unusually high. In fact, the bankruptcy rates in other lines of business in many cases were considerably higher than the rate of road haulage bankruptcy (Table 11-7).

Comparison of bankruptcy rates provides information on one type of exit. However, if the bankruptcy is used as a means of exit to about the same extent in all industries, the bankruptcy rates would provide a basis for estimating the overall exit rates for different industries. The average exit and bankruptcy rates by line of business were available for 1951–1955 (Table 11-8). The ratio of bankruptcy to exit rates shows considerable variation among industries. The bankruptcy rate alone, therefore, does not provide a satisfactory indicator for the overall exit rate of a particular industry.

[18] Ibid., p. 65.

Table 11-6

RETAIL LINES RANKED BY FAILURE RATE, 1973

Line of Business	Failure Rate per 10,000 Operating Concerns
Men's wear	103
Women's ready-to-wear	86
Gifts	82
Infants and children's wear	79
Books and stationery	63
Furniture and furnishings	60
Sporting goods	59
Cameras and photographic supplies	52
Shoes	41
Appliances, radios, and televisions	35
Toys and hobby crafts	30
Lumber and building materials	30
Dry goods and general merchandise	29
Bakeries	26
Auto parts and accessories	23
Women's accessories	22
Drugs	21
Eating and drinking places	21
Jewelry	17
Automobiles	17
Hardware	14
Grocery, meats, and produce	12
Farm implements	5

Source: Dun and Bradstreet, Inc., Business Economics Department.

Estimation of Exit Rates. Based upon our 1974 survey together with the 1961 survey of exempt motor carriers conducted by the U.S. Department of Agriculture, further analysis of exit rates can be performed if one is willing to make several, admittedly strong, assumptions.[19] The three most critical assumptions are as follows: (1) in cases where the needed information was not supplied by the 1961 survey, it is assumed that the response patterns in the 1961 survey

[19] The 1961 survey is described and the findings are reported in M. R. DeWolfe, *For-Hire Motor Carriers Hauling Exempt Agricultural Commodities: Nature and Extent of Operations*, U.S. Department of Agriculture, Marketing Research Division, MRR-585, 1963.

Table 11-7

PERCENTAGE OF BANKRUPTCIES IN SELECTED SERVICE INDUSTRIES PRIOR TO PASSAGE OF RAIL AND ROAD TRAFFIC ACT OF 1933, UNITED KINGDOM, 1921–1933

	Road Haulers						
Period	High estimate	Low estimate	**Butchers**	**Bakers**	**Green-Grocers and Fruiterers**	**Wine and Spirit Merchants**	**Confectioners, News Agents and Tobacconists**
1921–1924	0.43	0.31	0.32	0.82	0.42	0.28	0.39
1925–1929	0.31	0.23	0.49	1.03	0.44	0.23	0.42
1930–1933	0.30	0.26	0.53	0.76	0.47	0.36	0.55

Source: W. M. MacLeod and A. A. Walters, "A Note on Bankruptcy in Road Haulage," *Journal of Industrial Economics,* vol. 5 (November 1956), pp. 63-67.

Table 11-8

NUMBER OF DISCONTINUED AND BANKRUPT BUSINESSES PER 10,000 OPERATING CONCERNS BY INDUSTRY, 1951–1955 AVERAGE

Industry	Number of Discontinued Businesses	Number of Business Bankruptcies	Ratio of Bankruptcies to Total Discontinuances
Manufacturing			
Food and kindred products	450	57	.13
Textile mill products	910	76	.08
Apparel	1,080	116	.11
Leather and leather products	780	146	.19
Lumber and timber products	1,820	17	.01
Furniture and fixtures	660	174	.26
Paper and allied products	350	51	.15
Printing and publishing	330	21	.06
Chemicals and allied products	590	56	.09
Stone, clay, and glass products	640	38	.06
Metals, primary and fabricated	500	63	.13
Machinery, except electrical	690	57	.08
Electrical machinery	630	114	.18
Transportation equipment	550	85	.15
Retail			
Groceries	560	19	.03
Motor vehicles	1,080	26	.02
Automotive parts and accessories	600	17	.03
Shoes	540	47	.09
Lumber and building products	550	44	.08
Appliances, radios, and televisions	830	89	.11
Home furnishings	700	74	.11
Eating and drinking places	950	24	.03
Drugs	270	24	.09

Sources: B. C. Churchill, "Rise in the Business Population," *Survey of Current Business,* vol. 39 (May 1959), pp. 14-20; and data supplied by Dun and Bradstreet, Inc.

are the same as those in the 1974 survey; (2) mortality of firms is the function of age alone; and (3) the mortality function has remained constant over time.

These assumptions allow us: (1) to estimate the 1960 MCEAC* population and to test for the alleged bias in the 1961 survey results; (2) to estimate the mortality function; and (3) to compare the mortality function of MCEAC* firms with mortality functions of firms in other lines of business.

Estimation of the 1960 MCEAC population.* The master list for the 1961 survey was compiled from three separate sources: the Motor Carrier Bureau of the Interstate Commerce Commission, the National Agricultural Transportation League, and the records of the U.S. Department of Agriculture. The list contained 27,920 names.

From the above list, a 20 percent random sample was drawn for mailing a questionnaire. The outcome of the mailing is shown in the following tabulation:

	Number	Percent
1. Questionnaires used in the study	1,514	27.1
2. Questionnaires not returned	1,923	34.4
3. Questionnaires returned unopened	549	9.8
4. Responses from carriers having ICC operating authority	272	4.9
5. Responses from carriers out of business	690	12.4
6. Responses with no usable information and from those who were never in the trucking business	636	11.4
Total	5,584	100.0

Several adjustments were needed to estimate the 1960 MCEAC* population. In the 1961 survey the reasons for returning questionnaires unopened were not reported. In the 1974 survey 55 percent of returned questionnaires were undelivered because the addressee had moved and left no forwarding address. We assume that this reason accounted for the same percentage of questionnaires undelivered in 1961. Similarly, in the 1974 survey the ratio of nonusable to usable responses was slightly less than 6 percent. We assume that the ratio was the same in 1961.

The 1961 sample breakdown incorporating the above adjustments is shown in Table 11-9. We do not have any information about those who failed to respond, or about those who returned unusable questionnaires, or about addressees of questionnaires returned unopened for reasons other than moving. This group accounts for some 40 percent of the sample. An assumption about the proportion of MCEAC* among these nonrespondents, therefore, will have a significant effect on the population estimate.

Table 11-9

BREAKDOWN OF THE 1961 SAMPLE RESPONSES

Item	Number	Percent
Responses from MCEAC*	1,514	
Questionnaires returned unopened—addressee moved, assumed to be MCEAC*	300	
Total	1,814	32.48
Failed to respond	1,923	
Returned unusable questionnaires	89	
Questionnaires returned unopened—other reasons	249	
Total	2,261	40.49
Responses from carriers having ICC operating authority	690	12.36
Responses from carriers out of business	272	4.87
Responses from those who were never in the trucking business	547	9.80

We know for certain that this proportion is between 54.59 percent and zero. The former is based on the assumption that the proportion of MCEAC* among nonrespondents is the same as among those responding to the survey. The 1960 population of MCEAC*, therefore, must be between 9,068 and 15,239. The first estimate is biased downward since there are some MCEAC* among the nonrespondents. The second estimate is biased upward since we know from experience that the proportion among nonrespondents is usually smaller than among those responding.

The 1961 survey used only one mailing. In the 1974 survey there were three mailings. The responses from motor carriers of exempt agricultural commodities decreased from 92.34 percent in the first mailing to 57.02 percent and 45.86 percent in the second and third mailings, respectively.

For lack of a better alternative, we have assumed that the proportion of MCEAC* among nonrespondents is the same as the weighted average percentage of MCEAC* responding to the second and third mailings of the 1974 survey and the one-half of the third mailing response for those failing to respond after three mailings (that is, 30.87 percent). This gives us a population of 12,559.

Table 11-10

DISTRIBUTION OF MCEAC* BY YEARS IN BUSINESS, RESPONDENTS TO THE 1974 SURVEY

Years in Business	First Mailing		All Mailings	
	Number	Percent	Number	Percent
Fewer than 5	617	27.3	1,080	27.1
5 to 9	496	22.0	882	22.1
10 to 14	250	11.1	443	11.1
15 to 19	212	9.4	354	8.9
20 to 24	137	6.1	241	6.1
25 to 29	174	7.7	293	7.4
30 or more	373	16.5	689	17.3
Total	2,259	100.1	3,982	100.0

The above population estimate is still subject to two additional biases. Although the 1961 survey excluded motor carriers holding ICC operating authorities, it failed to exclude regulated intrastate carriers. In the 1974 survey these carriers accounted for about 21 percent of all exempt motor carriers responding to the survey. On the other hand, the list from which the sample was drawn may have represented an incomplete frame.

As was pointed out above, the 1961 survey used one mailing only. The author of that survey believes that the sample estimates on length of time in business are not representative of population because of the nonresponse bias; that is, responses tended to come from more successful operators.[20] To test this hypothesis we compared the distribution by years in business of MCEAC* responding to the first mailing of the 1974 survey with the same distribution of MCEAC* responding to all three mailings. As shown in Table 11-10, there does not appear to be any significant difference between the two distributions. Therefore, we reject the hypothesis that the 1960 survey results were biased.

The preceding steps allow us to estimate the distribution of the 1960 MCEAC* population by years in business. The estimates are reported in Table 11-11.

[20] Ibid., p. 2.

Table 11-11

ESTIMATED DISTRIBUTION OF MCEAC*
BY YEARS IN BUSINESS, 1960

Years in Business	Sample	Percent	Population
Fewer than 5	223	16.1	2,022
5 to 9	261	18.9	2,374
10 to 14	298	21.6	2,713
15 to 19	189	13.7	1,720
20 to 24	161	11.7	1,469
25 to 29	135	9.8	1,231
30 or more	114	8.2	1,030
Total	1,381	100.0	12,559

Estimation of mortality function. As the next step, a mathematical form for cumulative mortality function has to be selected. K. S. Lomax has experimented with various possible forms of business mortality functions. He has concluded that the hyperbola

$$F(t) = 1 - \left(\frac{a}{a+t}\right)^b$$

where a and b are parameters and t is age of the firm (F), gives the best fit in the retail trade and service industries, while the exponential function

$$F(t) = 1 - e^{a/b(e^{-bt}-1)}$$

gives a better fit for the firms in manufacturing industries.[21] Both alternatives conform to the desirable boundary conditions and monotonic behavior exhibited by the data.

After further experimentation with other functional forms, we chose the hyperbola. Given our initial assumption that mortality of firms is a function of age only, we are ready to estimate the parameters of mortality function for MCEAC*.

[21] K. S. Lomax, "Business Failures: Another Example of the Analysis of Failure Data," *Journal of the American Statistical Association*, vol. 49 (December 1954), pp. 851-52.

Suppose we have census of population and its distribution by year of entry at two different points in time, j and $j + L$. Then we have

$$n_{ij} = m_i \left(\frac{a}{a + j - i} \right)^b \tag{1}$$

$$\text{for } i = 1, 2, \ldots j$$

and

$$n_{ij+L} = m_i \left(\frac{a}{a + j+L - i} \right)^b \tag{2}$$

$$\text{for } i = 1, 2, \ldots j$$

where n_{ij} is the number of firms that entered in year i and survived to year j. The term $(j - i)$, therefore, is age of the firm. The term m_i is the total number of firms entering in year i.

Dividing equation 1 by equation 2 we have

$$\frac{n_{ij}}{n_{ij+L}} = \frac{\left(\frac{a}{a + j - i} \right)^b}{\left(\frac{a}{a + j+L - i} \right)^b} = \left(\frac{a + j+L - i}{a + j - i} \right)^b$$

or (3)

$$n_{ij} = \left(\frac{a + j+L - i}{a + j - i} \right)^b n_{ij+L}$$

$$\text{for } i = 1, 2, \ldots j.$$

In case we do not have the populations and thus do not know exact values of n_{ij} and n_{ij+L} for $i = 1, 2, \ldots j$, but we have samples drawn from respective populations instead, n_{ij} and n_{ij+L} can be estimated as follows:

$$n_{ij} = \frac{S_{ij}}{P_j} \times T_j \tag{4}$$

and

$$n_{ij+L} = \frac{S_{ij+L}}{P_{j+L}} \times T_{j+L}, \tag{5}$$

where S_{ij} and S_{ij+L} are the observed number of firms in the sample entering in year i and surviving to year j and year $j+L$, respectively. P_j and P_{j+L} are the sample sizes in year j and year $j+L$; T_j and T_{j+L} are the total population in year j and year $j+L$, respectively.

Table 11-12

DATA USED IN ESTIMATION OF CUMULATIVE MORTALITY FUNCTION FOR MCEAC*

Age in Years 1960	Number of Firms	Age in Years 1974	Number of Firms
2.0	223	16.0	289
6.5	261	20.5	246
9.0	298	23.0	256
11.5	189	25.5	146
13.0	161	27.0	103
15.5	135	29.5	90

Other information:

$T_j \ : T_{1960} = 12{,}559$
$T_{j+L} : T_{1974} = 10{,}968$
$P_j \ : P_{1960} = 1{,}381$
$P_{j+L} : P_{1974} = 3{,}671$
$L = 14$

Function to be estimated:

$$S_{ij} = 0.329 \left(\frac{a + j + L - i}{a + \ - j} \right)^b S_{ij+L}$$

Substituting equations 4 and 5 into equation 3, we have

$$\frac{S_{ij}}{P_j} \times T_j = \left(\frac{a + j + L - i}{a + j - i} \right)^b \frac{S_{ij+L}}{P_{j+L}} T_{j+L}$$

or (6)

$$S_{ij} = \left[\frac{T_{j+L} P_j}{P_{j+L} T_j} \left(\frac{a + j + L - i}{a + j - i} \right)^b \right] S_{ij+L}$$

$$\text{for } i = 1, 2, \ldots j.$$

For MCEAC* we know the values of T_j and T_{j+L}, as well as P_j and P_{j+L}, and we have two sets of observations for S_{ij} and S_{ij+L}. All of these are shown in Table 11-12. The parameters a and b are estimated using the method of nonlinear least squares.[22] The estimated coefficients are: $a = 736.0593$; $b = 61.1843$.

Comparison of estimated mortality functions. A problem was encountered in our attempts to compare the estimated cumulative mortality function of MCEAC* with a similar function for firms in

[22] BMD07R computer program was used for estimation.

Table 11-13

CUMULATIVE MORTALITY OF BUSINESS ESTABLISHMENTS BY MAJOR INDUSTRY DIVISION, POUGHKEEPSIE, 1844–1936

Age in Years	Manufacturing	Retail Trade	Services
1	24.0	32.5	32.9
2	27.1	45.8	47.2
3	49.8	55.0	56.8
4	57.8	61.1	63.7
5	63.2	66.2	69.0
6	67.7	70.4	73.0
7	70.4	73.5	76.3
8	73.3	76.3	79.3
9	76.0	78.6	81.5
10	78.7	80.8	83.4

Source: R. G. Hutchinson, A. R. Hutchinson, and M. Newcomer, "Study in Business Mortality," *American Economic Review*, vol. 28 (September 1938), pp. 497-511.

other lines of business. An exhaustive search of possible sources disclosed no contemporary data on business mortality. However, two earlier sets of data were available for comparisons. The first set consisted of data compiled by R. G. Hutchinson, A. R. Hutchinson, and M. Newcomer.[23] Their study covered experience of all business enterprises, except financial concerns and public utilities, in the city of Poughkeepsie, New York, for a period of ninety-four years, 1844–1936 inclusive.

Two definitions of mortality were used: (1) change of ownership was assumed not to terminate the business as long as its identity could be traced; and (2) change of ownership was assumed to terminate the business. The total number of observations were 11,222 and 10,033, respectively. The cumulative mortality estimates for manufacturing, retail, and services based on the second definition of mortality are shown in Table 11-13.

The second set consisted of the Office of Business Economics estimates of business life expectancy based on 1947–1954 experience.[24] Change of ownership was considered as termination of busi-

[23] Hutchinson, Hutchinson, and Newcomer, "Study in Business Mortality."

[24] B. C. Churchill, "Age and Life Expectancy of Business Firms," *Survey of Current Business*, vol. 35 (December 1955), pp. 15-19 and 24.

ness. The cumulative mortality estimates for manufacturing, retail, and services are shown in Table 11-14.

The estimated cumulative mortality function coefficients for all seven sets of data are reported in Table 11-15. To facilitate comparisons, mortality functions are shown graphically in Figures 11-1 and 11-2. The first figure contains mortality functions of MCEAC* and the three broad industry categories of the Poughkeepsie data. The second figure contains mortality functions of MCEAC* and the same industry categories of the OBE data. According to these functions, the MCEAC* firms enjoy a considerably greater probability of survival up to twenty-five years of age. Thereafter, the probability of survival is either the same as or slightly higher than in other industries.

The true shape of mortality functions was undoubtedly affected by extrapolation beyond the range of available data. The Poughkeepsie and OBE data covered periods of 10 and 10.5 years, respectively. On the other hand, the shortest period covered by MCEAC* data is 14 years. Thus, we do not know the true shape of MCEAC* mortality functions in prior years. Nevertheless, it is very likely that it is below mortality functions of other industries even in this age period. To be otherwise, given constraints that the cumulative mortality function has to go through the origin and be monotonically increasing, the MCEAC* mortality function would have to intersect other mortality functions very close to the origin. This would imply an implausibly high mortality during the first (and possibly the second) year, followed by implausibly low mortality during the remaining years. Therefore, it seems reasonable to conclude that MCEAC* firms enjoy a greater probability of survival than firms in broad industry groups for which we have data for comparisons.

Sensitivity of results. Probably the weakest input used in estimation of the MCEAC* mortality function is the 1960 MCEAC* population. If our 1960 and 1974 population estimates are correct, there must have been a decrease of 13 percent in the number of MCEAC* during the period from 1960 to 1974. No independent checks are available to evaluate the reliability of population estimates.

However, the available evidence suggests that the demand for truck transport services during this period should have increased. From 1960 to 1973 grain and soybean production in the United States increased by 42.6 percent.[25] The data on division of grain and soy-

[25] *Prelude to Legislation to Solve the Growing Crisis in Rural Transportation*, prepared for the U.S. Congress, Senate, Committee on Agriculture and Forestry, 94th Congress, 1st session, 1975, p. 72.

Table 11-14

CUMULATIVE MORTALITY OF BUSINESS ESTABLISHMENTS BY MAJOR INDUSTRY DIVISION, 1947–1954

Age in Years	Manufacturing	Retail Trade	Services
0.5	18	26	23
1.5	40	51	47
2.5	54	64	60
3.5	62	71	67
4.5	67	75	72
5.5	71	78	75
6.5	74	80	77
7.5	76	81	78
8.5	77	82	79
9.5	78	83	80
10.5	80	84	81

Source: B. C. Churchill, "Age and Expectancy of Business Firms," *Survey of Current Business,* vol. 35 (December 1955), pp. 15-19 and 24.

Table 11-15

ESTIMATED MORTALITY FUNCTION PARAMETERS, MCEAC*, AND COMPARISON INDUSTRIES

	Estimated Parameters	
Item	*a*	*b*
MCEAC*	736.0593	61.1843
Poughkeepsie Data:		
Manufacturing	7.3486	1.8412
Retail trade	1.9195	1.8412
Services	2.3443	1.0445
OBE Data:		
Manufacturing	1.2880	0.7294
Retail trade	0.9824	0.7822
Services	1.0543	0.7324

Figure 11-1

ESTIMATED MORTALITY FUNCTIONS OF MCEAC*
AND POUGHKEEPSIE DATA

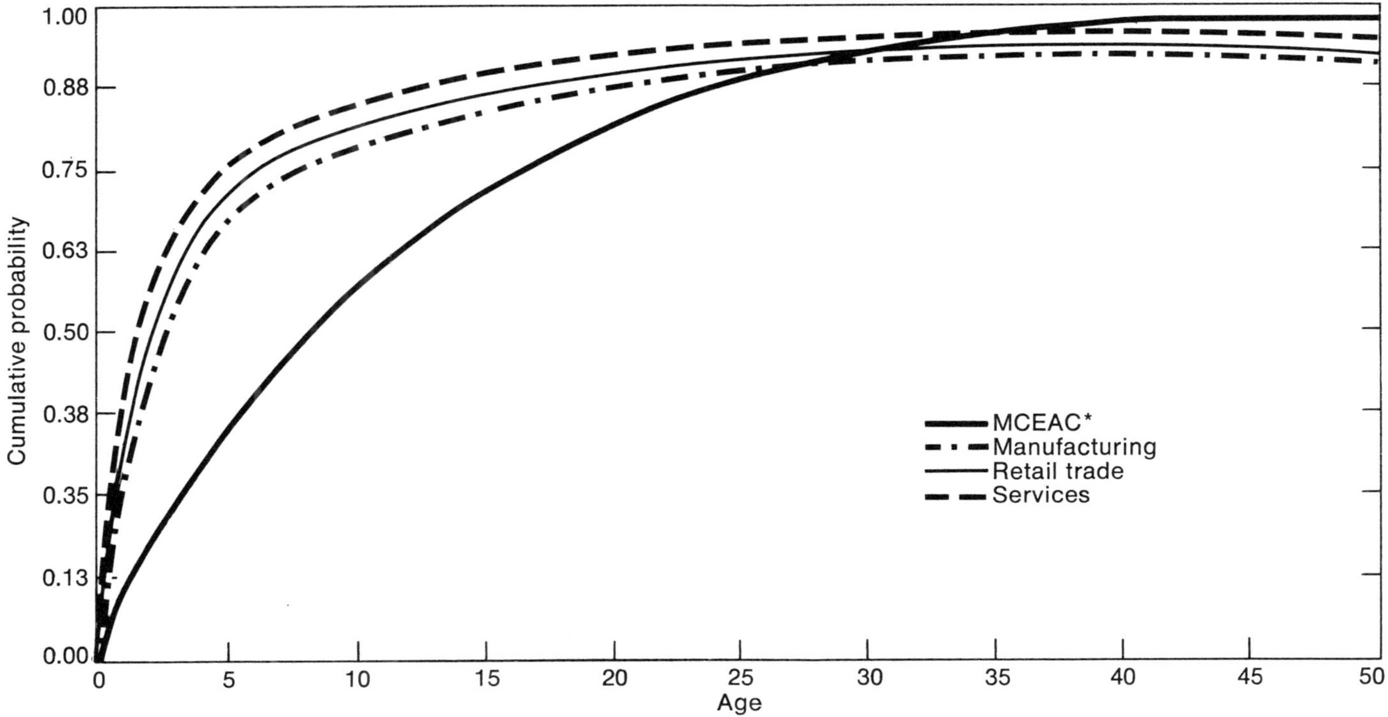

Figure 11-2

ESTIMATED MORTALITY FUNCTIONS OF MCEAC* AND OBE DATA

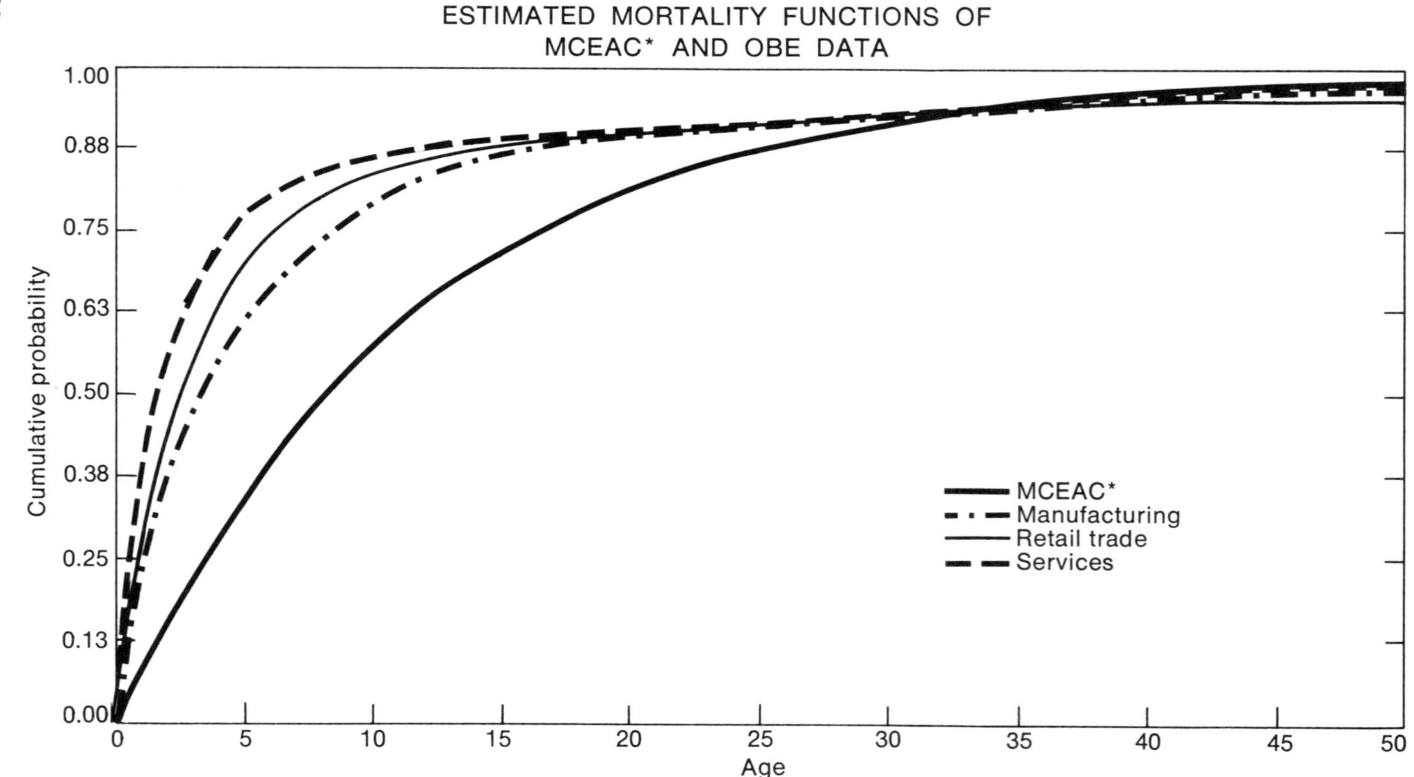

Figure 11-3

ESTIMATED MORTALITY FUNCTIONS OF MCEAC*, ORIGINAL ESTIMATE AND REVISED ESTIMATE

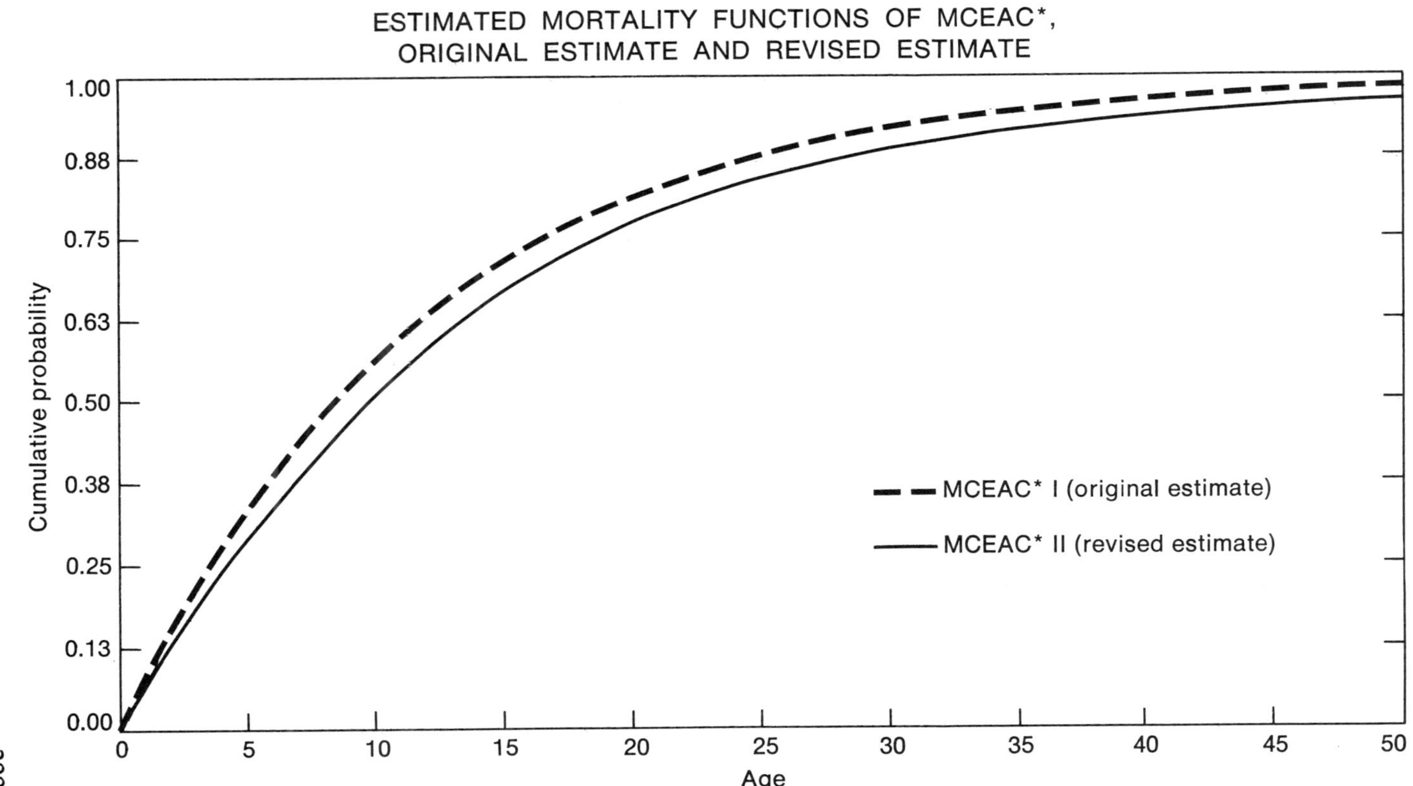

bean traffic by mode of transport are not available. But the receipts of grain and soybeans inspected under the U.S. Grain Standards Act at all areas provide an indicator. Between 1969–1970 and 1973–1974, the share of trucks in total receipts of inspected grains and soybeans increased from 12.7 to 18.5 percent.[26]

From 1962 to 1973 the truck share of fresh fruit and vegetable unloadings at forty-one major U.S. cities increased from 63.3 to 76.4 percent, although the absolute number of unloads decreased by 5.1 percent.[27] Similarly, in 1959 trucks handled an estimated 85 percent of all livestock movements. In 1974 they moved at least 95 percent.[28]

It may be argued that the increased demand for truck transport services was met by expanding capacity of existing firms rather than by entry of new firms. The available studies, however, found no significant economies of scale in the trucking industry. One would expect, therefore, the expansion of capacity to occur predominantly through entry of new firms.

Although none of the above is conclusive, it is more likely that the 1960 MCEAC* population has been overestimated than underestimated. If this is indeed the case, the mortality of MCEAC* has been overestimated. To test the sensitivity of our results, we have reduced the 1960 population estimate by 10 percent and reestimated the cumulative mortality function. As shown in Figure 11-3, the results are not sensitive to errors of this magnitude.

Conclusions

The purpose of the research effort, results of which are presented in this report, was to test the hypothesis that the entry and exit rates into and out of trucking of exempt agricultural commodities are significantly higher and the probability of survival is significantly lower than in other similar lines of business.

The available evidence is inconsistent with the hypothesis. The estimated 1973 entry rate appears to be within the range of historical entry rates into the restaurant business, but it is higher than entry rates into dry cleaning and auto repair. Furthermore, the 1973 entry rate may be atypically high as it may have been affected by the great surge in demand for truck transportation which followed the U.S. sale of wheat to the U.S.S.R. The bankruptcy rate of MCEAC* is lower

[26] Ibid., pp. 76-77.

[27] Ibid., p. 84.

[28] Ibid., p. 91.

than in any of the manufacturing industries and ranks with the lowest in the retail trade. This finding is consistent with the result of the study of bankruptcy rates in Great Britain. As indicated by the estimated cumulative mortality functions, the MCEAC* enjoy greater probability of survival than firms in industry groups for which we had survival data.

The results appear to be reasonable. Furthermore, the stability of mortality function coefficients between two sets of data derived from completely different sources and covering different periods is rather encouraging. The insensitivity of results to sizeable errors lends further support to our conclusions. Nevertheless, they should be considered as only tentative. The study was severely handicapped by unavailability of needed data. Thus, a number of assumptions, specified throughout the report, were required for estimation purposes. Unfortunately, only repeated surveys over time could provide data necessary for a conclusive verification of our results. The nature and mobility of MCEAC* population would make this a rather difficult, time-consuming, and costly undertaking.